Beginner's Guide to

Car Maintenance, Fault-finding and Repair

Denis Rea and Rodney Jacques

Guild Publishing
London

This edition published 1987 by
Book Club Associates by arrangement with
Heinemann Professional Publishing Ltd

© William Heinemann Ltd 1987

Printed in England by
Robert Hartnoll (1985) Ltd, Bodmin, Cornwall

Contents

Preface

Although modern motor cars are capable of very high mileages between major services, they should not be neglected altogether between these, and it's always worthwhile avoiding the high cost of a garage service. While the need for such servicing has decreased, labour costs and parts prices have risen considerably over the last few years. And garages will generally charge you much more for oil, filters, plugs and other parts than you would expect to pay when shopping around the High Street.

Also the occasional 'once-over' between major services may well spot – and nip in the bud – a developing fault that might otherwise be discovered months later, by which time it could itself be a major, and expensive, problem.

So, doing it yourself still offers the major attraction of cutting your annual motoring costs. But there is more to DIY than saving money. Once you've mastered the expertise – which anyone can do once he has the know-how – there's a tremendous satisfaction to be had from driving a sweet-running car which reflects entirely your own efforts. And not only is there the satisfaction. There is also the peace of mind in knowing not only that the job *has* been done, but that it has been done well.

For there *are* inefficient garages, that will neglect or skimp the servicing. And you find that, while paying out more than you can afford for professional maintenance, the car still does not perform as it should, costs you more to run than it should, lets you down when it shouldn't, and eventually wears out more quickly than it should.

The modern motor car is made up of thousands of individual parts, any one of which, in spite of quality-control checks during assembly and subsequent service inspections, can fail. This may be no more than an inconvenience in that the engine refuses to start one morning, in which case your priorities could well be to locate and rectify the fault. At the other extreme, however, a component failure could, in certain conditions, create a hazardous situation where your first priority should be to stop the car as quickly and safely as possible.

Part of this book is devoted to the first type of problem; tracing and rectifying faults which prevent the car from starting or running as it should. Sometimes doing so before the actual fault occurs. These sections also give some idea of what common everyday items may be of use in carrying out a temporary 'get you home' repair.

A failure of any sort when travelling at speed can be dangerous – all breakdowns are potential accidents. Advice is given on what to do in these and other emergency situations which could confront any driver at any time.

This book will provide you with the know-how to service and repair your car yourself, in your own garage. So get out and get under – and reap the benefits of more enjoyable motoring, and more money in your pocket!

D.R. and R.A.J.

Part One

Car Maintenance

1

The tools required

You may have some spanners already. But to tackle your own servicing and repair on a regular basis you will probably have to add to these, and buy some items of workshop equipment as well. What you buy will have to be of good quality, and won't be cheap. But a good toolkit is an investment, one that will eventually pay for itself many times over.

Remember, also, that some of these tools will be equally useful on other machinery, garden and household. In fact, there may be many odd jobs about the house, that you've had to refuse before, that once 'tooled up' you can now tackle.

The basic kit

Over the years there have been all sorts of nut/bolt/spanner designations, including British Standard Whitworth (BSW – or 'Whit'), British Standard Fine (BSF), United Fine (UNF) and United Coarse (UNC). Then, for many years until comparatively recently British cars standardised on A/F – a designation referring to the measurement 'across the flats' of the hexagon nut or bolt head.

But now, of course, we have gone 'metric', and these days you would be unlikely to find any new car – British or Foreign – using other than metric nuts and bolts. However, let's not forget that on the secondhand market there will still be many cars using A/F sizes – indeed, on some post-war models still running will lurk the odd 'Whit' size. If you're in doubt as to what your car uses, consult the local franchised dealer.

1

Incidentally, although we tend to think A/F or metric, more properly it should be 'imperial' or 'metric', since the latter type of nut or bolt is also measured 'across the flats'.

Types of spanner

The two common types of spanner are the ring and the open-ended. The ring spanner grips (almost) all round the bolt or nut, whereas the open-ended spanner merely straddles two flats. Where the nut or bolt is particularly tight the ring is preferable, for the open-ended could slip, and round off the edges of the nut. But the open-ended is often quicker and easier to use, once the nut has been loosened. So it makes sense to have some of each type. There are also 'combination' spanners (with a ring at one end, and an open end at the other) which are handy as well.

It's difficult to be precise on the sizes you may need, because the requirements will vary from car to car. However, the following sizes are usually basic needs for most cars. Note that most spanners (apart from combinations) will have a different size each end, and the A/F types commonly rise in sixteenths of an inch, the metrics by one millimetre:

A/F $\frac{3}{8} \times \frac{7}{16}$, $\frac{1}{2} \times \frac{9}{16}$, $\frac{5}{8} \times \frac{11}{16}$, $\frac{13}{16} \times \frac{7}{8}$

Metric – 10×11, 12×13, 14×15, 16×17

Larger – or smaller – sizes can be bought as and when the need arises. You will also want a proper brake adjusting spanner, suitable for the car.

And, once thought of as a luxury but now within reach of everyone's pocket, a socket set is well worth considering (Figure 1.1). In A/F or metric, an average set will cover all your basic spanner sizes, plus extras, and can often solve a difficult access problem, or provide the extra leverage required. Also practically a 'must' these days is a torque wrench, since the exact tightness of some nuts and bolts will be critical (Figure 1.2).

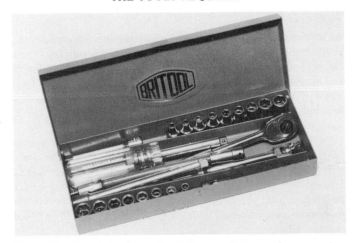

Figure 1.1. A socket set is well worth considering, and you can buy separate sockets and accessories as and when needed

Figure 1.2. Also practically a 'must' these days is a torque wrench, whether it's a basic needle and scale type or the more sophisticated 'breaker' type, as shown in use here

Additional tools

As well as the spanners, you will also require a few other tools. For instance you will need a selection of screwdrivers, both flat-bladed and cross-headed. A short 'stubby', a medium length and maybe a long slim example of both types are advisable. Then you will need pliers, and here you want 'ordinary' combination (or engineer's) pliers for general work, and 'long-nosed', for use, for instance, where access is tight.

Don't forget a plug spanner (but make sure it's suitable for the plugs used in your car) and also have a set of feeler gauges, and a wire brush. As well as ordinary feeler gauges, you can get an ignition set which includes feelers covering most plug or CB points gaps used, a tool for adjusting plug gaps, and a points file. You will want a hammer, with a 1 lb ball-pein type being a useful 'starter' here.

Apart from your basic set of tools, you'll want a grease gun, an oil can, and an oil funnel, a container of sufficient capacity into which the sump oil can be drained (Figure 1.3), and a drain plug key suitable for your car. Then you'll need wheel ramps or axle stands, and a small trolley jack, which is far preferable to the jack supplied with the car (Figures 1.4, 1.5). *Never venture underneath a car that is supported on a jack alone.*

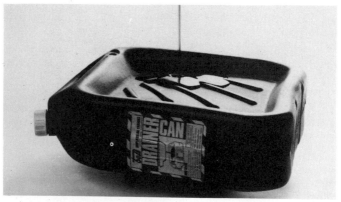

Figure 1.3. Engine oil drain trays can be anything that will do, or made for the job like this drainer/can example

Figures 1.4, 1.5. A trolley jack and axle stands are practically essential

Your toolkit is something you will always be adding to, and no doubt as the need arises you'll be buying different screwdrivers, some files, a copper hammer, hacksaws and some 'specials' (Figure 1.6). Some of these we will mention as and when the need arises as we progress through this book.

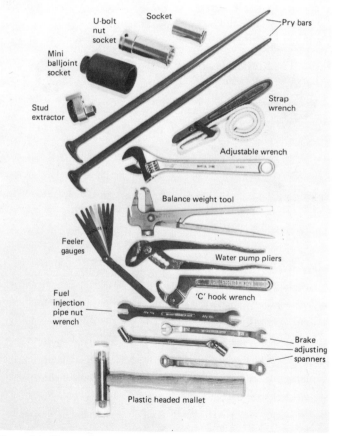

Figure 1.6. You might not want all the 'specials' shown here, but many of them, plus the more basic examples, can be very useful

Tuning aids

These, too, will be discussed more fully in the appropriate sections. Suffice now to say that there are instruments these days – affordable by the average motorist – that can be used for setting up ignition and carburation, whereas it was once assumed that this was work that had to be entrusted to a professional garage. These DIY tuning aids include a dwell meter for setting contact breaker points, a stroboscopic timing light ('strobe') for setting the ignition timing, and various carburettor tuning aids.

However, it is easier to understand them – and determine your choice – when describing them in action. This is why we will expand on such items as their need arises later.

To describe in detail the full range of tools you can choose from, and explain how they can help you, would take a separate book – and there is one! It's called *Questions and Answers Car Tools* by the same author and publisher.

2

Lubrication

Although modern cars cover incredible distances between specified engine oil-changes – often without the need even for topping up – neither the oil-change nor regular dipstick checks must be neglected. It's not that the oil wears out. But it does become contaminated, both with the by-products of the combustion process and with metallic debris worn from the moving parts. Eventually, despite the best efforts of the engine oil filter, this contamination builds to the point where the oil has abrasive rather than lubricating qualities.

Obviously the oil-change will be timed to be comfortably in advance of this state of affairs – though not to allow you to postpone the job indefinitely! Sometimes the oil and filter will be changed at the same time, sometimes there will be an intermediate oil change only. As to the regular dipstick check, oil may not wear out, but it can run out – either through external leakage, or leakage past pistons and rings into the combustion process. In severe cases the latter will be betrayed by a very smoky exhaust!

However, although this would normally indicate a very worn engine, even a healthy one sometimes consumes an appreciable quantity between oil-changes. And an engine low on oil risks metal-to-metal contact, over-heating and eventual seizure.

So the oil level should be checked least once a week if the car is used for fairly moderate, short journey work. If it gets much hard and fast, motorway type, use, it pays to check more often, maybe at the start of each journey. Obviously the car should be on level ground when you check the dipstick, and, to be sure you get the correct reading, withdraw the stick, wipe it, then re-insert and withdraw again.

There will usually be maximum and minimum marks on the stick, and your handbook may quote a specific quantity for the difference between the two. The lower mark is, of course, the danger level. But it could also be unwise to exceed the maximum mark – a shade over won't matter, but substantial over-filling can also lead to over-heating. If you need to top up, allow time for the oil to reach the sump before re-checking the level.

Changing the oil

As we said earlier, eventually the time will come when the sump will need to be drained and refilled with fresh, clean oil. At the same time as the engine oil change (or sometimes at every other change – check your handbook) the oil filter must be renewed. Basically, there are two types of oil filter – the older type has a separate element which has to be renewed, the other, more common these days, an integral, throw-away canister design. Some early engines had mechanical, centrifugal filters which needed occasional cleaning out. Still around are a number of VW air-cooled engines, which simply have a strainer fitted into the sump, though later versions did have a separate filter.

For newcomers to car maintenance this oil change procedure is usually the job they 'cut their teeth' on. Yet provided it's tackled with commonsense it's quite straightforward. The commonsense bit basically means buying the oil and filter in advance, making sure you have a tray or other receptacle of sufficient size into which the oil can be drained, making sure the shape is such that this will fit comfortably under the engine – and making sure you have the right tool for the sump's drain plug.

Maybe this will be a conventional spanner to fit a hexagon head. But maybe the plug has a recessed head requiring a special drain plug key. Attempt to use anything else and you could be in big trouble before you've even started, with a rounded out plug no tool will fit. Even with the correct tool you could have similar problems if you don't first make sure the plug recess is clean and the tool fitting snugly.

Commonsense comes into it again where access under the car is involved, and you need to have the drain plug at the lowest point on the sump. Most likely that is where it will be situated anyway, but if you need to jack up the car to gain spanner access to the plug, and have room for the drain tray, you'll need to ensure the plug is kept at this lowest point. So if you place axle stands or wheel ramps under the front of the car (and you must *never* venture under a car that is not so supported) then you may need to do the same at the rear. On the other hand, raising the front of the car may tip the oil even further towards the plug.

The best time to drain the oil is after a short drive, when the oil will be warm and will flow more easily. Before removing the drain plug, take off the oil filler cap to relieve any partial vacuum within the engine – the faster the oil can flow from the sump, the more debris it will drag out with it (Figure 2.1). On some engines, particularly where the oil also lubricates the transmission (e.g., transverse, front wheel drive units) a magnetic drain plug is fitted. This is designed to attract and collect any metallic swarf that might be drifting around in the sump. Make sure that any such build-up is thoroughly cleaned off.

With all plugs (other than taper fit) there should be a sealing washer which must be checked for soundness. Having cleaned the plug, washer, and seating on the sump, replace the plug as soon as you're sure the last drop has drained from the engine. It could cause problems if you neglected to do this now, and then forgot it later on.

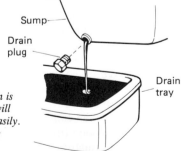

Figure 2.1. The best time to drain is after a short drive, when the oil will be warm and will flow more easily. Don't forget to replace the plug afterwards

Changing the filter

The oil filter might be a bowl-and-element type (Figure 2.2), or it could be a one-piece canister unit. With the former the element has to be renewed; with the latter the entire canister is discarded, and a new one fitted in its place. Often the easiest to remove is the bowl and element type. The bowl will be secured

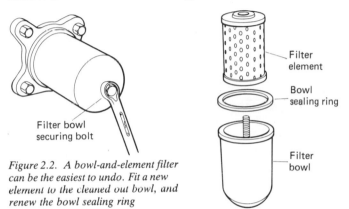

Figure 2.2. A bowl-and-element filter can be the easiest to undo. Fit a new element to the cleaned out bowl, and renew the bowl sealing ring

to the engine by a through-bolt, which can be undone with a suitable spanner. Have a container handy beneath it to catch spillage, and be careful if you up-end it not to let any of its components escape. Normally, any such components (like the metal base-plate, with spring beneath, on which the element sits) should be captive. You simply lift out the old element and swill or brush the bowl clean with petrol or paraffin. Dry it off afterwards with lint-free rag.

Although on the face of it there's nothing easier than discarding the old and fitting the new, in fact the canister filter (Figure 2.3) can set very tightly in service and be difficult to unscrew. Often a problem is getting your hands on it to apply sufficient pressure. Methods of overcoming the problem include buying a special filter strap (or chain) wrench, gripping it with abrasive paper (sometimes needed even with a wrench) or, if there's room, simply driving, say, an old screwdriver right through it and using this as a tommy bar (Figure 2.4).

Figure 2.3. The throw-away canister filter may not always unscrew by hand, although when fitting it should not be done up more than hand-tight

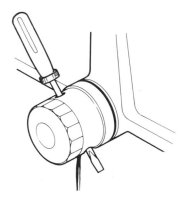

Figure 2.4. A tight canister can be undone with a strap wrench, or by driving a screwdriver through it and using this as a tommy bar

Refitting the oil filter

With the bowl type of filter, in the seating on the engine will be a rubber sealing ring. This must be hooked out with a slim screwdriver blade, scissor point or something similar, and the new seal – supplied with the element – fitted in its place. Then, when bolting the bowl back on, make sure it sits evenly on this seal. The bolt should be done up tightly, but not 'murdered'. The canister filter will include a sealing ring. Moisten this with clean oil, then, having also wiped its seating clean, screw on the canister hand-tight only.

Refilling with oil

Before refilling with oil, do make sure the sump plug has been replaced. Then fill with the correct grade and quantity of oil, checking that this corresponds with the correct mark on the dipstick. Afterwards run the engine for a few minutes while you check for leaks, looking in particular at the filter joint. Switch off the engine, allow the oil to settle for a while, then re-check the dipstick. Top up with more oil if required.

Transmission lubrication

With most cars it will be specified that the transmission oil levels should be checked and topped up as necessary at service intervals. Occasionally it will be recommended that the oil is changed at high mileages. Sometimes there will be separate gearbox and final drives to be serviced, sometimes a combined gearbox and final drive unit, sometimes, of course, the engine and transmission units will share a common supply of oil (Figures 2.5, 2.6). Mostly, the service requirement will be to remove a single filler/level plug and check that the oil level is up to this point. As with the sump plug, don't attempt to use anything other than the correct tool for the job.

Where topping up is required, your biggest problem is likely to be access to an in-line gearbox unit. You may have to decide whether it's easier to tackle the job from up above (from the

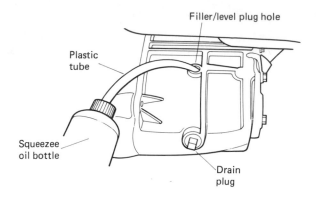

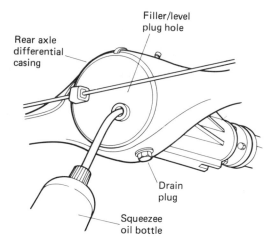

Figures 2.5, 2.6. The filler/level plug of a rear wheel drive car will often be found on the nearside of the gearbox, while front wheel drive vehicles may have a common transmission filler/level plug hole. Rear wheel drive cars will have a similar plug hole on the differential casing. Where access to either is difficult you may need extra lengths of plastic tubing. Also something like an old bicycle pump might be handier than the squeezee bottle. Note that not all transmission units will have drain plugs

engine compartment) or from below. Usually the oil will be supplied in a plastic 'squeezee' bottle, with a short flexible tube attached. If necessary, you can fit a longer piece of tubing. Or you can buy an oil gun, and, again, if necessary fit some tubing to this. Should you at any time need to drain a transmission unit, it's simply a case of placing a suitable receptacle underneath and removing the drain plug. As with the engine oil, it's best done after a run, when the oil will be warm and quick to drain. However, not only is this requirement comparatively rare, but some units will not even have a drain plug.

General lubrication

There are many moving parts on the car, such as door hinges (Figure 2.7), carburettor linkage, pedal pivots and linkage, that will benefit from regular lubrication. Use an oil can or general purpose aerosol lubricant as appropriate. Some dynamos, for instance, have provision for oil-can lubrication of their rear (bush) bearing.

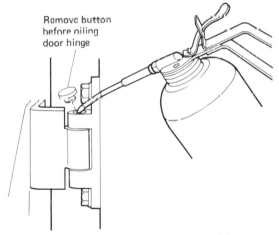

Figure 2.7. Door hinges, carburettor linkage, and pedal pivots, etc., need regular oil can lubrication

Although nowadays many components are sealed for life, you should check whether there are any grease nipples fitted to your car's steering (Figure 2.8), suspension or gearchange mechanisms. Sometimes (e.g., a suspension unit or drive-shaft) there may be a plug that has to be removed and temporarily replaced with a grease nipple. For most applications a lithium-based general purpose chassis grease will be specified. However, for

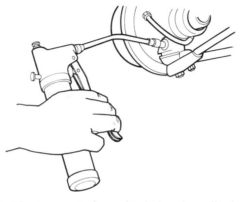

Figure 2.8. Where grease nipples are fitted, clean them off before applying the grease gun

specialist applications, where, for example, brakes or rubber components are concerned, there are specialist greases, and you should ensure you buy one suitable for the job. Always clean off the nipple first, to avoid forcing abrasive dirt into the joint. Then, generally speaking, three or four pumps of the grease gun should suffice.

Note, too, that sometimes the weight of the car needs to be off the joints (i.e., it must be jacked up) before grease will readily enter the joints. Where grease tends to escape between the gun nozzle and nipple, rather than enter the joint, a scrap of clean lint-free rag interposed between nozzle and nipple will often solve the problem.

3

The engine

Perhaps the best way to approach engine maintenance is first to clean both engine and under-bonnet area thoroughly. This may be particularly desirable if the car is a secondhand one that has seen a lot of mileage. Once clean, it should be kept that way. All this is more than mere fastidiousness – not only is a clean engine more pleasant to work on, but oil or coolant leaks are likely to be spotted earlier and rectified before too much harm is done. Also, an accumulation of grime can literally gum up the works, causing for instance, sticky throttle linkage, and abrasive grit will hasten wear.

Cleaning technique

There are aerosol and bottled engine de-greasers which are remarkably effective in softening the congealed grime. The more stubborn areas can be treated with brush and cleaner.

Typically, the cleaner is applied all over the engine, and then hosed off with water. But a wise precaution is to secure plastic bags over items such as the distributor, coil, carburettor and hydraulic reservoirs.

Service requirements

We have already dealt with oil-changing, and attention to the ignition and fuel systems will be covered in later sections of this book. Later in this section we will deal with a 'top overhaul', and basic engine overhaul as well. Which leaves the one specific item of regular engine maintenance – checking and adjusting (where necessary, and if possible) the valve clearances.

In a basic set-up, valve clearances are the gaps which are set between the valve stems and the mechanism which operates them. They are there to allow for heat expansion, which could otherwise make the engine try to operate with the valves pushed slightly open when they should be closed. Engines these days are virtually all 'overhead valve' units. That is, basically, the valves are on top of the engine, and not let into the side of it (side-valve). But depending on the type of valve mechanism some are referred to as OHV (overhead valve) others OHC (overhead camshaft).

The difference between the two is that the former are 'push-rod' engines, where the valves are operated by rods 'pushed' by a camshaft located further down in the engine – while the OHC unit has valves operated directly by the camshaft, mounted, with the valves on top of the engine. With the former the gap to be measured is maintained between the 'rocker arm', which the push-rod actuates in order to operate the valve, and the valve stem. With the latter, the gap is between the actual cam lobe and the valve stem.

Having said that, there are variations on the theme, with, for instance, some (indirect) OHC units which also use a rocker arm to actually operate the valve. There are also some hydraulically operated valve units, where no maintenance is necessary.

Checking valve clearances

In order to check the valve clearances, you will need the feeler gauges mentioned in the tool section. Each feeler will have its value stamped on it. Your handbook will probably quote the clearances in both Imperial and metric measurements so feelers of either value can be used. Traditionally the measurement (as with plugs and points) was quoted in thousandths of an inch – e.g., 'six thou' or 0.006 in. Nowadays this example would be given in your handbook thus: 0.006 in. (0.15 mm).

Not only do you need to know what your engine's valve clearances should be (and exhaust and inlets may have different gaps) but also whether the measurements are 'HOT' or 'COLD'.

'HOT' meaning the engine has attained normal operating temperature, and the valves checked/adjusted as shortly as possible after switching off. 'COLD' refers to a cooling off period of, say, six hours – so tackling the job after overnight garaging would make sense.

The procedure

First remove the valve cover (Figure 3.1). But before you do so, make a note of the positioning of any other parts you need to disturb – hoses, air cleaner, cables, etc. You will also need a

Figure 3.1. The rocker cover must be taken off for access to the valves, but if you need to remove hoses, cables, or linkage first, make a note of what goes where

replacement valve cover gasket. Each valve must be checked in its fully closed position which means you will have to turn the engine in its normal direction of rotation to ensure this is so. Depending on the engine, it may be easiest to turn it using a spanner on the crankshaft pulley nut, or maybe the generator pulley nut, perhaps leaning on the drive belt a little each time.

Alternatively you can jack up a driving wheel and turn this with the car in gear. Whatever method you use it will be easier with the sparking plugs removed.

Remember also that although most engines turn clockwise, a few – notably some Honda units – turn anti-clockwise.

As for ensuring the valve is fully closed, perhaps the most popular 'short cut', applicable to many four cylinder engines, is to use the 'rule of nine'. This has it that you get any valve in its fully open position, subtract that valve's number from nine, and the answer is the number of a valve that will be fully closed, and can be checked/adjusted. For example, if number three is fully open, number six will be fully closed. You must check with your handbook or dealer whether this will work with *your* engine. If it doesn't there may be another table recommended that will, and sometimes such tables will work on the basis of specific exhausts and inlets.

So you must identify your exhausts and inlets, and you must know also in what sequence (from which end of the engine) your valves are numbered. If you can't determine a short-cut system, the long way round isn't really that long. You simply start at one end with a valve fully open, then turn the engine one complete revolution – the valve will now be fully closed. To check the clearances, select the appropriate size of feeler and insert this between the valve stem and rocker arm – it should be a close sliding fit (Figure 3.2). If it won't go in at all, the clearance is too small. If it feels 'floppy', and with it inserted you can still move the rocker arm up and down, the clearance is too large.

Adjusting valve clearances

With a conventional push-rod engine, adjusting the clearances is usually fairly straightforward. But although some OHC engines are provided with similar adjustment, many will have a more complicated 'shim' adjustment that could call for further dismantling, and maybe the use of a micrometer or other special tools. Happily, with fewer moving parts in the valve gear to wear, an OHC engine usually runs for a considerable mileage

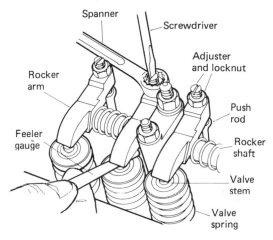

Figure 3.2. Adjustment is correct when the appropriate size feeler gauge is a close sliding fit

before attention to the clearances is needed. The job is then best left to the professionals.

The most common type of adjuster on push-rod engines consists of a ball-ended screw and locknut at the push-rod end of the rocker arm, and usually the screw will be slot-headed. But sometimes it will have a flat on its top end, in which case a small adjustable spanner or self-made tool will be required. To alter the clearance, the locknut must be slackened (preferably with a ring spanner which can then be left in place) and the adjuster screwed up or down with a screwdriver (or other suitable tool) until the clearance is correct. It might take practice to get the hang of it, particularly holding the adjuster still and avoiding altering the clearance again as you tighten the locknut.

The job is easier on some engines – notably a few Ford units – where, instead of having a rocker shaft, each rocker arm pivots on a pedestal and its single self-locking nut is screwed up or down to alter the adjustment (Figure 3.3). With the job done, and after reassembly, run the engine for a while to ensure all is well and that the valve cover joint is oil-tight.

THE ENGINE

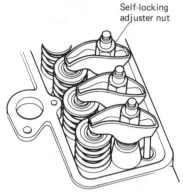

Figure 3.3. Some engines have self-locking adjuster nuts, with each rocker arm mounted on a separate pedestal

Top overhaul

Regular maintenance apart, there is still one job that you might need to tackle sooner or later on a high mileage engine. This is variously described as a 'Top Overhaul', or 'Top Job', but better known to older motorists as a 'Decoke'. The latter term relates to the days of less sophisticated fuels and oils, when engines tended to carbon up their combustion chambers relatively quickly, so the decoke (or decarbonisation) was almost part of regular maintenance. These days, at much higher mileages, the job relates more to a need to clean up and re-seat the valves. The symptoms are poor performance, difficult starting, and increased fuel consumption. A garage compression check (unless you have your own compression gauge) will confirm the need for the job, and pin-point the faulty cylinder if one valve in particular has 'burned out' (Figure 3.4).

From the DIY point of view we can only really deal with the push-rod OHV engine. But a typical top overhaul calls, again, for the valve cover to be removed, the valve gear to be taken off, and the cylinder head to be unbolted and lifted off the engine block. You will need a 'de-coke' set of gaskets, which as well as a

Figure 3.4. A compression check can confirm the need for a top overhaul, and pin-point the faulty cylinder

gasket for the head, should also include enough to cater for any auxiliary components (i.e., carburettor, manifolding, thermostat housing) that might also need to be removed.

With the head on the bench, the valves are removed and everything cleaned up. Finally, any badly burned valves will have to be replaced, otherwise the process of 'grinding-in' each valve will smooth out both the valve face and its seat, so that it will again form a gas-tight seal.

Dismantling procedure

Start by draining the coolant. There may be drain taps (or plugs) on the radiator and cylinder block, or you may need to disconnect the bottom hose and let the coolant out there. If the coolant contains reasonably fresh anti-freeze, you may wish to retain it by draining into a suitable container.

The battery must be disconnected to guard against accidental 'shorts', all hoses should be removed, and you need to work round the engine taking off the cables, linkage, petrol pipe (plug this) and any components that either have to come off or would be better out of the way. Disconnect the exhaust system at the head or down-pipe, as required. Make notes as necessary, so you'll know exactly what goes where on reassembly.

Head removal

With the valve cover off, you may find that some of the cylinder head retaining nuts (or bolts) are hidden beneath the valve gear. In this case the rocker shaft must be unbolted first – slacken all pedestal bolts evenly. The push-rods come out next. (If the rocker shaft is still in place, slacken the adjusters so the rods can be freed). Twist each rod sharply as you lift it, to free it from its cam follower. (The film of oil between the two tends to stick them together). The rods should be kept in order, and an easy way to ensure this is to locate them in numbered holes punched in card.

Check your handbook for the cylinder head tightening sequence, and follow the same order as you slacken off each nut/bolt in turn, just a little at a time. If any bolts are longer/shorter than others, note their positioning. Should the manifolding have been left on, incidentally, you may find it's the ideal answer to the problem now of how to lift the head off.

Note there are precautions you need to take with a 'wet liner' engine – e.g., some Renaults. Wet liner engines are so named because they have removable cylinder bores (the liners). Steps must be taken to prevent the liners becoming dislodged and breaking their bottom seals, which would cause the coolant to leak into the sump. First, when removing the head (which

normally clamps the liners down) leave in a central bolt –
loosened off – and pivot the head about this to break the head
joint before removing this bolt and lifting the head up. This
prevents the head from dragging the liners up with it. Then, with
the head off, use distance pieces and large washers on a couple of
head bolts, temporarily replaced so each bottom washer overlaps
a pair of liners, thus holding them down.

Decoking

The cylinder head has now been removed and is on your
work-bench. The first job is to remove the light coating of
carbon you'll find in the combustion chambers and on the piston
crowns. Tools for the job include a wire brush (rotary type in an
electric drill is handy, Figure 3.5) a scraper, maybe some emery
cloth, and plenty of rag. To avoid the danger of scratches, the

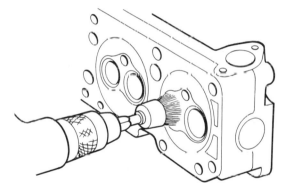

*Figure 3.5. .A rotary wire brush in an electric drill can speed the
'de-coking'*

scraper should be something like a blunt screwdriver, or a
sharpened piece of wood. When working on the block –
including scraping away all traces of gasket or sealant – work on
a pair of pistons brought to TDC (top dead centre) at a time. Use
rag stuffed into the other bores, and all other apertures, to keep
out stray debris.

Valve removal

When all parts are thoroughly clean, remove the valves with a valve spring compressor – often referred to in workshop manuals as a 'special tool'. It is, in fact, a sort of large G-cramp. To some extent these compressors are adjustable, but if you need to buy one (all accessory shops sell them) make sure it is suitable for your particular head. The forked end of the tool locates on the valve spring, straddling the valve stem, and the screwed end goes against the valve head. Having checked that it is securely located, tighten the screw until the spring compresses sufficiently to expose the collets (a pair of semi-circular sleeves) which seat around a recessed section of the valve stem. These collets sit down inside the valve spring cap, but cannot pass right through it – the spring slightly compressed even 'at rest', thus holds the valve firmly against its seat.

Pick out the collets (Figure 3.6) and carefully unscrew the compressor – do not at any stage allow this tool to slip off, since spring, cap, and maybe those collets, will be violently propelled into space, possibly never to be seen again. The collets (easily lost) can be collected together in a tin, but keep the valves,

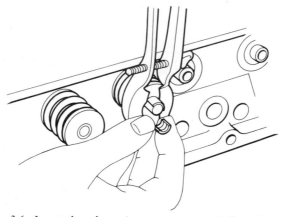

Figure 3.6. Locate the valve spring compressor carefully and tighten just sufficiently to squeeze down the spring and expose the collets. These should be extracted and placed carefully on one side

springs and caps strictly in order of removal. Note also whether any oil seals (small rubber O-rings slipped over the valve stem) are used, and if so exactly where on the valve stem they are positioned (Figure 3.7). And make a note, too, of which way round the valve springs are fitted – possibly they will have a 'closed-coiled' end which fits next to the head.

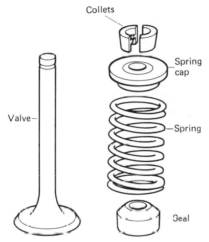

Figure 3.7. Note what goes where, and where – if fitted – the oil seal (often just a rubber O-ring) is located on the valve stem

Grinding-in the valves

In essence, grinding-in the valves is a very simple operation, but a rather tedious one. The 'special tool' for this job is basically a stick with a different sized rubber sucker at each end. These valve grinding sticks are available quite cheaply at most accessory shops. You also need a tin of grinding paste – usually sold in double-ended versions with fine paste at one end, coarse the other. If any of the valves are badly 'pock-marked' or burned, they might need replacement out of hand. But if they are salvageable you'll need the coarse paste to start with. Minor imperfections can be dealt with using the fine paste.

Unfortunately, if any valve seats are badly burned or otherwise damaged you might need to take the head to a machining specialist, who will re-cut or renew the seats. Alternatively, you might be able to hire some valve seat cutters and re-face them yourself.

Presuming things are not too bad, smear a little of the appropriate paste around the seating edge of the valve, and attach the appropriate end of the grinding stick to the valve face. Then replace the valve in its correct guide and start grinding – using a boy-scout fire making action on the valve stick. It might take you a while to get the hang of twisting that stick between the palms of your hands, while at the same time maintaining a light pressure on the valve (Figure 3.8). Eventually, however, you'll

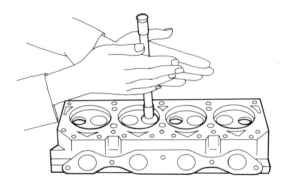

Figure 3.8. Grinding-in may be tedious but it is vital to the success of the job

get the knack, including the need to occasionally lift the valve and rotate it a quarter turn or so to keep the paste and the action evenly distributed. Some 'old hands' position a light coil spring under the valve head to assist this lift and turn procedure.

Continue the grinding operation (adding more paste as necessary) until you obtain an unbroken matt grey ring on both valve and seat. One way of checking this out is to make a number of radial pencil marks around the valve face, then rotate the

valve a few times on its seat. If the job has been successful, all
the lines will have been cut through, showing that the mating
surfaces are in perfect harmony. When all valves are successfully
ground-in (not having skimped anywhere) it is essential that all
traces of grinding paste are cleared from valves and combustion
chambers. Also remove any carbon left in valve ports or
anywhere else on the head you couldn't get at previously with
the valves in place.

Reassembling the valves

As you reassemble, check that all valves and parts are in their
original order, and don't forget to fit (where used) the valve stem
oil seals. New ones should have been supplied in the decoke set.
Again be careful that the spring compressor is securely located
and ensure that the collets are properly positioned. You should
also coat the parts in clean engine oil as you reassemble them, to
provide lubrication when the engine is first started, for it will be
a while before oil is pumped to the valve gear.

Finally, some mechanics of the old school 'clout' the valve
stems with a soft hammer after reassembly, to settle the parts
and reassure themselves things are properly located.

Refitting the head

Make sure both head and block faces are clean (no stray bits of
grit or gasket) then position the new head gasket on the block.
Unless otherwise stated, most head gaskets these days are
'coated' and should be assembled dry – no grease, no sealant. It
will probably also be marked 'Top' so you should get it the right
way round. Incidentally, although a bolted head is sometimes
easier to remove than one which has to be freed from studs,
replacing is not always so easy. For with nothing to locate them
initially, it can be difficult getting head, gasket and block into
perfect alignment so the bolts can be inserted and pick up their
threads cleanly. One answer is to obtain (or make) a couple of
studs having the correct thread size, so these can be screwed in

temporarily, and then gasket and head lowered into place and some bolts located.

Tighten all nuts/bolts progressively, in the sequence given, and to the recommended torque (Figure 3.9). Replace and/or re-connect all other parts, and remember to refill the cooling system. Don't forget, also, that although the valve clearances

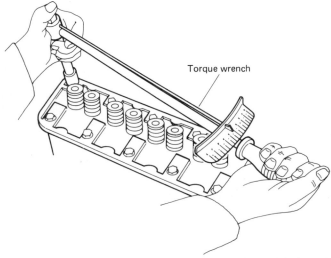

Figure 3.9. Use a torque wrench to tighten the cylinder head bolts to the correct setting, and follow the tightening sequence recommended by the manufacturer

will have had to be re-set, at this stage, particularly if the settings are normally 'Hot', they can only be rough and ready. You can re-check them after you have run the engine for a while, and assured yourself all is well, with no oil or water leaks.

It will be a while before everything settles down, and it's usually recommended that after, say, 100 miles or so, the head bolt torque should be rechecked – to do this properly, incidentally, each should be slackened a little first. At the same time, the valves can be re-set, and possibly the carburation and ignition settings will also require re-adjustment.

Bottom end overhaul

As the terminology suggests, a bottom end overhaul is literally the opposite of a top overhaul, in that it deals with the bottom of the engine, specifically the crankshaft main bearings and connecting rod big end bearings. Generally the pistons and piston rings would be dealt with at the same time.

The problem is that very often this kind of work demands that the engine must be removed from the car. This can be a daunting task, although it is not impossible if you have a strong enough garage beam, and also possess (or can hire) a suitable hoist. If there is not a handy garage beam, it may be possible to rig a tripod or gantry of some sort.

Some engines will lift away from the transmission, some will require the engine and transmission to be removed as a unit, and with others it may be possible, or desirable, to first remove the transmission – e.g., on an in-line engine, rear wheel drive car, unbolt and withdraw the gearbox backwards from the engine. There are so many possible variations from car to car that it is impossible to be specific. But it is as well to appreciate the likely problems before embarking on an overhaul of this magnitude.

Limited overhaul

A possibility that can be borne in mind is that limited overhaul is sometimes possible with the engine *in situ*, provided the sump can be removed. In this case at least the connecting rod bearings (the 'big ends') can be renewed, but rarely all the crankshaft main bearings. Also, with the cylinder head off, the pistons can be removed, for attention to the rings or renewal of the pistons.

Exchange engines

If your engine does require complete overhaul, you need first to look at the price of reconditioned exchange engines. This is a flourishing, competitive market these days, and bearing in mind the time and effort involved in a DIY overhaul, as well as the high cost of parts, you may well feel an exchange unit is the more sensible course.

4

The cooling system

Although we call it the cooling system, its function is not only to stop the engine getting too hot, but at the same time to prevent it getting too cool! In fact, the nearer to boiling point an engine can be run the better its efficiency will be.

There are some critical requirements for the cooling system to consistently tread the thin dividing line between too hot and too cold – and also avoid the extreme disasters of boiling or freezing. Let's look at some.

Coolant level

The level must be maintained as marked on the expansion tank of a semi-sealed cooling system, or just below the filler neck on the radiator of an unsealed system – or wherever else your handbook specifies. It should be checked at least once a week, when the engine is cold.

But note that it's a level that drops. When it continues to drop that is cause for worry. Some engines seem determined to set their own level – always quickly dropping back to this, no matter how often you top up. However, a level that continues to fall demands urgent investigation. The more likely causes will become apparent as we deal with the various components of the cooling system (See Figure 4.1).

The fan belt (or drive belt)

We are talking of the belt that drives the water-pump and generator and maybe the fan blades as well. If the pump stops,

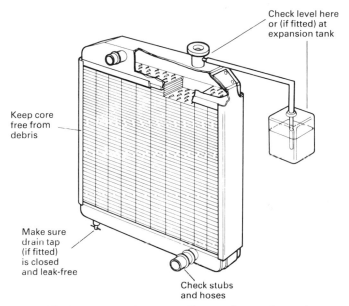

Figure 4 1 This rather schematic radiator and expansion tank set-up serves to highlight important check-points

through belt breakage, the coolant circulation stops, and over-heating will soon follow. Also a worn or badly adjusted belt may slip (accelerating its wear) and fail to turn the pump fast enough for efficient circulation.

Where the belt does drive the fan, as well as the water-pump and generator, it's still a fan belt. But many modern engines have thermostatically controlled electric fans. These are switched on or off by a heat-sensing switch mounted within the cooling system and – in theory at least – maintain the engine at a more efficient operating temperature than the constantly rotating mechanical fan. In this case the belt, still driving generator and water pump though not the fan, is more likely to be called just a 'drive belt' or sometimes 'generator drive belt'.

Note, incidentally, that we're more worried about the belt than the fan. For instance, should an electric type fail, it could be some time (depending on weather and traffic conditions) before serious overheating occurs – witness the fact you'll rarely hear your thermo fan operating. And how long a system with a mechanical fan could survive without the fan blades turning would vary a lot from engine to engine. Indeed, in winter some motorists used to remove the fan blades anyway.

However, it's all rather academic if the base problem is a broken belt, for no engine is going to last long without a water pump – and eventually you're going to run out of electricity, too. Belt adjustment or renewal is dealt with later, in the 'Electrics' chapter.

The hoses

If you're losing coolant, the hoses are prime suspects. These harden with age and can develop cracks. Conversely, if attacked, say, by oil, they may soften and blow-out under pressure. Hose securing clips must be sound and properly tightened (Figure 4.2). But as hoses harden with age, their joints become less sound, and tightening their clips may only aggravate the problem. Look for cracks at the bends in hoses – straightening out the hose at this point may reveal a myriad of tiny cracks, which, if not leaking now, soon will be.

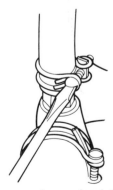

Figure 4.2. Hoses must be sound and their clips secure

Fitting new hoses

Having loosened off its clips (if necessary soak these in penetrating oil first) the old hose may need some forceful twisting to break its seal at the stubs, but take care not to fracture the stub. If necessary, split the hose with a sharp knife, and peel off the remains – being careful with that knife. The next job is to thoroughly clean up those stubs, filing off any imperfections and finishing off with emery cloth.

Don't forget to position the clips (new ones, preferably of the flat, 'worm-drive' type) on the new hose before you position this on the stubs. Check, too, that these clips are the best way round for easy screwdriver access to their tightening screws. If necessary, smear some washing-up liquid on the stubs to help the hose slide home. Afterwards tighten the clips firmly, but not to the extent that they bury themselves in the hose.

The pressure cap

The pressure cap allows pressure from the coolant expanding as it heats up within the cooling system to rise to a predetermined point – say 7 or 13 PSI. The reason is that the pressurised coolant can reach a higher temperature (better for engine efficiency) without actually boiling. The pressure cap is fitted to the radiator of a basic cooling system, or on the expansion tank of a semi-sealed system. Beyond the predetermined point the cap will vent to atmosphere. There is a secondary valve which allows air back into the system, to prevent a vacuum forming as the engine cools down. Obviously if the cap starts venting below its intended pressure, the coolant will escape.

The cap should never be removed while the engine is hot, or a nasty scald could result from escaping steam. If an emergency means the cap *must* be taken off before the engine is completely cool, wrap rag round it and your hands, and open the cap in two stages – the first half turn or so to allow internal pressure to escape.

If you suspect the cap may be faulty, your local garage will have the equipment to run a pressure check on both this and, for that matter, the cooling system as a whole.

The radiator

The heart of the cooling system is the radiator itself, and to do its job properly air must be able to pass through it, and water circulate within freely. And, of course, it must be free from leaks.

Ensuring an unrestricted air-flow involves keeping the cooling fins (the core, mesh or matrix, as this section may be called) free from accumulation of summer flies, autumnal leaves and congealed oil. Leaks within the matrix often require professional repair. There's little the DIY motorist can do other than add a proprietary sealing compound to the coolant, and hope for the best – and, to be fair, if the leak is relatively minor these sealants often do work.

Leaks in the top (header) or bottom tanks (usually on a seam, or around a hose stub) can sometimes be tackled with a small blow-torch and solder produced for this purpose – obviously the radiator would have to be drained first. Alternatively the sealant might cure these leaks, too.

(Incidentally 'top' and 'bottom' tank doesn't always apply these days, since in some modern cars the radiator is mounted on its side.)

Back-flushing

Particularly on older cars, the build-up of sediment or sludge within the radiator may slow circulation to the point where the cooling action is practically inoperative, and the engine overheats.

Flushing by means of simply opening the drain tap or – preferably, and maybe necessarily – removing the bottom hose, and running the garden hose into the filler neck *may* clear the system. But bearing in mind the sludge has circulated with the coolant in its normal direction of flow before ending up somewhere, what is often needed is flushing in the *opposite* direction to shift it. This is known as back-flushing.

The procedure

Follow this procedure, and the engine block can be similarly flushed at the same time:

● Drain the system (filler cap removed) and disconnect the top and bottom hoses. Remove the thermostat housing on the engine and withdraw the thermostat (more of this unit later).

● Careful tapping with a soft hammer, and maybe a liberal dose of penetrating oil down the locating studs, may be necessary to shift stubborn thermostat housings.

● Wrap rag around the end of your garden hose so that it is a tight fit in the *bottom* hose stub of the radiator. Run the water (preferably mains pressure) until the overflow from the filler neck looks to be clean and free-flowing. In some cases it may be preferable to remove the radiator, and invert it while flushing.

The same procedure can be used on the engine, by sealing the hose this time into the thermostat bowl.

Afterwards both radiator and engine can be flushed in the normal direction, until you're happy with both the rate of flow and the cleanliness of the overflow. For systems which are really badly clogged with scale, there are flushing compounds which are poured into the radiator and the engine run for a while before embarking on this hose-flushing procedure.

The thermostat

It is the thermostat that allows the engine to reach its designed operating temperature as quickly as possible, and maintain it there.

In effect, it is a temperature-sensitive valve which closes off the coolant flow to the radiator until the engine has heated up the relatively small amount of water in the cylinder jacket. When the requisite temperature is reached (say, 88°C) the expansion of a wax pellet or of bellows (depending on the thermostat type) forces open the valve, allowing normal circulation of the coolant throughout the system.

When the engine runs persistently cool – shown on the temperature gauge, or by poor heater output or increasing fuel consumption – or overheats with no sign of coolant leaks or slipping fan belt, suspect the thermostat (Figure 4.3). The

Figure 4.3. The thermostat must help the system warm up quickly and then maintain it at the designed operating temperature

bellows type will usually fail in the open position (over-cooling) while the wax type can fail open or closed (the latter causing over heating).

If there is any doubt about its condition, or if it is anyway an elderly unit, it should be renewed as a matter of course when servicing the cooling system.

Fitting a new thermostat

First remove the old unit, as described under 'back flushing' – note that as a rule you would need to drain the coolant to a level only just below that of the thermostat housing.

Clean up the housing and flange faces thoroughly, and when installing the new unit note it should have an arrow or some indication on it which should face towards the outlet to the radiator. Use a new gasket, smeared with grease or an appropriate sealant. Particularly with an alloy top cover, it may pay to 'scrub' this on emery paper laid on a flat surface (e.g. plate glass) until, checked with a straight-edge, it is seen to be perfectly true.

Anti-freeze

The anti-freeze will have to be renewed anyway if you have drained the system for flushing out. Also, the corrosion inhibitors in anti-freeze do weaken eventually, as does the anti-freeze/coolant mixture strength after a long period of regular topping up of the radiator – unless an anti-freeze/coolant mixture is used for this topping up.

Check your car's coolant capacity in the handbook and buy sufficient anti-freeze of reputable make to allow a mixture of the recommended strength. For example, if your coolant capacity is 12 pints, a recommended 25 per cent mixture – usually the minimum – would require three pints of anti-freeze, 33 per cent four pints (probably the safest average) and 50 per cent six pints. Often litres and pints are quoted – if litres only are quoted, the principle is the same, but the arithmetic may be harder.

There are two ways of adding the mixture to the system. Either mix up the required quantity of coolant/anti-freeze (e.g., 12 pints) first, then pour this into the radiator or pour the anti-freeze (e.g., four pints) into the radiator, then pour in water until the required level is reached. Make sure the drain taps are closed, and pour slowly to minimise the chance of air locks. A ready-mixed solution should also be added to the correct level in an expansion tank.

When the level appears to be correct, run the engine for a while with the radiator cap off. The level may settle as minor air locks disperse. Top up as required, stop the engine, and if all appears to be well, replace the cap. Where air locks persist, however, the coolant may threaten to overflow – replace the cap quickly, and switch off the engine.

Bleeding the system

Some cars have a complicated anti-air lock procedure, which can only be followed using the car's workshop manual. However, the following procedure will generally work, particularly with the problem of an air lock in the heater system. This is betrayed by poor heater output or heater hoses which remain cool to the touch with the engine running and otherwise at correct temperature. Be careful how you approach the hoses, and first make an initial check on the radiator top hose – you should feel this warm up as the thermostat opens.

● Loosen the heater return hose (the one that leads to the radiator bottom hose, or adjacent stub at the water pump) then restart the engine.

● Now, with the engine running, pull the hose off its stub completely and wait until water flows freely from it.

● Replace the hose, keeping the engine running, and hopefully both heater hoses should now be felt to be getting well and truly hot, showing that the air lock has been dispersed. Switch off the engine.

● Make sure all hose clips are secure, and when the engine has cooled down, recheck the coolant level.

General

Over the next few weeks keep a particularly wary eye open for leaks. There is a myth that anti-freeze causes leaks. It doesn't – it finds them. Because it has a lower surface tension than water, anti-freeze will flow out through gaps or holes which are too small to let ordinary water through. It's possible you might need to tighten the odd hose clip here or there. Remember that when you need to top up the system it's best to do so with a ready-mixed solution kept handy for this purpose. Using water alone dilutes the content, and weakens the frost protection. Remember, too, that anti-freeze is a good paint stripper – if any gets spilt on the bodywork, wash it off immediately.

To sum up the possible causes of leaks, apart from failing hoses there are various possibilities. The pressure cap on the radiator or expansion tank could be faulty, the radiator itself could be leaking, so could the water pump, or a faulty cylinder head gasket could be letting coolant escape into the engine. The latter can be the most puzzling, since there will be no signs of coolant 'escape' under the bonnet.

There is also the possibility of a cooling system fault (like a partially blocked radiator) causing over-heating, and the coolant boiling off via the pressure cap. Or the fault could, again, be that cylinder head gasket, for this can work two ways: the coolant could be escaping at the head joint, or the hot combustion gases could be escaping into the coolant, causing it to boil.

The water pump

On some older cars there may be a grease nipple, or a plug on the water pump which at service intervals must be removed and substituted by a grease nipple (Figure 4.4). But most pumps these days have sealed-for-life bearings, and rarely will any overhaul kit be available. Should the pump bearings fail (betrayed both by noise and the ability to rock the fan blades or pulley) of if it starts to leak (both problems often going hand-in-hand) the only cure is to take off the old and bolt on a new.

Figure 4.4. The only cure for a faulty water pump these days is to renew it. This is an older example, fitted with a grease nipple – most modern units have sealed-for-life bearings

5

Ignition

More and more cars these days are fitted with electronic ignition as standard. But even where their maintenance requirements are practically nil it's prudent to cast a regular eye over them, checking, for example, that the component parts are clean and dry, and that all insulation and connections are sound. Even where the system is electronic there are still the sparking plugs to consider, and of course many of you will also have vehicles fitted with conventional ignition systems. Eventually, of course, we may have to refer to the electronic systems as 'conventional'.

Sparking plugs

Many service schedules will suggest you clean and regap the plugs at, say, 6000 miles, and renew them at 12 000. The HT (high tension) leads should also be checked. Pull off the HT lead caps carefully, and if necessary use numbered clothes pegs or tags to identify the leads. It's also a good idea to use something like a small paintbrush to clear away dirt from around the plug before removing it, to prevent any abrasive debris from falling into the cylinders. See Figure. 5.1.

Be careful to seat the plug spanner squarely on the plug, since if the tool tips to one side there is a risk of cracking the ceramic insulator. The rubber inset on many plug spanners guards against this, and will also grip the plug stem so you won't drop the plug into the depths. Always use one of these when working on the VW Beetle and other VWs using the air-cooled engine, since the plugs are hidden beneath the engine cowling.

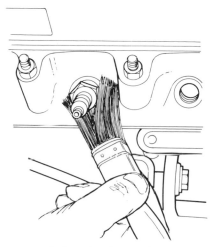

Figure 5.1. It is a good idea to brush away dirt before removing sparking plugs

Cleaning the plugs

You can have your plugs sand-blasted clean at your local garage. But, provided the plugs are not too carboned up (incidentally, soaking in vinegar overnight will soften such deposits) or oiled up – in which case maybe the engine is in need of overhaul – most motorists will manage quite satisfactorily with a wire brush sold for the purpose. Purists sometimes argue that this risks depositing metallic traces on the insulators that could cause shorting out, nevertheless it is a method that has been used by motorists since the early days to good effect.

Use a piece of folded fine-grade glasspaper passed between the plug electrodes to clean these up. If necessary a points file can be used to square up the edges of the side electrode, since sharp edges allow a better spark. However, it could be argued that if the plugs require attention to this extent they are probably in need of renewal. If the plugs are taken out one at a time, this not only avoids the risk of mixing up the cables, but also allows you to check the individual performances of the cylinders, by looking at the condition of the plug electrodes. When a plug has been operating normally in an efficient engine, with the carburettor delivering the correct mixture, the centre electrode insulator and the inner body of the plug will bear a powdery, chestnut brown deposit. The deposits to beware of are black, especially if they appear to be oily. The latter is the result of too much oil finding its way into the cylinder, either from below (e.g. via worn piston rings) or from above (via worn valve guides or stems, etc.). It means that the engine needs an overhaul. A fluffy black deposit usually indicates that the mixture is too rich, and that the carburettor needs adjustment. However, on odd occasions the cause can be incomplete combustion of the mixture, possibly as a result of some ignition fault, or due to the engine being allowed to 'tick-over' for long periods. Or the air cleaner may be choked with dirt.

A whitish centre electrode which appears to be slightly blistered indicates that the engine has been running too hot. Where a vehicle is driven consistently at high speeds, and loaded up well, this overheating may be inevitable. On the other hand it might be due to something amiss in the cooling system, or to the ignition timing being wrong, or the fuel mixture being too weak.

Adjusting the plug gap

To check the plug gap, select a feeler gauge of the appropriate value as specified in your handbook (e.g., 0.025 in., or '25 thou') and check that it is a close sliding fit between the electrodes. Should adjustment be required, carefully bend the side electrode until the gap is correct. An 'ignition set' comprising a number of commonly used feeler gauge sizes for both contact-breaker points and plug gaps, and a points file, will also usually incorporate an electrode bending tool (Figure 5.2).

In service, erosion of the electrodes widens the gap, so adjustment will require the side electrode to be bent towards the centre electrode. Careful tapping with a hammer can also be used to achieve this.

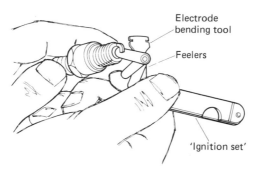

Figure 5.2. An 'ignition set' contains appropriate feeler gauges and plug side electrode bending tool

You should also ensure that the plug stems are clean, since any dirt here, particularly oily dirt, can encourage the HT current to 'track' to earth.

If there is a sealing washer fitted, check that this is not excessively flattened. Plugs having a taper seat (without a washer) must not be over-tightened, or next time you may find it impossible to remove them. Although as a rule-of-thumb plugs should be screwed in hand-tight, then nipped up a further quarter of a turn ($^1/_{16}$th of a turn for tapered plugs) using the spanner, it is as well to check whether a specific torque is specified on your engine. See Figure 5.3.

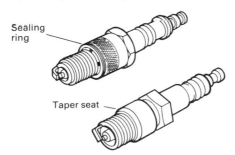

Figure 5.3. The plug at the top is a traditional example, having a sealing washer, while the lower one is of the more recent taper seat type

Both the threads in the engine and on the plug should be clean
and free from carbon. And with aluminium cylinder heads it is
vital that you ensure the plug does not enter cross-threaded,
since with the latter it is easy to strip the threads in the head – a
particularly expensive mistake on VW air-cooled engines. With
these I always smear the plug threads with something like
Copaslip or graphited grease, and make absolutely sure that the
plug is screwing in easily by hand before proceeding too far.

HT leads

Examine the HT leads and ensure that the insulation looks
sound, and all connections are clean and secure. The modern
suppressed, carbon-cored leads tend to deteriorate faster than
the old copper-cored types, and after extended mileage it's
advisable to renew them. Replacement plug lead sets of both
types are available, though remember the copper cored ones
need resistive plug caps and an in-line suppressor in the lead
from distributor to coil, to prevent radio interference. Incidentally, misfiring caused by HT current tracking through poor (or
damp) insulation or bad connections can often be pin-pointed by
opening the bonnet after dark and watching for the sparks.

Contact-breaker points

The contact-breaker (CB) points must be sound, clean and
properly adjusted. Typically, they would be serviced at 6000
miles and renewed at 12 000 miles. Since sooner or later the CB
points must be renewed, and this also entails obtaining the
correct adjustment, it is necessary to understand both operations. However, as distributor layout and contact-breaker
components may vary from make to make, I can only suggest a
general procedure. To gain access to the points, the distributor
cap (held by clips or screws) must be removed, then the rotor
arm, and possibly a dust shield as well. See Figure 5.4.

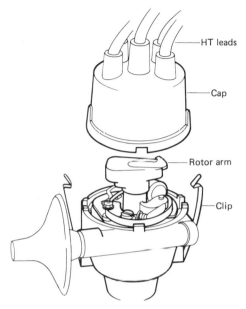

Figure 5.4. In a basic distributor set-up the cap may be held by clips or screws, and there might be a dust shield between the rotor and points

Cleaning the CB points

The points can be cleaned, rather like the spark plug electrodes, by passing a points file, or folded piece of glass paper, between them a few times. However, if this procedure fails to remove any suggestion of a 'pit' that may have formed on the one and a corresponding 'pip' on the other, then they are due for renewal whatever the mileage.

Renewing the points

Note the various LT (low tension) connections to the contact-breakers may consist of a tag (maybe shared also with the condenser lead) secured by a nut and insulating sleeve on a post at the far end of the moving contact's spring blade, or the lead may be bolted to an insulated block on the side of the distributor (the moving contact spring blade also bolted or slotted in at this point). There may be a lead, integral with the contact set, which pushes into a terminal at the side of the distributor, with, again, the spring blade slotted into an abutment at this point.

Examine the set-up on your distributor closely, and preferably make notes and/or a sketch so you can be sure of getting it all correctly reassembled. See Figures 5.5 to 5.7. With the end of the spring blade disconnected, the moving contact may now be free to be lifted away, or it may still remain attached to (but insulated from) the fixed contact plate. Generally, whether of this one-piece design, or where the two contacts are separate items, there will be a single screw securing the fixed contact to the distributor base plate. Remove this screw, and the points can be lifted away.

Before fitting the new points make sure the distributor base plate and the cam lobes are clean – a fresh smear of HMP grease

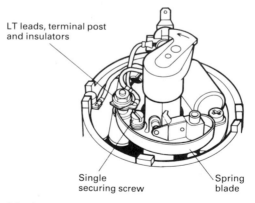

Figure 5.5. A common set-up will have the spring blade of the moving contact and the LT connections held by a nut on a terminal post, but insulated from it – it is vital that you note the position of insulators, leads and washers. Quite often this will be a one-piece contact set, held by a single screw through the fixed plate

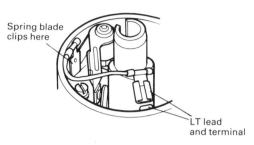

Spring blade
clips here

LT lead
and terminal

Figure 5.6. Here the LT lead pushes onto a terminal and the spring blade clips on at the side

should be given to the lobes. In fact, if your service schedule suggests a few drops of oil for the distributor (usually through apertures in the base plate) it would be convenient to do this with the points out of the way. Wipe away any surplus afterwards. It would also be wise to wipe the contact faces of the new points with petrol or paraffin, since sometimes these will have a protective coating while in stock.

Note also that the fixed contact securing screw can be awkward, particularly during reassembly, and may try to

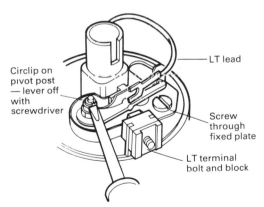

LT lead

Circlip on
pivot post
— lever off
with
screwdriver

Screw
through
fixed plate

LT terminal
bolt and block

Figure 5.7. The LT lead and spring blade are held by the nut and bolt through the terminal block, and the points assembly is secured by the screw and circlip

'escape' into the works. A wise precaution, therefore, is to temporarily block off those apertures in the base plate with tissue. Once this screw has been located in its threaded hole it shouldn't be tightened right up at this stage, since the fixed plate must be free to slide (just) for the adjustment procedure.

Adjusting the points gap

A typical points adjustment procedure requires that the fixed contact's securing screw is slackened just sufficiently so it will slide, but stay put wherever it's moved to, as suggested above. First, of course, the points should be fully open. This is done by turning the engine until the moving contact's fibre heel is on the peak of one of the cam lobes.

Then a feeler gauge of the appropriate value (e.g., 0.016 in.) is entered into the gap between the contacts and checked for a close sliding fit. If adjustment is required, slacken that screw and – usually by inserting a screw-driver blade into a slot provided for the purpose – the fixed contact is levered towards or away from the moving contact until the gap is correct. The screw is then tightened – and the gap re-checked, since the clearance has a habit of altering as the screw is done up.

Dwell angle

Often these days the handbook will specify a 'dwell angle' sometimes as well as, sometimes instead of a CB points gap. Measured, with the engine running, by a form of voltmeter known as a dwell meter, the dwell angle is the number of degrees through which the distributor cam rotates from the point at which one lobe allows the points to close to the point where the next lobe opens them again. It is during this 'dwell' period that the magnetic field in the coil builds up in order to generate the spark at the points.

It can be argued that the dwell angle is itself determined by the points gap. But the advantage of having a measurement which is checked with the engine running is that it eliminates the slackness between parts that exists with the engine at rest, and which can cause a static setting to become inaccurate once the engine is moving, and the slackness is taken up.

Multimeters

At one time measuring the dwell angle was a job that had to be left to professional garages having specialised equipment. But these days most accessory shops will have a number of both individual dwell meters, or – better still – engine 'analysers' or 'multimeters' at a price that most DIY motorists can afford. The latter unit, which combines dwell meter, voltmeter, high and low rpm scales, and ohms and amps measurement, puts precise engine tuning well within your grasp.

Measuring the dwell angle

A typical dwell angle might be quoted in your handbook as 55 ± 5 degrees. To measure this the leads of your dwell meter (or multimeter) would be connected between the distributor low tension terminal or coil CB (or 'neg') terminal and earth (chassis). Now start the engine and let it idle – a reading on the dwell scale of between 50 and 60 degrees would be within tolerance.

If adjustment is required, unless your distributor has the rare luxury of an exterior points adjuster, the engine must be stopped, the distributor cap removed, and the points gap increased or decreased. Note that closing the gap increases the dwell angle, widening the gap lessens the angle.

Ignition timing

Once the points have been correctly set, the ignition timing must be checked – and, as with the dwell angle, more often than not these days your handbook will specify 'stroboscopic' ignition timing, with the engine running, rather than a static setting. Like the dwell angle, it is a progression from 'static' to 'dynamic' setting that, again because it overcomes the backlash problem, allows far more precise tuning.

The setting requires the use of a stroboscopic (strobe) timing light connected to the plug lead of the cylinder used for timing – usually No. 1. With the engine running, the strobe flashes each time the plug fires. This happens briefly but so often at high speed that the light appears to be continuous, and when pointed at the timing marks it has the effect of 'freezing' the moving mark. So it is easy to check its position in relation to the fixed timing mark, and any adjustment necessary can be made with the engine running.

Various strobe lights are also sold by the accessory shops, ranging from cheaper neon types to the more expensive but usually much brighter xenon strobes. Some have a spacer connection that fits between the spark plug and the plug cap, while more expensive models have an inductive pick-up that is simply clamped over the plug lead. There are also types that draw their power from the car battery, and some that have their own internal batteries.

Using a strobe

As well as noting the stroboscopic ignition timing (sometimes both static and strobe figures are given, and sometimes the figure will be the same for both) your handbook should also state whether (as is often the case) the vacuum pipe between carburettor and distributor should be disconnected, to avoid the vacuum advance coming into play and confusing the setting. A typical specification might be ten degrees Before Top Dead Centre, at 850 rpm with a tolerance either way of 50 rpm (expressed as 10°BTDC at 850±50 rpm) with vacuum disconnected.

You also need to know where the timing marks are on your engine, and – if there's a choice, which might occur when basically one engine serves a range of cars – which ones apply to your model. See Figure 5.8. Typical marks would consist of a notch in the crankshaft pulley and a ridge or pointer on the engine, or there might be a series of pointers. There might even

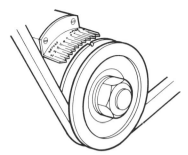

Figure 5.8. There could be a choice of timing marks on the engine and a notch on the crankshaft pulley, or a choice on the pulley and a single mark on the engine

be just the one fixed pointer, and a choice on the pulley. Having noted which marks you need, it might pay to pick them out with a touch of white paint. It's simply a case then of connecting your strobe – usually, as suggested earlier, to No. 1 spark plug lead – starting the engine (vacuum pipe off) and adjusting the carburetter idle screw to get the specified engine rpm. If your car doesn't have a rev-counter, here's a case in point where the rpm scale on a multimeter can assist you.

Now point the light at the timing marks. If the right marks align with each other, all is well. If they don't, adjustment is required.

Adjusting the timing

First stop the engine. Then loosen the distributor clamp bolt just sufficiently so the unit can be turned by hand. Start the engine again, then turn the distributor slightly, grasping its base rather than the cap, to avoid the risk of any shocks from leaking HT. As you turn the distributor you should see the timing marks move either closer together, or further apart. Adjust until they align, then stop the engine and tighten the distributor clamp nut. Finally, start up again and re-check the timing. Afterwards, re-connect the vacuum pipe, and if necessary adjust the idling speed.

Static timing

If your car data allows only for static ignition timing, the procedure is simple enough. First you need a 12 volt bulb with two leads attached to it, either via a holder or soldered directly to the bulb. (Some motorists save old headlamp bulbs, on which only one filament has blown, for this purpose.) Connect the bulb between the distributor low tension terminal (or coil CB/neg) and earth (Figure 5.9). Slacken the distributor clamp bolt. Vernier adjusters (if fitted) should be on their central setting.

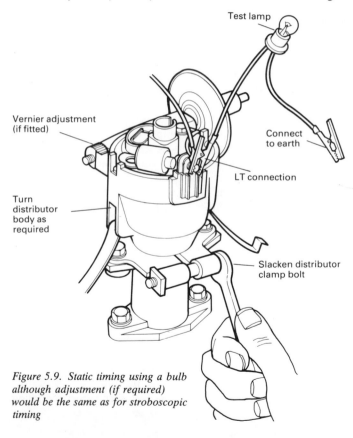

Test lamp

Vernier adjustment
(if fitted)

Connect
to earth

LT connection

Turn
distributor
body as
required

Slacken distributor
clamp bolt

Figure 5.9. Static timing using a bulb although adjustment (if required) would be the same as for stroboscopic timing

Remove the distributor cap and then turn the engine (easier with the plugs removed) until the timing marks are aligned and the rotor arm is pointing towards the segment in the distributor cap for number one spark plug lead. Leave the cap off. Switch on the ignition and turn the distributor body slightly in the direction of rotation of the rotor arm. Turn it back again until the bulb lights, which indicates the CB points have opened.

The timing should now be correct, but turn the distributor back and forth a couple of times until you're certain you have the exact point where the bulb lights. Tighten the clamp bolt.

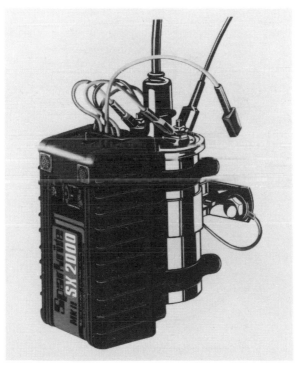

Figure 5.10 If your car doesn't have electronic ignition as standard, you can buy DIY conversion kits from accessory shops

Double check then by turning the engine over a few times, ensuring the timing marks are exactly aligned when the bulb lights. If your distributor does have a vernier adjuster, any fine adjustments needed after road test can be achieved using this.

Electronic ignition

Maintenance requirements here depend largely on the type of system fitted. See Figure 5.10. If your car has an accessory-type electronic ignition system, this may or may not still retain the contact breakers. They will not be carrying as high a current as is the case with conventional ignition, and consequently will not suffer the arcing that causes the pits and pips referred to earlier.

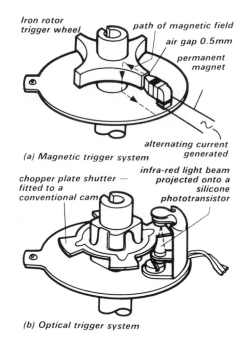

(a) Magnetic trigger system

(b) Optical trigger system

Figure 5.11. Contactless electronic ignition may use magnetic (top) or optical (bottom) triggering systems

But although the gap may no longer be as critical as previously, it is as well to remember that wear of the contact breaker heel will still take place, and unless attended to as normally the gap will eventually close.

Most cars fitted with electronic ignition as standard will have contactless systems (Figure 5.11). Here all that is required is wiping the outside and inside of the distributor cap, plus lubrication as specified previously. With some of the latest systems there are no centrifugal weights, either, the advance and retard also being controlled electronically.

Remember that with most electronic ignition systems the HT output is greater than with a conventional system. Therefore, not only are precautions like keeping all units clean and dry more important (to prevent leakage of the current) but also the system is capable of giving you a more severe shock. So those with weak hearts, or pacemakers fitted, should be particularly cautious.

6

The fuel system

It is true to say that modern carburettors are finely calibrated both for economy and with greater emphasis on restricting the amount of carbon monoxide (CO) emitted by the exhaust, and that they do normally stay in tune longer than did older designs. However, it is *not* true to say that it's impossible for the DIY motorist to tackle any work on them, or that the European Emission Regulations say you mustn't tamper with their adjustments. In fact the Regulations have resulted in all carburettors since about 1977 having mostly tamper-proof adjustment points, to discourage anyone not having the special tools or equipment from tinkering with them.

The EEC regulations

In fact, also, what EEC Regulation 15 says is that the carbon monoxide level in the exhaust gases emitted at idling speed should not exceed 4.5 per cent by volume. This is not enforced in the UK, although many car manufacturers operate on an even lower percentage. There is no law here or on the Continent that says you mustn't tamper with the adjustment, although exhaust spot-checks on the Continent could result in a fine for exceeding that 4.5 per cent.

The myth

As far as the UK is concerned, on the one hand there is the myth that you mustn't 'break the seals' and adjust your carburettor, while on the other some surveys have shown that as many as seven cars out of ten are running around with over-rich adjustments, wasting petrol and exceeding the EEC pollution standard.

However, it must be admitted that the individual complexity of today's carburettors makes it impossible for a book of this kind to cover specific mixture adjustment – although there may be other general possibilities (e.g., choke and idle speed) which we will discuss later.

Sources of information

If you can obtain the information on your individual carburettor, perhaps from its maker, or the car manufacturer (and we have covered some in *Motorist* magazine) then there are also DIY tuning aids you can use to obtain the correct adjustments. Note that there are service kits available from auto accessory and carburettor factors that should also contain the relevant data.

The tools

For removing the seals, usually no more that a sharp screwdriver or scissors point should be needed to prise out the plastic or wax plug, or lever off a metal cap. Beneath the seal will often be a conventional screw adjuster, or perhaps an unorthodox screw head demanding, say, a two pronged 'tool' easily cobbled up from your scrap-box. A number of firms (the carburettor manufacturer, even) will market the hexagonal or bladed tools required on some constant-depression carburettors having internal adjustment. Look for these tools in auto accessory shops.

The tuning aids

For getting the idling speed right there is the rpm scale on the multimeter which we have mentioned earlier on, in the Ignition chapter. Then there are piston (or valve) lift gauges and air intake gauges for 'balancing' twin or multiple carburettor installations.

As far as the mixture is concerned there are DIY CO meters with which you can measure the exhaust emission. There is also a

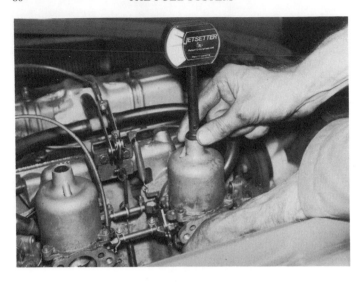

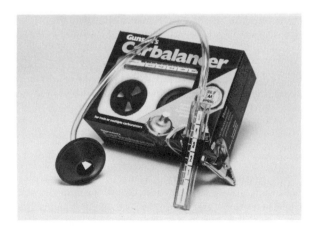

Figures 6.1, 6.2. Tuning aids for balancing twin or multiple carburettor installations include devices for measuring piston (or valve) lift and for balancing their air intake

novel glass-topped sparking plug (called Colortune) that enables you to see the colour of the burning gases and adjust accordingly, having temporarily fitted the device in place of the conventional sparking plug. And not to be overlooked is the humble vacuum (or performance) gauge that invariably comes with instructions that include how to set up the carburettor. So, although this book cannot give you the specific adjustment procedure for your car, at least you know that the possibilities for doing it yourself still exist (see Figures 6.1 and 6.2).

General

On some carburettors it might be easy enough to make basic adjustments to the idle (tick-over) speed and sometimes, also, to the fast-idle setting.

Idle adjustment

Other than on the more complex units, the idle adjustment screw will be found very close to the spindle on the carburettor which operates the throttle valve. It bears on the throttle linkage in such a way that screwing it up or down simply closes or opens the valve a little.

The engine should be at normal operating temperature before attempting any adjustment, and ideally you should have a multimeter with an rpm scale to obtain the specified idling speed – typically, around 800 rpm.

If you lack this meter, all you can do is seek the slowest, smoothest idle that won't have the engine stalling on you in traffic situations. See Figures 6.3 to 6.5.

Fast idle

For the choke-fast-idle adjustment look in the vicinity of the idle screw for a similar screw, probably with a locknut. Typically, this screw will bear on a cam which is part of the choke linkage. Normally, with the choke pushed in there should be a gap between the screw and cam – a workshop manual would usually specify a feeler gauge measurement for the gap. There should be an initial movement when the choke knob is pulled out that opens the throttle slightly *before* it starts to operate the choke flap itself. Typically, this arrangement comes into its own after a cold start when the engine will no longer run on choke, nor will it keep going when the choke is pushed right in. But that initial movement of the choke knob (trial and error will find it) simply speeds up the idle until the engine is warm enough to tick over normally.

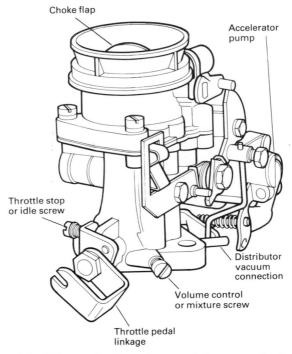

Figure 6.3. Older-type fixed-jet carburettors had an exposed volume (or mixture) screw, usually screwed inwards to weaken the mixture or outwards to enrich it, and balanced against the throttle stop screw for the smoothest tickover. Adjustments on modern units are often more complex and usually sealed

Sometimes there will be a tab instead of a screw that can be bent carefully to obtain the same result. If further information is unavailable, remove the air cleaner so that you can see the choke flap, and adjust so a comfortable fast idle is obtained before the flap starts to move.

A variation on the theme occurs with some variable jet (or variable choke) carburettors (such as the SU) where a rich mixture for starting is obtained by the choke linkage lowering the jet away from the throttle needle. Here you watch for the initial movement of that jet, rather than a choke flap.

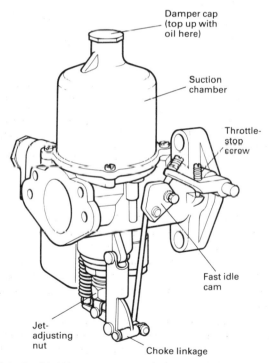

Figure 6.4. On this older type SU variable-jet carburettor the jet adjusting nut would be turned down to richen the mixture, up to weaken it – note also the fast idle adjustment

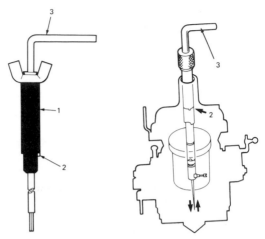

Figure 6.5. On some Zenith-Stromberg CD (constant depression) carburettors, it is the needle height that is altered to vary the mixture. This requires a special tool (available to the DIY motorist at auto accessory shops) to be inserted through the damper orifice. This tool is shown separately (left) and (right) in use: (1) Outer barrel; (2) Locating pin; (3) Allen key – note, the tool must be the right one for the particular carburettor, since the means of locating on the needle varies

Air cleaner

The air cleaner that sits on top of the carburettor will normally contain a filter element which is simply discarded and replaced by a new one at normal service intervals. Note that a dirty element restricts air-flow, and may cause the engine to run as if the choke is in permanent operation, causing sooty spark plugs, rough running, accelerated engine wear, and excessive fuel consumption.

The element can be found under a lid in the air cleaner body, the lid secured maybe by a central wing nut or bolt, or a number of bolts, or simply by spring clips. Note the lid's exact positioning on the body before removing it. See Figure 6.6. There may be separate 'summer' and 'winter' settings for the air cleaner, possibly changed by swivelling its intake away from or nearer to

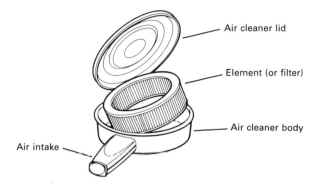

Air cleaner lid

Element (or filter)

Air cleaner body

Air intake

Figure 6.6. The air cleaner element lives under a lid in the air cleaner body

the exhaust manifold, sometimes by swapping a flexible section pipe from one intake to another, or maybe there's an adjustment lever on the body itself.

As well as lubrication of linkage points, some carburettors have a damper which must be topped up with a light oil at regular intervals. Finally, check whether there are any in-line fuel filters in the fuel pipes which should be renewed at specified intervals.

7

Transmission

As well as checking and topping up oil levels as described in the Lubrication chapter, there will usually be other regular service requirements for the transmission system. For instance, if your car has a hydraulically operated clutch, the reservoir on the master cylinder will also require regular checking for fluid level, and topping up as necessary. The fluid used is the same as for the brake hydraulics. If the clutch is mechanically operated, there is usually provision for adjustment of pedal free play which needs to be checked, and maybe reset, at regular intervals. Some early hydraulic units (specifically Mini and other related BL front wheel drive models) also incorporate adjustment points.

Some of those early cars (e.g., the Mini) also have grease nipples on their gearchange linkage. Others (rear wheel drive) will have grease nipples on their propellor shaft universal joints (UJs) or maybe plugs that you remove and temporarily replace with a grease nipple. More recent models will have sealed-for-life UJs. But on all modern front wheel drive models the drive-shaft joints will have gaiters that need to be checked regularly. Should one of these split, and remain unnoticed for long, the joint lubrication can escape, and abrasive road dirt can enter, with speedy ruination of the joint as a sure consequence.

Some rear-engined, or rear transmissioned cars will have similar joints to check on the rear drive shafts.

Clutch free play

Returning to the clutch free play mentioned earlier, this may be referred to in your handbook as 'clutch adjustment'. However, strictly speaking it isn't the clutch itself that is adjusted, but the free play in the pedal-to-clutch linkage. There usually has to be some free play to guard against the clutch running partially disengaged, slipping and eventually burning itself out, or the release bearing rubbing continuously and wearing out prematurely. That said, there are some cars with what are known as 'constant contact' release bearings which have to be set up so there's no free play at all.

Where free play is specified the usual need for adjustment is caused by wear in the linkage, or cable stretch, resulting in so much free play that full pedal movement barely operates the clutch. The problem is usually highlighted by difficult and noisy gearchanges. There will be variations from car to car in where the free play is actually measured. For instance, your handbook may specify a degree of free pedal movement (e.g., an inch) before the pressure of releasing the clutch is felt. In some cases (e.g. 'constant contact') it may be stipulated that the clutch and brake pedals should be level, or that the clutch pedal should be a specific distance from the floor, or even from the steering wheel.

In other cases the free movement may be measured at the clutch operating fork, under the car or in the engine compartment, according to whether the vehicle is front or rear wheel drive, and in still more instances the measurement may be where the clutch cable meets the engine bulkhead.

Adjustment procedure

Mechanical linkage

A typical adjustment on a rear wheel drive car would be underneath, at the clutch operating (or release) lever which protrudes from the clutch housing at the front of the gearbox – where the free play would also be measured as suggested earlier. Here the clutch linkage may terminate in a threaded portion passing through the lever (or 'fork'). There will probably be a nut and locknut, and having pulled the lever away from the nuts (i.e., taking up its free play) you measure the distance between lever and nuts. See Figure 7.1.

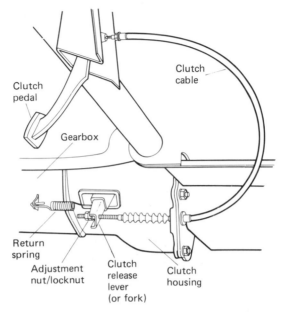

Figure 7.1. Typical rear wheel drive clutch adjustment would be at the release lever (or fork) where this protrudes from the clutch housing and connects to the clutch cable

If adjustment is required to obtain the specified distance, you simply unlock the nuts and turn them in the appropriate direction. Before doing this – or moving the lever – you may need to unhook a lever return spring. Variations on the theme include pulling the cable through the lever until all slack is taken up and then measuring between the nuts and lever, or pulling the cable outer sleeve away from an abutment on the clutch housing and measuring the distance between the abutment and the adjuster nuts.

There may be similar set-ups on the transmission housing under the bonnet of front wheel drive cars. Where adjustment is made at the cable abutment on the engine bulkhead there may again be adjuster nuts, or – simpler – a C-clip in a choice of grooves: typically there should be 5–6 grooves between the clip and its abutment when the cable outer is pulled away from the bulkhead. See Figures 7.2 and 7.3.

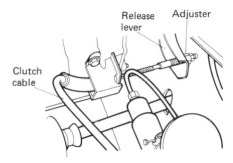

Figure 7.2. Front wheel drive cars may have an adjustment set-up similar to rear wheel drive, but found probably on top of the transmission housing under the bonnet

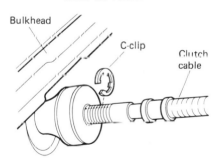

Figure 7.3. Sometimes adjustment will be at the bulkhead, with locknuts or a clip in a choice of grooves

Hydraulic linkages

In the rare event that adjustment is provided on a hydraulic linkage, it could be similar to that described at the clutch operating lever on mechanical linkages (Figure 7.4). Here the push-rod from the clutch hydraulic slave cylinder would act

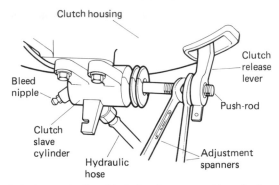

Figure 7.4. A typical adjustable hydraulic set-up, with nut/locknut on the slave cylinder push-rod where it meets the release lever – note the return spring has been removed

directly on this lever, and the push-rod would have a threaded portion and adjuster nuts.

Probably the most common of hydraulic clutch adjustments is that found on the earlier BL front wheel drive cars, typically – of course – the Mini (Figure 7.5). Here there is a clearance

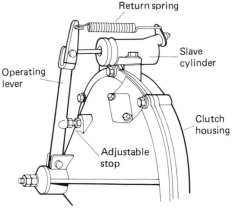

Figure 7.5. On early BL front wheel drive set-ups (e.g. Mini) the clearance is measured with a feeler gauge between the operating lever and an adjustable stop on the clutch housing

prescribed between the clutch operating lever and an adjustable stop on the clutch housing. A typical measurement (using a feeler gauge) would be 0.060 in. on very early cars, 0.020 in. on later ones (1969 onwards) and to check this unhook the spring from the clutch operating lever, pull the lever back, away from the housing and insert the feeler between the lever and the stop. If adjustment is required, slacken the locknut and screw the stop (in effect a bolt) in or out as required. Don't forget to replace the spring afterwards.

Clutch drag

Mechanical

If your clutch adjustment appears to be correct, but you are still getting difficult and noisy gearchanges, and provided you are sure the gearbox is not at fault, it could be that you have a problem known as 'clutch drag. In other words, the clutch is still not clearing properly.

With a mechanical linkage the problem is most likely due to cable stretch, or other wear in the components leading to 'lost motion'. This can be pin-pointed by asking someone to operate the clutch pedal while you examine the linkage, looking for undue delay in one component passing the movement to another. Prime culprits apart from a stretched cable are worn clevis pins and/or the pin holes. If there is no apparent lost motion even as far as the clutch operating lever, it's possible the clutch release bearing is worn. This is the component that actually presses against the clutch to release it. Sometimes this will be a ball-race unit (as it will be in a 'constant contact' set-up) or a ring of carbon in a metal housing.

It is not unknown for the carbon type to wear down to the extent that the pedal linkage will run out of movement before the lever and bearing can exert any force on the clutch. Unfortunately renewal of either type of release bearing calls for the same major dismantling as does the renewal of the clutch itself.

Note, incidentally, that the ball-race unit does not usually wear in this way. But should it start screeching, particularly when the pedal is operated, it may be a warning of wear and loss of lubrication which could eventually cause it to collapse. Other causes of clutch drag (and/or judder) include congealed or burnt oil on the clutch friction lining. Alternatively this oil may cause the clutch to slip (as will a badly worn lining) the symptom being the engine going faster but the car going slower. The oil could be escaping from the gearbox or the engine into the clutch housing. Obviously, again, major dismantling for investigation will be called for.

Clutch drag

Hydraulic

The same problem can occur with a hydraulic unit, although obviously there's less linkage to examine for lost motion. However, you can, again, ask a helper to press the pedal while you watch that push-rod from the slave cylinder. If it barely moves, or fails to move at all, you have a hydraulic fault.

The possibilities include external fluid leaks (which you should be able to see) failure of internal seals in either the master or slave cylinder, or simply air in the system. If pumping the pedal restores clutch movement, albeit temporarily, the latter could be the problem. In this case, provided all seals are sound, you can deal with the problem yourself.

Bleeding the clutch

There should be a bleed nipple on the slave cylinder, to which you can attach a length of rubber or plastic tubing. Immerse the other end of the tube in a little clean hydraulic fluid in a glass jar. See Figure 7.6.

It's preferable to have a helper for the next stage of the operation, for it really needs one person now to use a spanner to carefully open the bleed nipple, while the other briskly presses

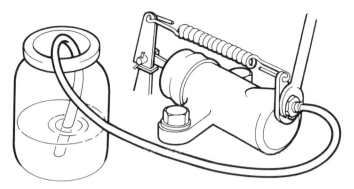

Figure 7.6. Lost motion can be caused by bubbles of air in the hydraulic fluid, in which case bleeding the system may effect a cure

the clutch pedal to the floor and releases it a few times. Bubbles of air should be seen emerging from the tube into the fluid in the jar. Keep the level in the master cylinder topped up, and when bubbles give way to fluid alone, pump the pedal a couple of times more to be sure, then hold it down while your helper tightens the bleed nipple again. If this operation fails to provide a permanent cure, new seals or – if it's a high-mileage car – new components are the only answer. Start with the slave cylinder, in the hope that this more easily overhauled, or less expensive to renew, unit is the faulty one!

Clutch judder

Apart from oil on the friction lining (this unit is also sometimes called 'centre plate' or 'driven plate') clutch judder can also be caused by a centre plate which is badly worn, weak or warped. See Figure 7.7. Note also that the problem can be caused by weak engine or gearbox mountings, or – particularly with BL front wheel drive models – worn engine tie-rod bushes. You can solve this one yourself simply by unbolting the rod between engine and bulkhead and renewing the bushes.

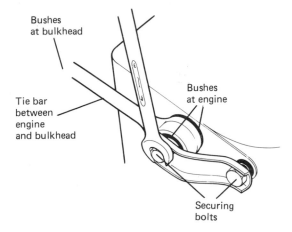

Figure 7.7. Clutch judder can be caused by worn engine tie-rod bushes

Drive shaft checks

As far as front wheel drive is concerned, if you suspect drive
shaft wear, or hear occasional knocking sounds from the front
end, the possibility of worn joints can often be confirmed by
driving the car with the steering on full lock, first one way then
the other. This action will often aggravate the problem, causing
the knocking to be loud and clear.

Renewal or overhaul of the joints is the only cure, as is the
case with rear engine, rear wheel drive, and, for that matter,
with also the joints on the propellor shaft of a front engine, rear
wheel drive car. But with the latter set-up symptoms of wear
include a 'clonk' as the drive is taken up, from rest or from
over-run, and sometimes a vibration felt throughout the car.

You can often detect wear in these propellor shaft universal
joints (U/Js) by grasping the shaft on either side of the joint and
twisting it in opposite directions. Or you can insert a large

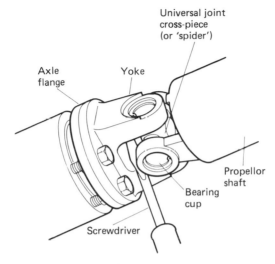

Figure 7.8. You can test for wear in a universal joint (U/J) by levering with a large screwdriver

screwdriver between the central cross-piece (the 'spider') and the yokes of the joint and attempt to lever them apart (Figure 7.8). Any movement perceived with either test points to wear.

Clutch renewal

Rear wheel drive

Whether the car is front wheel drive or rear wheel drive, the work involved in gaining access to the clutch – and whether it's a DIY proposition – will vary from car to car. All this book can do is suggest what may be a reasonably typical procedure. Basically, the gearbox must be withdrawn from the engine, to expose the clutch unit, which will be bolted to the engine flywheel.

To start with, the battery should be disconnected to guard against accidental shorts. Then in most cases the starter motor should be removed, since usually its retaining bolts also help to hold the clutch housing (or bellhousing) to the engine. Also remove the speedometer drive at the gearbox, and any wiring, such as to a reverse lamp. And the clutch linkage and gear stick will also have to be dismantled.

The propellor shaft has to be removed, but before unbolting the rear flange scribe marks on this and the axle flange to ensure exact reassembly. Failure to do this could result in imbalance, and prop-shaft vibration. Then, as soon as the shaft is pulled away at its front end, tie a plastic bag over the gearbox tailshaft to prevent oil loss during subsequent operations.

Since the gearbox rear mounting (effectively the engine rear mounting) will need to be unbolted from the underbody, an additional support must be placed beneath the engine. Ideally, a trolley jack or bottle jack under the sump – with a square of timber against the sump to spread the load – should be used, as you may need to raise or lower the engine/transmission to facilitate both access to clutch housing bolts and eventual removal of the box. But note also that this movement could strain such items as the top hose or exhaust system to the extent that it might be wiser to disconnect them first.

It is also wise to leave a couple of clutch housing bolts (top and bottom, or one each side) loosely in place so you can take stock before actually withdrawing the box. And, of course, you do need to check carefully that *all* bolts are accounted for, and that all necessary bits and pieces have been disconnected.

Removing the gearbox

What you need to consider now is the size and the weight of the box – can you manage it single-handed? Remember it must neither be allowed to hang on the shaft that passes through the clutch, nor must it crash to the ground. So it might be an idea at this stage to re-arrange things to leave the trolley jack free to take the weight of the gearbox and ease the job of pulling it backwards (don't forget those remaining bolts) and wheeling it out from underneath. In point of fact, the box may need some heaving and general persuasion (careful levering, even) before it will part from the engine.

Release bearing

At this stage the release bearing should be inspected for signs of wear. When you consider the work involved thus far, you might well feel it's worth renewing this bearing now as a matter of course, rather than face repeating this dismantling procedure all over again at a later date.

The location of the release bearing in the operating fork in the clutch housing is usually fairly straightforward. Typically, the carbon thrust type sits in half-sleeves at the end of the fork, and is held there by spring clips, while a ball-race type might simply slot into a cut-out on the operating arm, and slide on a guide sleeve. On a front wheel drive assembly, the ball-race may be pressed on to a spigot in the clutch housing cover plate.

The clutch unit

The clutch assembly is usually secured to the flywheel by six or more bolts, and will probably be located also on a couple of pegs (Figure 7.9). If the clutch cover and pressure plate assembly (which may be a coil or diaphragm spring unit) is to be retained, it's good practice to note (or make) alignment marks, so it may be returned to the flywheel in the same position. As with the propellor shaft, this precaution is to avoid causing any imbalance.

You will probably find you need to prevent the flywheel turning while you undo the bolts. This can usually be done by jamming the blade of a large screwdriver in the flywheel ring gear teeth, the screwdriver wedged in the starter motor aperture or against the floor. Loosen all bolts progressively. Then, when you withdraw the clutch unit (it can be quite heavy, incidentally) be careful not to let the centre plate fall, because – even though it may be marked – it's sensible to note which way round it faces. You may note, for instance, that the hub protrudes further one side than the other. Somewhere on its face it may be marked 'flywheel side'.

If there are signs of oil, wet or burned, on the clutch plate, then obviously the cause must be found and rectified before you fit a new clutch and reassemble. Typical suspects are either the

Figure 7.9. The clutch assembly of a rear wheel drive car is secured to the flywheel by six or more bolts and located on dowels

oil seal at the front of the gearbox or at the engine rear main bearing.

If the plate is so badly worn that the rivet heads are exposed, check that the pressure plate and the flywheel face have not been badly scored. Should this be the case, then the pressure plate (or cover plate) assembly must also be renewed, and the flywheel will have to be removed and taken to a machine shop for refacing. Even if the pressure plate looks sound, it's arguable that after long service the diaphragm or coil spring will have weakened, along with other parts, and it might be sensible to renew the assembly out of hand.

Clutch alignment

The most difficult part of reassembly is entering the gearbox first motion shaft through the splines in the centre plate hub, and into the spigot (or pilot) bearing in the flywheel. The problem is making sure the clutch plate is central before you finally tighten the clutch unit bolts. The easiest way is to enter a dummy shaft, which can be a commercial 'mandrel', or an old first motion shaft, from a breaker's yard perhaps (Figure 7.10). Alternatively you can make up your own dummy shaft, using maybe a grinding stick, or length of turned down broom handle, or a socket set tommy bar – wrapping tape round as required to bring it to the right diameter for the centre plate hub.

Figure 7.10. Note the use of a 'mandrel' to centralise the clutch plate when the unit is bolted back on the flywheel

It will help if you put a smear of HMP grease on the gearbox shaft, but rarely will the gearbox slide home without some sweat, and trial and error regarding height and angle. As soon as you achieve even partial success, get a couple of bolts in, both to stop the box sliding away again, and also for possible use – by careful tightening – to help draw the box fully home.

Front wheel drive

With a front wheel drive car, sometimes the complete engine and/or transmission unit will have to be removed for clutch renewal. There are cases, however, where there's room – sometimes by using a jack to tip the engine – to do the job *in situ*. The Mini is a case in point, though note in particular with this one that before removing the flywheel the engine must be at TDC, otherwise a clip on the shaft can slip and jam the engine.

Typically the clutch housing is unbolted and removed, having first unbolted the engine mounting at that end, which is often attached to this housing, and having removed any auxiliary components in the way, as well as the starter motor. The flywheel must be removed because in this transverse engine set-up, the clutch assembly straddles the flywheel, with the spring unit on the outer face, and friction lining and pressure plate on the engine side. Once the spring unit has been unbolted, other bolt holes will be exposed to which a flywheel puller must be attached in order to withdraw this component. Suitable pullers can be bought quite cheaply from auto accessory shops, or perhaps hired from your local garage or tool hire specialist.

Renewing U/Js

With earlier U/Js, the bearings are secured in the yokes with circlips, so renewing them isn't too much of a problem. Some more recent prop-shafts, however, have 'staked' joints, often considered unrepairable, so the expensive answer to worn bearings would seem to be a complete new shaft. But there are now specialist kits, complete with necessary instructions, for the DIY renewal of these joints. The firms making these also market centre bearing kits for split prop-shafts. So check with your auto accessory shop before being persuaded that you need a new shaft.

A typical procedure for renewing conventional U/Js is as follows:

● First remove the shaft as described for clutch renewal, earlier in this chapter. Then take the shaft to the bench. Clean the joints with brush and paraffin, then use proper circlip pliers (pointed pliers may do at a pinch) to remove the circlips from each joint.

● Support one end of the propellor shaft on the bench or a sturdy vice, then use a copper or soft-faced hammer against one side of the swivelling yoke in order to drive out the bearing cup from the shaft on the opposite side. In effect you're using the centre crosspiece of the joint (known as the 'spider') as a drift.

● Turn the shaft over (through 180°) and repeat the operation to drive the other bearing cup from the shaft; where there is insufficient travel of the spider to drive the cups right out of the shaft, use gas pliers (or the vice jaws) to complete their removal. With both cups out, it will be possible to disengage the spider from the yokes on the shaft.

● Now clamp the spider firmly in the vice and use the hammer to strike the yoke downwards so as to drift out the top cup. Turn the yoke and spider over and repeat the process to remove the remaining cup.

● Use a screwdriver blade or similar to clean out the circlip grooves in each yoke, and carefully file away any burrs. Remove two of the cups from the new spider and position their journals in the swivelling yoke – ensure there is sufficient grease in the cups to retain the needle rollers.

● Position the yoke in the vice with a bearing cup each side and use the vice to squeeze the cups into place, checking all the while that the spider journals enter the cups without dislodging the needles. See Figure 7.11.

● Repeat the process in the shaft end yokes, then use a suitable-sized spacer between the vice jaws and each yoke to ensure the cups go far enough in for the new circlips to be located in their grooves. When all circlips have been fitted, tap the joint at each end to drive the bearing cups hard against the clips, so ensuring correct free movement of the joint. Having overhauled both ends of the shaft, oil the splined end before refitting the shaft to avoid possible damage to the oil seal in the gearbox tailshaft. If necessary top up the gearbox oil level.

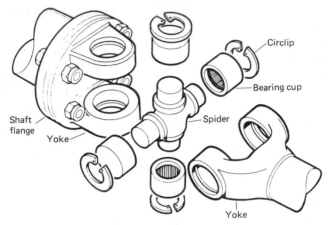

Figure 7.11. This is an exploded view of a universal joint (U/J) for which overhaul kits are available

Joint lubrication

Most replacement U/J kits will have ready-greased, 'sealed-for-life' bearings. However, should a spider having a grease nipple be supplied, when positioning the spider (nipple removed) note that the nipple should be angled away from the body of the propshaft. In some cases, the spider might just have plugs which can be removed at service intervals, and a temporary nipple inserted for greasing. Or, there may be a plug simply to allow charging with grease at this overhaul stage, with no subsequent servicing required. This type of joint will include rubber seals on the legs of the spider.

Drive shafts

(Transmission to road wheels)

The drive shafts to road wheels, as opposed to the gearbox-to-rear-axle propellor shaft, also have various types of universal

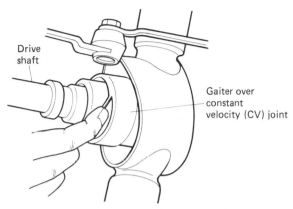

Figure 7.12. Check for split gaiters on the constant velocity (CV) joints of road wheel drive shafts. The loss of lubrication and entry of dirt will hasten the wear that is betrayed by knocking sounds, particularly on lock

Figure 7.13. The rubber 'spider' joints found on the inner end of some drive shafts (e.g. Mini) swell and rot with oil contamination, and in this condition can be heard chafing or knocking on the transmission casing. Some overhaul kits will have a plastic replacement spider

joint. These include rubber 'spider' cross-piece joints, as used on the inner ends of Mini FWD drive shafts (there are 'plastic' replacement kits for these) or the rubber 'doughnuts' used, for instance, on the Hillman Imp and some Triumphs. See Figures 7.12 to 7.14.

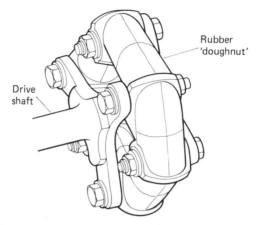

Figure 7.14. This is the rubber 'doughnut' joint found on some Triumph and Hillman Imp cars

On these joints regular checks should be made on the security of U-bolts and general nuts and bolts, and also on the condition of the rubber.

Probably most common these days on front or rear wheel drive shafts, but particularly the front, where they can cope with the steering angles involved, are the constant-velocity (or CV) joints.

The need to check their gaiters, and how to pin-point the knocking noise they make when worn or lacking lubrication was mentioned earlier.

Unfortunately, renewal of joint or gaiters demands removal of the shaft from the car. The procedure will vary from car to car, and the relevant workshop manual will need to be studied.

8

The braking system

General maintenance of the braking system includes keeping an eye on the hydraulic fluid level in the master cylinder, and at service intervals checking on the depth of friction lining remaining on disc pads and brake shoes, and adjusting the latter and maybe the handbrake as required. See Figure 8.1. Front disc

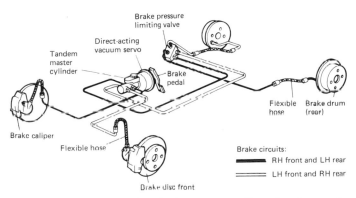

Figure 8.1. A typical modern braking system will employ discs at the front, drums at the rear, and will have a dual (split) hydraulic feed: in this example, the circuit has a diagonal split, so that failure of one circuit will leave one front and one rear brake operating, on opposite sides to retain balance

brakes are self-adjusting as, indeed, are many modern rear drum brake systems. And, of course, some cars have disc brakes front and rear. Note that with a disc brake system, a gradual fall in the hydraulic fluid level is perfectly normal, and is a result of the pistons in the calipers moving further out of their cylinder bores as the pads wear, in order to maintain the close contact between disc and pads that is a feature of this system.

A sudden fall in the fluid level, however, points to a leak somewhere in the system. Prime suspects include master cylinder or slave (wheel) cylinder seals, faulty unions, perished flexible hoses, or rusty metal pipes. These are all faults to look out for during routine servicing where hopefully impending trouble can be spotted before fluid (and braking) loss occurs. Obviously such faults must be rectified as a matter of urgency.

Brake adjustment

Where a disc front and drum rear system incorporates self-adjustment on the rear shoes, something like a ratchet and pawl system will be linked to the handbrake (sometimes the foot brake) mechanism. Each time the brakes are operated any undue shoe clearance will be taken up automatically. Where the system is not self-adjusting, a means will be provided for manually adjusting the shoes closer to the drums. If you're not sure what system your car has, check with your handbook or car dealer. Since handbrake cables may stretch in service a means of adjusting (shortening) these, too, will be incorporated.

As mentioned earlier, disc brakes are self-adjusting. So if inspection of a disc brake system shows a marked gap between the pad and the disc, there could be a problem. Check by having an assistant press the brake pedal. If the pad doesn't move (presuming the system to be otherwise working correctly) the caliper piston has seized, and the brake unit will have to be dismantled to deal with the fault. Abnormally heavy disc pad wear may mean the caliper piston has seized in the 'on' position, so the pad is pressed perpetually hard against the disc (Figure 8.2). Another possible cause of either no pad contact or perpetual hard contact against the disc is where a moving caliper is used. Various types include 'floating', 'sliding' or 'swinging'. Basically, though one or more pistons may be used, only one piston will actually operate a pad. Reaction from the force of this piston, or direct pressure from another piston, then causes the

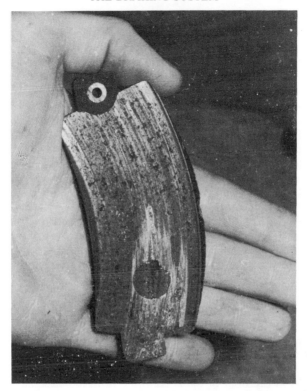

Figure 8.2. Abnormally heavy disc pad wear can result from a seized caliper piston, or sheer neglect . . . .

caliper to slide sideways or pivot on a pin so the opposing pad is also clamped against the disc.

Obviously, if the caliper fails to move freely the opposing pad will either fail to operate, or will remain in perpetual hard contact with the disc. Again the unit must be dismantled and the fault rectified. The ideal adjustment for drum brake shoes should leave each shoe almost touching the drum, so that the slightest touch on the brake pedal simultaneously brings all shoes into instant contact with the drums. If some shoes fail to contact the drum at the same time as others, unbalanced braking will result, as one or more wheels will attempt to 'stop' before the others. This could cause the car to skid dangerously.

In practice, it is permissible to adjust until the faintest of 'rubs' is heard occasionally as you spin the brake drum. Although there are exceptions to the rule, where manual adjustment of drum brake shoes is provided there will normally be two adjusters (one for each shoe) on two leading shoe arrangements, normally used for front drum brakes, and one adjuster for leading and trailing shoe set-ups, commonly used on the rear wheels. You can check by looking at the back-plate, behind the wheel and drum. If there are two brake pipes, or a bridge pipe running across the backplate it is probably a two leading shoe unit, with a separate hydraulic cylinder operating each shoe. In this case look for two adjusters. If there is only one brake pipe it means there is just one cylinder operating both (leading and trailing) shoes. Therefore look for one adjuster.

Typical adjusters

The adjuster will normally be a squared protrusion on the backplate. However, this shouldn't be confused with the large hexagon head of a friction device that is part of the self-adjustment system used, for instance, on some Fiats. A rarer form of adjuster is a toothed wheel accessible through a hole either in the front of the brake drum or in the backplate. The former may align with a hole in the road wheel, accessible once the nave plate had been removed: or you may need to remove the wheel. The latter will be covered usually with a rubber plug.

The toothed wheel adjuster is used particularly where a double acting wheel cylinder (instead of a single acting but sliding cylinder) operates rear leading and trailing shoes. On this set-up look for two such adjusters, fairly close together.

Adjustment procedure

You would be well advised to buy a sturdy 'brake spanner' (available from auto accessory shops) for the squared adjuster.

Anything else may just slip and round off the adjuster. It is also a good idea to give these adjusters a squirt of penetrating fluid before attempting to turn them – and thereafter to keep them clean and lubricated. Being exposed to road dirt they are prone to seizure. The toothed (or 'star wheel') adjuster is turned with a screwdriver blade.

Raise one end of the car and chock the wheels that are on the ground, then release the handbrake. If you need to get under the car to reach the adjusters use axle stands – never rely on the jack alone. You need to remove the road wheel only if you cannot otherwise reach the adjuster with your spanner.

Looking at the brake backplate, squared adjusters are turned clockwise normally to tighten up the shoe adjustment, anti-clockwise to slacken it off. It is not quite so easy to relate to the toothed adjusters, which are viewed edge on. Although the opposite assumption probably applies here, it may be easier to remember to move the screwdriver blade upwards to tighten on the right-hand adjuster (again, looking at the back-plate from behind) and downwards to tighten on the left-hand adjuster. See Figure 8.3 and 8.4. These adjusters travel on a screw thread, and turning one towards the shoe allows the threaded stem and the

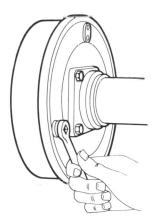

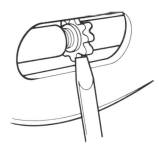

Figure 8.3. Use a sturdy brake spanner on squared adjusters

Figure 8.4. A screwdriver can be used to turn toothed-wheel adjusters

shoe to retract away from the drum. Slackening the adjuster has the opposite effect.

Squared adjusters may turn a 'snail' cam inside the drum, which bears against a peg on the shoe. Similar in shape to the shell of a garden snail, the larger section would push the shoe towards the drum, the narrower part should allow it to move away from the drum. More likely to be found on the rear drum brakes, another type of squared adjuster has a tapered inward end which, depending on whether it is screwed in or out, forces wedges apart, or allows them to move closer together. The wedges bear against the brake shoes, so again these are moved nearer the drum, or allowed to retract away from it.

If you are unsure which way to turn the adjuster, simple trial and error will soon solve the problem. Then the adjustment procedure is the same for all types. Working on one adjuster at a time, turn it while rotating the drum (or wheel) until the shoe (or shoes) is hard against the drum. Then slacken off until the drum just starts to spin freely. As mentioned previously, an occasional slight rub is permissible. Remember that the driven wheels will not spin as freely as the undriven ones, since you will also be turning part of the transmission.

Serrations on snail cams and a form of ratchet on toothed wheel designs mean these adjusters will remain exactly where you turn them to. On wedge type adjusters, however, it is possible to obtain a position on one of the 'ridges' of the square tapered end. Therefore once you have obtained the required adjustment, always rotate this type back and forth until you are sure it has settled properly on a squared face. A definite 'notchiness' should be felt.

Finally, after adjustment press the brake pedal several times to centralise the brake shoes, then re-check the adjustment.

Adjusting the handbrake

When you have adjusted the main brakes, check that the handbrake is hard on after the recommended number of clicks of its ratchet – usually somewhere between three and five. If it isn't, the handbrake cable probably requires adjustment to compensate for its having stretched in service. Again the type of adjuster may vary, but the end result, shortening the effective length of the cable, will be the same. Both rear wheels (front, where these are the handbraked wheels) must be clear of the ground.

If you're not sure of the set-up on your car, first look for an adjuster adjacent to the handbrake lever – you may have to lift a rubber gaiter, or the floor-covering. If there's none there, look for one on the cable beneath the car floor (bear in mind the car must be securely supported before you venture underneath) or adjacent to one of the (handbraked) wheels, or on a bracket fixed to the rear axle.

Generally speaking where two handbrake cables are used (one on each wheel) the adjusters (one for each cable) will be adjacent to the handbrake lever (Figure 8.5). Each cable will

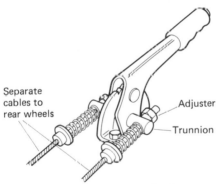

Figure 8.5. A twin cable handbrake set-up

have a flat which can be gripped with a spanner (or a screwdriver slot in its end) to stop it turning during adjustment, and then a threaded length passing through a trunnion or other abutment on the hand-brake lever. Adjustment is made by screwing a nut down this threaded portion to draw more of the threaded length through the trunnion, thus shortening the length of the cable. Sometimes there will be a single nut which registers in the trunnion, so it cannot turn between adjustment, or a nut and locknut may be used. With the latter system the two nuts must be turned away from each other to break the 'lock' before adjustment can be made, then turned against each other to re-lock after adjustment.

Similar adjustment at the handbrake may apply to single cables which run from the handbrake lever to a central yoke or equalising stirrup towards the rear of the car. Each end of a single cable from this point will go to a rear wheel, free to move in the yoke so each provides an equal effort when the handbrake lever pulls on the single cable. Quite often, however, the adjustment will be in the cable length or at the yoke (Figure 8.6).

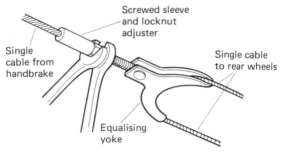

Figure 8.6. A single cable and equalising yoke set-up

The former may consist of a screwed sleeve with locknuts which effectively divides the cable into two lengths – tightening (i.e., shortening) the sleeve draws the ends of the cable closer together to shorten the overall length. Or there may be a Bowden cable set-up, where an outer cable terminates at a bracket under the car, the inner cable continuing via an equalising yoke to the wheels. This set-up is adjusted just like a bicycle brake, a screwed sleeve and locknut on the end of the outer cable being screwed in or out of the bracket to shorten or lengthen the outer cable, thus adjusting the tension on the inner cable.

Adjustment at the yoke will be similar to that described at the handbrake lever, with a threaded end to the cable being pulled further into the yoke by a nut and locknut. As a rule of thumb these adjustments should be carried out with the handbrake on about its third notch, and continued until each raised wheel can be only just turned under heavy hand pressure.

This procedure varies on some cars with self-adjusting rear brakes – e.g. Ford Cortina and current Escort models. On these a plastic abutment stop will be found sticking out on each rear brake backplate. When the handbrake is adjusted correctly it should be possible to push each stop in no more than approximately ⅛ in (3 mm). If the stop moves further with no resistance it means the actuating arm in the drum has started to move, and the brakes may be partially applied. On some cars (again the Escort is an example) instead of using a locknut the cable adjuster (a knurled plastic unit) under the car has a taper which is plugged into a bracket. In other instances, there will be primary and secondary cables, each adjustable, with the former running from the handbrake lever to a relay lever, and the latter then running from the relay lever to an equalising unit.

Where the adjustment is on the equalising unit mounted on the rear axle, or on the rod or cable just before it attaches to the lever protruding from the brake backplate, there is a different rule of thumb (Figure 8.7). Here, the split pin should be removed and the clevis pin linkage disconnected from the backplate lever. Next, with the handbrake lever on its first notch, adjust until the clevis pin holes in cable/rod end and backplate lever just align, with neither under tension. Then replace the clevis pin, using a new split-pin.

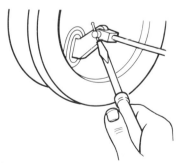

Figure 8.7. Adjustment at a rear-mounted equaliser bracket often requires the cables (or rods) to be disconnected from the backplate levers

Renewing disc brake pads

Some cars use a sensor system linked to the disc brake pads which lights a warning lamp on the car facia to alert the driver when pad thickness has been reduced to the point where the pads should be changed. But otherwise there should be a recommendation in your handbook as to the minimum permissible pad thickness. Recommendations vary – perhaps from $\frac{1}{16}$ in (1.5 mm) to exactly double this at $\frac{1}{8}$ in. (3 mm). Many would prefer to work on the higher figure, since it's a relatively short step from $\frac{1}{16}$ in (1.5 mm) to no brakes and a ruined disc because the pads have worn to their metal backing.

Sometimes the pad thickness can be checked without needing to remove the road wheel; sometimes a viewing aperture is let into the caliper body. At worst the wheel will have to be removed. Often, the pads will be retained by pins passing through them and the caliper body, with the pins themselves secured by 'hairgrips' (Figure 8.8). Once all these have been removed (and be absolutely sure to note what goes where) you may need grips to withdraw the old pads. If you can use two pairs of pliers, gripping top and bottom of the pad backing plate to

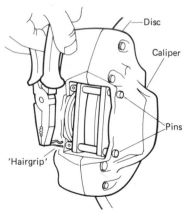

Figure 8.8. Disc pads may be retained by pins and 'hairgrips', or split pins, or roll pins

maintain an even pull, so much the better. Otherwise use one pair of pliers, maybe alternately gripping top and bottom of the pad to rock it free.

If they are very tight you may need to use a slim drift from the other side of the caliper, again alternating between top and bottom, to tap the pads out. Alternatively there is now a DIY pad pulling tool available, which is basically a type of slide hammer. On calipers which swing down, or are removed completely for pad renewal, the pads normally are just lifted from their housings. In all cases it is essential to note how the pads (and any spring clips, or metal shims) are positioned (Figure 8.9). In some the pad to one side of the caliper may be a different shape to that on the other side.

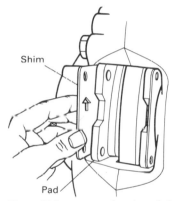

Figure 8.9. Note which way round pads and shims are fitted

Once the pads have been removed, their housings and the exposed portion of the piston(s) must be cleaned thoroughly, both to allow room and freedom of movement for the new pads, and to ensure dirt on the piston is not forced back into the cylinder bore, with possibly ruinous consequences. The worst of the dirt can be scraped out with a screwdriver blade, then a small paint brush or a toothbrush dipped in methylated spirits or proprietary brake cleaning fluid can be used to get the parts spotlessly clean. Be very careful not to damage the surface of the piston or any dust seal that may be fitted around it. Also, on no account should you attempt to blow away brake dust – inhaling it cound be harmful.

If there is excessive rust build-up on the edge of the brake disc this can often be removed by inserting a screwdriver through the caliper so it bears against the edge of the disc, then spinning the disc by hand. A lint-free rag moistened with methylated spirits (or cleaning fluid) can be used to ensure the disc faces are thoroughly clean. Some pistons can be quite difficult to push back into their bores. Where pad renewal demands the removal of the caliper cylinder unit, it may be possible to use a G-cramp (a valve spring compressor, perhaps) or hub-pulling device such as a flat bar drilled to take a central sturdy bolt, to squeeze the piston back.

When working on a caliper that remains *in situ* for pad renewal, there is a way round the problem of avoiding damage while levering, and that forcing one piston in may cause an opposing piston to move further out – even to eject completely. The answer is, after cleaning, to reinsert the old pads temporarily. Then leverage can be applied between the disc and the old pad, using, perhaps, a large screwdriver. And working on one pad aperture at a time means the other old pad will prevent the opposing piston moving out. Incidentally there are brake toolkits that include a suitable lever.

Note that you need to allow for the displaced fluid when pushing a piston back into its caliper bore. You can use a dip tube to draw off some fluid from the master cylinder reservoir, or simply wrap rag round its neck to mop up the spillage. Or you can open a bleed nipple on the caliper, closing this while fluid is still emerging, so that air cannot enter and necessitate bleeding the brakes when the job is finished. Try each new pad in its housing, ensuring that it moves freely. If it doesn't, and you are sure the housing is clean and that the piston is sufficiently retracted, you may need to remove the paint carefully from the edges of the pad backing plate.

When the fit is satisfactory, lightly smear the rear face of the pad's metal backing plate and (if fitted) the faces of anti-squeal shims with brake grease, or a recognised anti-squeal lubricant.

Be extremely careful not to get grease on the pad friction lining. Where pins are used to retain the pads, use something like a slim electrical screwdriver blade to ensure that the pinholes in the caliper body and those in the newly-fitted pad backing plate are aligned. If pad wear sensors are fitted, do not forget to reconnect their leads.

When the job is completed, press the brake pedal several times to position the pads and restore correct pedal travel. Then check hydraulic fluid level and top up as necessary. Allow time (maybe some hundred of miles) for the new pads to bed in properly and give maximum efficiency.

Variations on the theme

Some calipers require a different procedure for pad renewal. An example found on some is a single piston unit which is free to slide in a bracket that is bolted rigidly to the hub assembly. When the piston acts directly against one pad, pushing it against the disc, the cylinder reacts, sliding in the opposite direction and pulling the other pad against the disc.

Pad renewal here starts with the removal of the split pins from the wedge-shaped guides (Figure 8.10). Then pull (or carefully

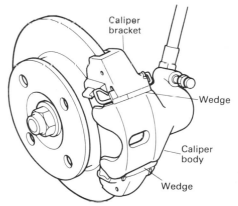

Figure 8.10. In this example the wedges are knocked out and the body removed (see text) for access to pads

drift) these guides from the caliper bracket. It will help if at the same time you push down the cylinder body. Next, push down again on one end of the body and lift the other end clear. Then slide the pads clear of the bracket. Note the springs located on the edges of the pads nearest to the caliper bleedscrew. On reassembly, ensure the holes in the guides and cylinder body are aligned and that the split pins are fitted securely, with their bent-over ends well clear of the road wheel.

Another caliper design is the Girling 'Colette', also built under licence by other manufacturers, including the Japanese, and increasingly used on both European and Japanese cars.

This unit has a single-piston body which slides on sealed guide pins housed in a rigidly mounted bracket. The piston pushes the inboard pad against the disc, the body then sliding and pulling the outboard pad against the disc. See Figure 8.11.

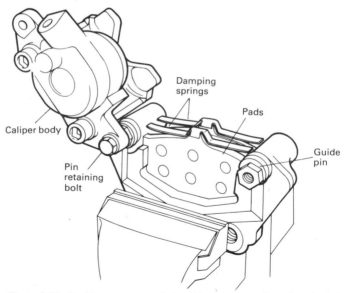

Figure 8.11. In this more recent design (shown mounted in a bench vice) the body moves on guide pins. Removing a pin retaining bolt allows the body to be swung out on the other pin to expose the pads

To change the pads, hold one of the guide pins steady with an open-ended spanner held across the flats provided. The pin must not be allowed to rotate in case this should damage its seal. Then use a ring or open-ended spanner to remove the guide pin retaining bolt. The caliper body can now be rotated on the other guide pin (do not strain the flexible hose) until the pads are accessible. Remove the pads. Note that some pads have a separate damping spring fitted over them, while others have built-in springs. Where a pad incorporates a wear sensor lead, note which side it is fitted.

A not dissimilar unit to the Colette is used by Ford on the new Escort. But this needs dismounting, and is secured by 'female' socket headed bolts, requiring the use of a 7 mm Allen key.

Drum brakes

The friction linings in drum brakes may be riveted or bonded to the metal brake shoe. Riveted shoes must be renewed before the lining is worn down to the level of the rivet heads, otherwise the exposed rivets will score, and possibly ruin, the friction surface of the brake drum. While bonded linings can be permitted to wear down further than rivets would allow, as with the disc pads covered earlier, it is safer to double the $\frac{1}{16}$ in (1.5 mm) minimum permissible thickness that is quoted normally.

As with disc pads, brake shoes must be renewed in axle sets to maintain balanced braking. For example, if you have to renew the lining on, say, the rear offside wheel, you must also renew that on the rear nearside wheel. This rule applies even if one set of linings has to be renewed because of oil or hydraulic fluid contamination, and you feel the opposing set of linings still has thousands of miles of wear left in it.

On more recent cars a plugged aperture may be provided on the brake backplate, through which the brake shoe lining thickness can be examined. If there is no aperture the brake drum must be removed in order to determine the lining thickness. This is a routine check which will be specified in the servicing schedule for your car, and which may be required once a year, or every 12 000 miles, whichever is the sooner. Some motorists may prefer to make this check twice a year. And even where an aperture is provided on the backplate they may prefer to remove the drum, which allows detection of hydraulic fluid leaking from a wheel cylinder – perhaps in time to save the brake shoe linings, as well as ensuring you are not caught out by unexpected brake failure.

Removing the drum

It usually makes life easier if, on a manually adjusted drum brake system, the brake shoes are retracted ('de-adjusted') before attempting to remove the drum. On an automatically adjusted system, generally there is no need to retract the shoes, nor will a means of readily doing so be provided. Only occasionally will there be a hole in the face of the brake drum through which screwdrivers can be inserted, one to lift the actuating lever from the ratchet wheel (in a typical system) the other to turn the ratchet wheel to retract the shoes. Sometimes the brake drum will be a separate component (Figure 8.12), sometimes there will be a combined drum/hub unit. Where it's a separate component, it may be secured to the wheel hub (axle flange) by one or two set-screws, or there may be no screws, but just a spring clip over one of the wheel studs. Sometimes the drum will be retained merely by having the wheel bolted on.

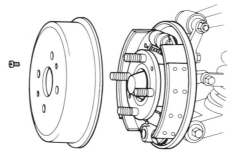

Figure 8.12. Where the drum is a separate component, it may be secured to the axle flange by one or two set screws, a spring clip over a stud, or be held merely by the road wheel

Before attempting to pull off the drum, blobs of paint on a wheel stud and adjacent area of the drum, or scribe marks should be used to ensure the drum will be refitted in its former position. This will help to retain overall balance.

If the drum refuses to budge, corrosion (or paint) could be causing it to stick on the wheel studs or where it centres on the axle flange. Careful use of a copper-faced hammer, tapping around the circumference (not the lip) of the drum, in an outwards direction, should jar it free. If this doesn't work, however, penetrating oil should be dribbled around the studs and flange joint and left awhile to do its job. Another method that can be tried is to wrap the drum in rag, and then pour boiling water on to the rag: the heat expansion may break the seal. Don't be tempted to lever between the lip of the drum and the backplate, as this may very easily cause serious damage. So, too, could attempting to hit the lip of the drum with the hammer.

Drum hub units

Where the brake drum is integral with the wheel hub, the grease cap (or dust cap) must first be removed. Sometimes this can be done simply by levering between the hub and the lip of the cap with a screwdriver blade. But lever evenly around the cap, to prevent it tipping and jamming. Alternatively you can use a hammer and chisel, tapping the chisel carefully round the lip – in fact, sometimes the action of forcing the chisel blade between the hub and the lip will start the cap moving outwards. Carefully tapping the cap outwards with the copper hammer, as was described for tight drums earlier on, may also work.

Occasionally, however, the cap can prove extremely obstinate, and might also lack a lip to provide any leverage. One answer could be to drill the end of the cap and insert a self-tapping screw on which you can pull with a claw hammer, or slide hammer. Sometimes a worm-drive clip tightened around the cap can be used as a lip. On the other hand, you may find the cost of a replacement cap is cheap enough to allow for brutal, but quicker removal with the hammer and chisel, or hammer alone. The wedge end of an engineer's hammer is particularly useful here.

Hub removal

Removing the cap should reveal a large castellated nut, or castellated cap over a plain nut, with a split pin located through the castellations and the stub axle. Straighten the legs of the pin and pull it out with pliers or side cutters. The pin may need starting with a hammer, or extra leverage may be obtained by bearing the pliers or side cutters against the nut. Once the pin has been removed, it may be found that the nut is little more than finger tight. Or it could be very tight indeed – something in the order of 200 lb ft. torque (or more) can be the case on some cars. In these cases a length of pipe is often needed on the socket extension bar to obtain sufficient leverage to loosen the nut. And you may need an assistant to sit in the vehicle and apply the footbrake firmly.

Note that sometimes the nut may have a left-hand thread, and obviously this must be ascertained beforehand.

The nuts which appear to be comparatively loose will have a torque or drum turning force specified as part of correct bearing adjustment. With the nut removed (note carefully the positioning of any washers that may be fitted) the drum/hub unit (Figure 8.13) may simply pull off by hand. But first spread clean rag on the ground, since sometimes a bearing may fall free as the unit is

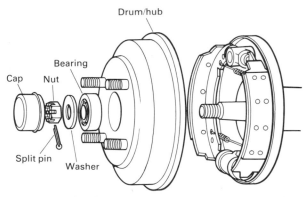

Figure 8.13. Combined drum/hub units present more of a problem – see text

removed. In some cases a hub puller suitable for the vehicle may have to be bought or hired to draw the drum/hub off the axle. Check first whether temporarily replacing the wheel will provide sufficient leverage to withdraw the unit. A puller may be required in any case to remove the inner track of the inner wheel bearing, which is sometimes left on the axle, probably along with the grease seal. Occasionally it may be found helpful to position a worm-drive clip around or behind this track to provide better location for the puller legs.

Note the layout

Once you have removed the drum, stop and note very carefully how all the components on your vehicle are positioned. A sketch (or maybe a Polaroid picture) showing which way round the shoes fit, where the pull-off springs are located, the disposition of shoe retaining pins, automatic adjustment components, and so on, will prove invaluable when you come to reassemble the parts. See Figures 8.14 and 8.15. For example, it may not be enough to note just that each shoe pull-off spring hooks into a hole on the web of the shoe. There may be two or three holes in each web.

Sometimes the springs may stretch from one shoe to the other, sometimes from the shoe to some point on the brake back-plate. The springs may have a long leg at one end, and a short leg at the other. Note which end goes where, and whether it hooks over the front face or the rear face of the shoe web. On some shoes (e.g., a two leading shoe layout) the lining will appear to have 'slipped', being closer to one end of the shoe than the other. Note that it should appear to have slipped in the forward direction of rotation.

Incidentally, although removing an integral brake drum hub unit is more complex than simply pulling off a separate drum, the former does have the advantage of leaving a more open backplate. It is easier to see where the parts fit, and access for the tools required to remove the parts is better. Where the drum is separate, the wheel flange obscures the backplate, and hinders the use of tools.

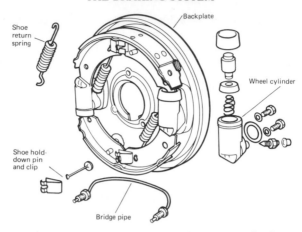

Shoe
return
spring

Backplate

Wheel cylinder

Shoe hold-
down pin
and clip

Bridge pipe

Figure 8.14. Note the layout – this 'exploded' view is of a front wheel design with single-piston fixed wheel cylinders

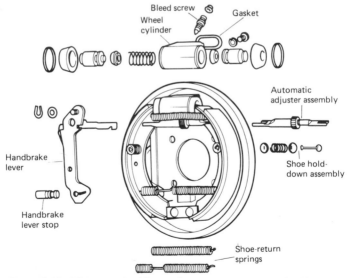

Bleed screw

Gasket

Wheel
cylinder

Automatic
adjuster assembly

Handbrake
lever

Shoe hold-
down assembly

Handbrake
lever stop

Shoe-return
springs

Figure 8.15. This rear wheel layout features a twin-piston, double acting fixed wheel cylinder and automatic brake adjustment

Removing the shoes

Having made your sketch and notes, hopefully now you're ready
to remove the brake shoes. And on a typical system the first task
usually is to remove the shoe hold-down springs. These may be
small coil springs or spring clips located on pegs (one on each
shoe) which pass through the back plate and shoe web. The coil
spring will have a dished cap with a slot in it. The cap must be
gripped with a pair of pliers, pushed in against spring pressure,
and turned until the slot aligns with the flattened top of the pin.
The cap can then be drawn off the pin, releasing the coil spring,
and a mating version of the cap at the shoe end of the spring. The
dished portions of the caps face into the spring. See Figure 8.16.

Removing the springs can be a fiddly operation, requiring
much patience because of the difficulty of maintaining a grip
with the pliers, and of turning the cap without the pliers fouling
the edge of the brake shoe. The spring clip design has to be
depressed with the pliers until its forked end can be pulled clear
of the flattened end of the pin. Again, the proximity of the shoe
edge may hinder the operation. With both types, it may help if
the pin (which is free to be withdrawn once the spring cap is
removed) can be kept pressed in from behind the backplate.

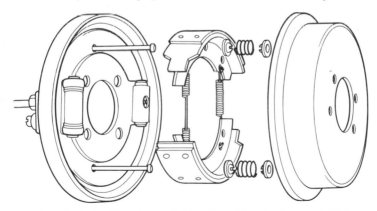

*Figure 8.16. In this typical brake shoe disposition the shoes are held down
by pins, coil springs and caps*

Having noted where the pull-off springs fit, it is not necessary normally (indeed it could be very difficult) to detach the springs in order to remove the shoes. Mind you, they may drop off during the operation, and must anyway be taken off and located on the new shoes. However, their prior removal is required where on some cars (e.g., Fiat 127/128 models) the axle flange is too large and too close to the backplate for the shoes to be pulled far enough outwards to draw the springs over the flange. A strong hook is handy for this job. You can make one using a T-handled bradawl or auger with its end bent over. This end is then slipped under the spring hook, and the handle assists the considerable pull that may be required to both remove or refit the spring at the shoe end.

Be prepared for some initial juggling with pliers and screwdriver blade to persuade the hook eye in or out of the hole on the shoe web, but note that there may be a cut-out in the rim of the axle flange which can be positioned to provide better access.

Shoe horn

A 'shoe horn' is required to lever off the shoes (Figure 8.17). This can be the commercial article, often sold as part of that brake overhaul tool-kit mentioned earlier, though an adjustable spanner or self-grip wrench will also do the job. Use the shoe horn as shown on a typical front brake two leading shoe layout to lever one of the shoe webs out of the angled abutment slot in the wheel cylinder body. Allow the shoe to collapse inwards, over the top of the wheel cylinder, unhook its pull-off spring from the backplate, and remove the shoe entirely. Repeat the operation for the second shoe. As soon as the shoes are off, fit strong rubber bands over the wheel cylinders to guard against accidental ejection of the pistons.

On a typical rear brake leading and trailing shoe layout, lever the trailing shoe from the wheel cylinder abutment slot. This should relieve the spring tension sufficiently for both shoes to be removed as a pair, the pull-off springs normally stretching from one shoe to the other. See Figure 8.18. Note that the leading

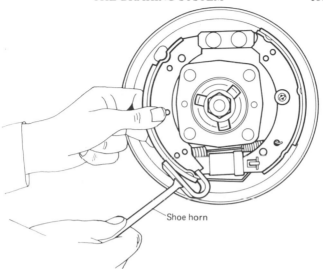

Figure 8.17. *You can buy a 'shoe horn' or improvise – see text*

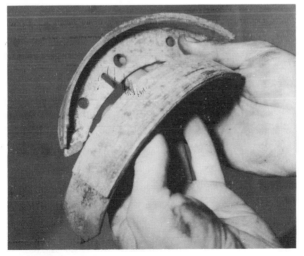

Figure 8.18. *Note which shoe is which – see reference to 'slipped linings'*

shoe will also appear to have a slipped lining, and that one end will probably be slotted over the handbrake lever. There may also be a support plate let into this slot. Retain the plate for fitting to the replacement shoe. Sometimes the replacement shoes may be interchangeable (e.g. on the layout just described, both will have 'slipped linings') and sometimes they will be 'handed' – that is, one will definitely be the leading shoe, the other the trailing shoe.

On some layouts (apart from automatically adjusted types described later) there will be a handbrake cross-lever, stretching from shoe to shoe, and operated by the lever protruding through the backplate. The Mini Metro is an example. In other examples, the cross-lever may be connected to a vertical lever, to which is linked (inside the drum assembly) the handbrake cable.

It may be advantageous (and occasionally necessary) to remove the appropriate split pins and clevis pins or 'C'-clips to disengage the handbrake cable and allow the cross-linkage and operating lever to be withdrawn also.

Cleaning up/reassembly

Before fitting the new shoes, the backplate should be cleaned up. Once all loose dirt has been scraped off, surface corrosion can be scrubbed off with a wire brush. Afterwards finish off with rag and a proprietary brake cleaning fluid. Use the wire brush on the outside of the brake drum, and the rag and cleaning fluid on the inside – never attempt to blow away brake dust from the drum backplate, since if inhaled asbestos dust can be dangerous to your health. (Note that nowadays asbestos-free brake linings are available.)

You should also check that manual brake adjusters are working freely. The threaded stem and component parts of a wedge type adjuster can be removed for cleaning, and then smeared with brake grease before reassembly. Sometimes a semi-seized snail cam (or 'eccentric') type adjuster can be redeemed by dosing it with penetrating oil, then carefully rotating it backwards and forwards until it moves freely. Afterwards wipe away the surplus oil, and if possible work some brake grease around the stem, beneath the cam and where it protrudes through the backplate. But if the adjuster is seized or otherwise damaged beyond redemption, or on the other hand moves so easily it will be rotated by the strength of the shoe pull-off springs, it must be replaced. Repair kits are marketed both by makers of the braking system, and by other manufacturers of brake components.

Check-points

Lift the rubber boots on wheel cylinders and ensure there is no sign of escaped fluid: if there is, the cylinder must be replaced. Push the piston/s in and check that they are moving freely. This point can be checked again later on, when the shoes have been replaced, by pressing the brake pedal and observing whether the shoes move outwards, and are afterwards retracted properly. Do not press the pedal while the brake shoes are off, or there is a real risk of the cylinder pistons, seals and other components, being ejected.

On the typical rear brake leading and trailing shoe layout described earlier, when the foot brake is pressed the single piston in the wheel cylinder moves the leading shoe on to the drum. At the same time the cylinder body reacts by sliding on the backplate to operate the trailing shoe. Check that the cylinder does move freely. Use something like a feeler gauge to work some brake grease between the backplate and the flanges of the cylinder. Should the parts need dismantling for thorough cleaning and lubrication, or in the event of an hydraulic leak having been discovered, follow the procedure described for wheel cylinder renewal later on in this section.

The raised abutments on the backplate on which the brake shoes rest and slide should be smeared lightly with brake grease, as should the tips of the new shoes – but be extremely careful not to get any grease on the linings, and never handle new linings with greasy fingers. Fit the new shoes and their pull-off springs, and the hold down pins and springs, reversing the dismantling procedure described previously. Afterwards check that the brake adjusters work properly, but then leave them so the shoes are fully retracted.

Ask an assistant to press the brake pedal and afterwards operate the handbrake while you observe that the shoes expand and retract correctly, and that sliding wheel cylinders move freely. If necessary, use a soft hammer to centralise the shoes on the backplate before replacing the drum. If it is a drum/hub unit, ensure the wheel bearings are adjusted and the hub nut tightened to the correct torque – see Steering and Suspension, Chapter 9. Finally, adjust the brakes as described earlier in this section, but note that after a hundred miles or so, the new linings will have 'bedded in' and may need readjusting.

Automatically adjusted rear brakes

Brake shoes having automatic adjustment are removed in much the same way as just described, and of course it is vital to note how the components are assembled. See Figure 8.19. The adjustment will have to be retracted fully before the drum can be replaced, and afterwards reset before the car is driven on the road. Typically, the handbrake (usually, though sometimes the footbrake) should be operated 20 to 30 times, causing the automatic adjuster to 'wind itself up' until the correct shoe-to-drum clearance is obtained.

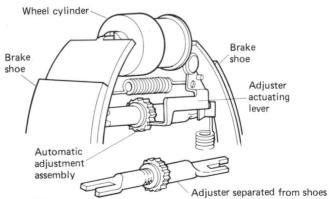

Figure 8.19. A typical rear shoe automatic adjustment set-up – as the linings wear the lever pivoting on the trailing shoe actuates the toothed wheel on the adjuster, lengthening the rod and pushing the shoes outwards, closer to the drum

Wheel cylinders

Before removing a wheel cylinder (or 'slave' cylinder) it is a good
idea to apply a clamp to the adjacent flexible hose to minimise
fluid loss and simplify bleeding the system on reassembly. See
Figure 8.20. A sheet of cellophane slipped over the neck of the
hydraulic reservoir with the cap then screwed on over this will
also restrict fluid flow by shutting off the air and creating a
vacuum in the reservoir.

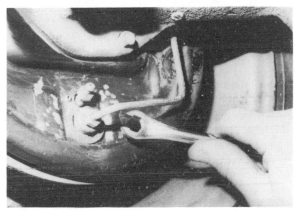

*Figure 8.20. Removing a wheel cylinder: scrub the hydraulic pipe and
union clean and ease the union nut carefully – note that the flare nut
wrench shown is ideal for this application*

A trick worth remembering is that where there is a flexible
hose connection it is sometimes possible to reduce the work
involved by pulling the wheel cylinder clear of the backplate (on
the drum side) and then unscrewing the cylinder from the
flexible hose. However, this method does rely on the new
cylinder tightening on to the hose at more or less the same point,
so that the hose is not put under any strain. Failing this, the
locknut must be slackened and the flexible hose disconnected at
its location on the car chassis before it can be unscrewed from
the wheel cylinder. A flexible hose feeding metal brake pipes

attached to a live axle should also be clamped, but also have a rubber plug or plastic bag and elastic band handy to seal off disconnected metal pipes.

Scrape or brush dirt off the backplate, then use the wire brush to scrub the brake pipe union and locknuts really clean. If it is a metal brake pipe, be particularly careful to ensure that the length of pipe over which the union sleeve nut must travel is clean and smooth. Remove the brake drum and shoes as described earlier in this section. Now disconnect the hydraulic feed pipe. Note that the sleeve nut on a metal pipe should be eased back very carefully – check that it is actually rotating on the pipe, and not just twisting it. In some cases a bridge pipe connecting two cylinders will also have to be removed.

The wheel cylinders may be secured to the backplate by a single bolt, or a stud and nut, with a pin or raised abutment locating in the backplate to stop it attempting to turn on its seating. It may have a circlip (or E-clip) securing a projection through the backplate, plus a locating pin, or it may be secured with two bolts. Watch out for a paper gasket fitted between the cylinder and backplate, particularly where a circlip retainer is used. The circlip can be levered out with a screwdriver, and both clip and gasket should be renewed.

It can be tricky fitting the new clip when reassembling. One method is to spread it (concave face first) on the end of the wheel cylinder projection, then drive it home along the projection and into its groove using a tubular drift. Alternatively, it could be levered back into position with careful use of screwdrivers.

Where a sliding wheel cylinder is used, the cylinder will be retained by opposing spring clips locating between the flanged projection of the cylinder and the backplate. The clips may have dimples and pips on their legs so they interlock with another, and they are usually U-shaped. There should be a dust cover over the clips. Having pulled the cover back, use a hammer and screwdriver, bearing against each leg in turn, to drift out the outer clip. The inner clip can then be slid out from the opposite direction. The clips can vary in shape and sometimes a one-piece spring plate is used to secure the two separate clips. In this case, first slide one clip as far as possible towards the handbrake lever, then slide the opposite clip inwards until its end lug can be eased under the spring plate. Then press down on the first clip until the second can be removed completely. The plate and first clip can then be lifted off to free the cylinder.

When reassembling this type do not slide the cylinder more than is absolutely necessary until the shoes and drum have been refitted, or the clips and plate may become disengaged again. Incidentally, in some instances the bleed nipple and handbrake lever may also need to be removed before you can detach the cylinder from the backplate.

When fitting a new sliding cylinder, first clean both sides of the backplate where it slides, and smear with brake grease. On reassembly ensure the dust cover is located properly over the parts. Screw the brake pipe unions together finger tight, ensuring they are not cross-threaded before final tightening with the spanner. When the job is done, you will of course have to bleed and adjust the brakes.

Master cylinder removal

The master cylinder will be mounted normally on the bulkhead between the engine compartment and car interior, or on a vacuum servo unit which in turn is mounted on the bulkhead. See Figure 8.21. More often than not it will be secured by just two nuts and studs or nuts and bolts. Sometimes (the Triumph Dolomite is an example) there will be an additional fixing to a bracket on the wing valance. In some cases, particularly where the car was designed originally for left-hand drive or perhaps where space is insufficient for both a master cylinder and a servo unit, these units will be mounted in tandem on a bracket fixed to the bulkhead on the nearside of the car. A rod running across the bulkhead will link the pushrod and brake pedal arm. Where the unit is mounted on the bulkhead, its pushrod will protrude into the interior of the car and be linked to the brake pedal arm, usually by a clevis pin.

If you prefer to empty the master cylinder before removing it, this can be done by pumping fluid from the offside front wheel

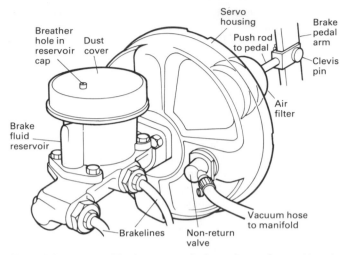

Figure 8.21. A typical brake master cylinder and servo set-up. Note that there may be an air filter on the servo (see text later in this section) which should be renewed at long service intervals

bleed nipples, and also the nearside rear on a tandem system – open both inboard bleed nipples on a four-pot tandem system. Pump the fluid through the bleed tubes(s) into a jar, but do not re-use it. However, the master cylinder can be left full, although it is wise to seal off the breather hole in the reservoir cap with adhesive tape, or place cellophane over the reservoir neck before replacing the cap, in order to minimise the fluid loss. Have a receptacle handy into which you can empty the master cylinder, and pack plenty of rag beneath the unit and the brake lines to catch spillage. Note that brake fluid will ruin paintwork if not wiped off immediately and thoroughly.

Incidentally with some units it is possible that the reservoir itself can be unplugged from the master cylinder body. As a rule the master cylinder pushrod is fixed into the cylinder body, and before the cylinder can be dismounted this rod must be detached from the brake pedal. Often this can be the most difficult part of the operation. Sometimes the parcel shelf or other interior fitting will have to be removed to gain access to the brake pedal linkage, and even then it can be difficult to extract or replace the clevis pin that links parts together: the clevis pin will be retained by a split pin, or similar locking device.

Sometimes space is so tight that it is difficult to get fingers and pin into place. Here a tip worth trying when reassembling is to push the pin through a strip of adhesive tape and then wrap the tape around a finger. Just one finger is all that is needed then to locate the pin initially through pedal arm and pushrod. A typical example where this trick may be the answer is the Leyland Mini, one of the worst models for access.

Before disconnecting the linkage, note which hole in the pedal arm is used (there may be more than one) and the positions of any washers, bushes or pedal return springs. If your car has a tandem master cylinder, make a careful note of which goes where before uncoupling the brake lines. Similarly, make a note of any wiring (to stop lamp switch or fluid level warning light) that must be disconnected. With the pushrod detached from the pedal, the brake lines uncoupled and any wiring disconnected (also any unrelated items likely to impede the work – such as choke or throttle cables) the master cylinder can now be unbolted and lifted away.

Exceptions regarding the pushrod fixture include the VW Golf range and Beetle, where the pushrod can be left attached to the pedal, and the master cylinder withdrawn from the rod. The procedure for detaching the master cylinder from the bulkhead also differs on the Beetle. Here you work first from within the front offside wheel arch. Having removed the road wheel, first the tube(s) from the reservoir in the front luggage compartment must be unplugged from the master cylinder – either the tube(s) must be sealed off to prevent spillage, or the fluid can be allowed to drain into a jar. Then a brake line(s) must be uncoupled and the wiring detached from the stop lamp switch. The bolts securing the master cylinder are removed from inside the car, taking care not to drop any washers into the space below.

On all models, after reassembly, the master cylinder reservoir must be topped up with fresh brake fluid and the system bled as described earlier on in this section. If necessary, on the VW models the locknut must be slackened and the pushrod length adjusted until the free play between the ball end of the rod and its seating in the cylinder piston is approximately 1 mm. It is also important on the VWs with a tandem master cylinder that the pedal stop adjustment allows the pedal to move far enough inwards, in the event of circuit failure, to operate the other circuit.

Removing the servo unit

Like the (unservoed) master cylinder, a servo unit will be mounted in much the same way, either directly on the bulkhead, or on a bracket bolted to the bulkhead. The master cylinder will then be bolted to the other end of the servo. The procedure for removing the servo unit will be almost identical to that described for the master cylinder. The latter must be dismounted from the end of the servo, and the servo pushrod must be detached from the brake pedal. Then the servo unit can be unbolted and dismounted from bulkhead or bracket, having also disconnected its vacuum hose.

Occasionally the length of the pipes fitted to the master cylinder will allow sufficient movement for this unit to be merely dismounted and moved to one side so the servo unit can be withdrawn. Therefore there would be no need to drain off the hydraulic fluid, or to bleed the system after reassembly.

Many servo units will have a felt air filter fitted on the rear of the unit, encircling the pushrod. This filter should be changed approximately every three years, or 36 000 miles. Normally you don't have to dismount the servo in order to renew the filter. It will be accessible either between the rear of the unit and the bulkhead, or on the driver's side of the bulkhead. To renew the filter, pull the rubber boot off the rear end of the servo and slide back along the pushrod. Then prise the filter from the rear of the servo – sometimes a cap will have to be removed first. Using a sharp knife, slit the new filter across its radius and at an angle of 45 degrees. The filter can then be slipped over the pushrod and positioned in its housing. Afterwards replace the rubber boot.

Brake bleeding

Bleeding is the term given commonly to the procedure used for the purging of air from the hydraulic system. The presence of air is betrayed by a 'spongy' brake pedal action and diminishing braking effect. See Figure 8.22. Strictly speaking bleeding should

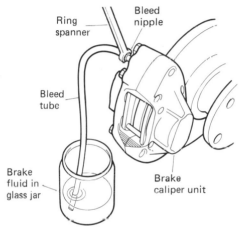

Figure 8.22. The basic brake bleeding set-up involves fitting one end of a bleed tube to the bleed nipple(s) and immersing the other end of the tube in a small quantity of clean brake fluid in a glass jar

be necessary only when some part of the system has been disconnected for repair. And provided you have used a clamp on the flexible hose feeding the disc or drum under repair, or have taken the various other precautions mentioned, bleeding should be required only at the wheel where the dismantling has taken place.

However, strange as it may seem, it is possible for air to enter an apparently healthy hydraulic system. Both air and moisture can find their way past seals or through flexible hoses that are still capable of keeping the fluid in. This is more likely as the seals and hoses age, so it could be argued that preventive maintenance, in the form of fitting new seals or hydraulic components, is overdue.

On earlier cars, bleeding used to be a relatively straight-forward operation. However, with the advent of more sophisticated braking systems it has become more complicated although there is no technical difficulty involved. The basic operation involves fitting a rubber (or plastic) tube to each bleed nipple (or bleed screw) in turn and immersing the other end of the tube in a small quantity of clean brake fluid in a glass jar. The nipple is then opened (unscrewed) – about half a turn should be sufficient – with a spanner and the brake pedal pressed. As the fluid flows from the nipple through the tube and into the jar, any air in that line will emerge as bubbles. The pedal may need 'pumping' several times to purge all the air. When the bubbles cease to appear, pump the pedal once or twice more to be sure, then with the pedal held down at the end of its last stroke the bleed nipple is closed. Holding the pedal down during this operation guards against any air being drawn back in.

Air can also be drawn back in if the bleed tube fits slackly on the nipple, or if the nipple is unscrewed too far, so on the downstroke of the pedal fluid may pump out past the screw threads rather than through the nipple, and on the upward stroke air will re-enter past the threads. It's also imperative that you keep the master cylinder reservoir topped up during the operation – air will enter again if the level drops too low.

Use a close-fitting spanner on the bleed nipple, preferably a ring spanner that can be left in place during the operation. It will be easier to fit the bleed tube first, then thread the ring spanner over the tube. Use a wire brush to clean around the nipple first, and where the nipple has not been disturbed for some considerable time be very careful with the spanner. It is fatally easy to snap off a nipple that is corroded into the wheel cylinder or caliper. If, after wire brushing, the nipple resists reasonable spanner pressure, apply some releasing fluid then try to ease the nipple back and forth carefully with spanner.

Another problem that might arise under these circumstances is a blocked, or partially blocked bleed nipple. However, it's no use trying to overcome this problem by simply opening (unscrewing) the nipple further. This will only aggravate the leakage past the screw threads mentioned earlier. The answer is to remove the nipple and poke it clear with a piece of wire. Fluid loss and further entry of air can be kept to a minimum by first applying a clamp to the flexible hose feeding the wheel in question. It is also worth noting that a set of bleed nipple dust caps (available from accessory shops) would help largely to prevent these problems. Also available in accessory shops are automatic or one-man bleeding units. However, particularly if you haven't attempted this operation before, you may prefer to have some assistance. Normally, one person operates the brake pedal and keeps the master cylinder reservoir topped up, while the other opens and closes the bleed nipples. Make sure beforehand that each understands the commands to be given – such as, 'pump' and 'hold'.

The sequence

On an all drum or all disc brake set-up, normally bleeding would start at the rear nearside wheel (the furthest from the master cylinder) and end at the offside front wheel (the nearest to the master cylinder). But these days a front disc rear drum set-up is more likely. Here both the front wheels should be bled first, starting with the wheel furthest from the master-cylinder. At the rear, again start with the wheel furthest from the master cylinder.

If the car has dual-circuit brakes, with a tandem master cylinder, the sequence is different again. Here both rear wheels should be bled first, starting with the nearside, then the front wheels, again nearside first. A variation here, calling for some dexterity and long bleed tubes (and a close eye on the reservoir level!) is to bleed a front and rear simultaneously. There is also a variation for certain 'four-pot' divided systems (the Leyland Princess and Austin Mini Metro, for example) where front wheel braking is retained whichever circuit fails. On these cars the front disc brakes have four pistons, each set of two pistons working as a separate pair.

The system here requires the use of two bleed tubes. Start with a single tube on the nearside rear wheel and then the offside. Then move to the nearside front, and attach the two tubes to the inboard bleed nipples. Having bled these two, move on to the single outboard bleed nipple, then repeat this process on the offside front wheel.

A variation on this is to bleed a rear then the front on the same side, bleed the rear again, then repeat the process on the other side of the car.

It is generally recommended that the handbrake should be left off (but the car wheels chocked securely) during the bleeding operations.

Pumping action

The recommended brake pedal pumping action varies according to the type of master cylinder fitted. Basically, these fall into two types – the aluminium bodied centre valve (CV) design and the cast-iron bodied compression barrel (CB) unit.

Where the CV design is used, the pedal should be pushed down through its full stroke, followed by three short rapid strokes, then allowed to return quickly by sliding the foot off. With the CB type, push the pedal down slowly through its full stroke, allow it to return slowly, then pause for three or four seconds before repeating the action.

Bleed each nipple until no more air bubbles appear, and on completing the entire sequence check the feel of the brake pedal. It should move very little before firm resistance is felt. However, if the pedal pressure still feels unsatisfactory the process must be repeated, maybe trying some of the other sequence variations mentioned, and possibly even reversing the pedal technique. If you've tried everything, but still with no success, try looking elsewhere for the problem – such as faulty seals, sticking pistons, or even incorrect brake adjustment.

9

Steering and suspension

With many systems having sealed-for-life components requiring no lubrication, it is tempting to assume the steering and suspension systems need no maintenance. As far as actual service operations are concerned this may be largely true. However, part of regular maintenance is keeping an eye (or ear) open for signs of impending trouble.

When you check round the car, look out for damaged gaiters on a steering rack: they will let lubricant out and abrasive dirt in. Obviously such damage must be rectified immediately – basically that means fitting a new gaiter – and you might bear in mind that such a fault is an MoT failure point. See Figure 9.1.

You should also ask an assistant to rock the steering wheel to and fro (wheels on the ground) while you watch underneath the car for 'lost motion' on the way from the steering rack or box to the road wheels. Don't forget to check any universal joints in the steering column. As well as sloppy movement at steering or suspension ball joints or swivel pins, look also for looseness at rack, box, or steering idler mountings. Jacking up a road wheel and rocking it top and bottom may show up worn suspension ball joints, or king pins. It can also pin-point worn or slack wheel bearings – here you watch for movement between the brake drum or disc and the backplate.

Slack bearings might be cured by adjustment. Worn bearings, particularly if noisy or 'gritty' when the wheel is spun, must be renewed. Worn steering ball joints may be detected by rocking the wheel laterally, rather than vertically (Figure 9.2).

Sometimes wear at leaf spring shackle pins, or suspension arm bushes or ball joints will only show up by using a sturdy bar to lever between the various components. Remember that on the

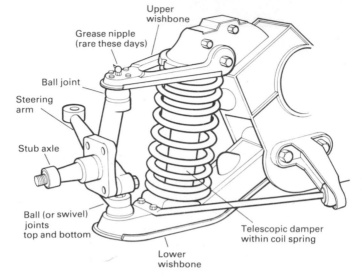

Figure 9.1. A typical front suspension set-up

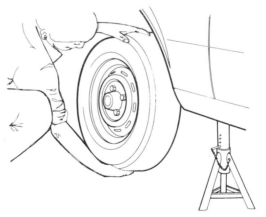

Figure 9.2. Rocking a front wheel vertically can show up slack wheel bearings, while rocking it laterally can pin-point worn steering ball joints

road the weight of the car will be applying rather more leverage
than you will be with that bar (Figure 9.3). Check that all
suspension dampers are tightly mounted, with no signs of
movement or deterioration of rubber bushes (Figure 9.4). Look
for signs of fluid leaks, or of severe rust, or cracks in leaf or coil
springs.

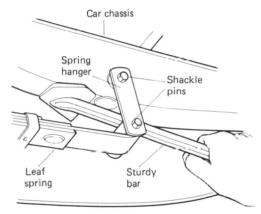

Car chassis

Spring
hanger

Shackle
pins

Leaf
spring

Sturdy
bar

*Figure 9.3. You may need a sturdy bar to show up wear at leaf spring
shackle pins or other suspension joints*

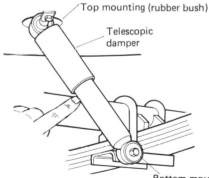

Top mounting (rubber bush)

Telescopic
damper

Bottom mounting (rubber bush)

*Figure 9.4. Check dampers for leaks and for security of their mountings,
ensuring also that their rubber bushes are sound*

Keeping an eye open also means more than simply checking your tyres for tread wear or damage. Bear in mind that abnormal tyre wear can often be the first sign of steering or suspension trouble. For instance, severe wear on one side of the tread only could indicate incorrect wheel alignment (i.e., toe-in or toe-out) or some other steering or suspension fault. Intermittently uneven wear around the tread circumference can indicate similar problems, or out-of-balance wheels, or grabbing brakes. Excessive wear of the centre tread only may be caused by over-inflation of the tyres, while excessive wear of the outer edges only points to the opposite. Buy yourself a good quality tyre pressure gauge, and believe this rather than the average garage airline gauge.

Keeping an ear open means noting undue noise, or deteriorating ride comfort. Persistent moaning, growling, squealing – possibly altering in character as you turn corners – suggests worn wheel bearings. Crashings and bangings, excessive bounciness, uncertain steering or unbalanced braking can all reflect worn suspension.

Judder at the steering wheel, perhaps disappearing at certain speeds, may be caused by out-of-balance wheels. This can be due to worn tyres, new tyres, a lost balance weight, or swopping wheels around (front to rear and vice versa) to even out tyre wear. Note also that while the fronts are chief culprits, unbalanced *rear* wheels can also cause the problem.

Tyre law

As well as being correctly inflated according to the manufacturer's recommendations, the tyres must be free from lumps, bulges, cuts or splits in the tread or sidewalls. All tyres must have a tread depth of at least one millimetre throughout a continuous circumferential band of at least three-quarters of the tread width. In addition, there must be a visible tread pattern over the remaining one-quarter of the tread width, and there must not be the smallest bald patch on the tread area.

Radials and crossplies must not be mixed on the same axle, and if you have this mix of types, the pair of radials must be on the rear, the crossplies on the front. Tyres on the same axle must be of the same size, and pressures all-round must be as recommended by the manufacturer.

Maintenance

As suggested earlier, the predominance nowadays of 'sealed-for-life' steering and suspension joints means that greasing is largely a thing of the past. Do be sure, however, that your car does not have the odd grease nipple that needs occasional attention (see 'Lubrication' earlier) or maybe a steering box, steering idler, or shock-absorber that needs topping up with the recommended fluid.

If your car has lever arm shock absorbers (rather than telescopic units) these may have a filler plug allowing them to be topped up with damper fluid at regular intervals. Check these units for signs of leakage and (particularly rear ones) for security of their mounting nuts and bolts. Even slight looseness here can cause quite an insistent, and elusive knocking noise. Leaking units can only be replaced.

The same checks apply to telescopic units, although these rarely provide for topping up. Points to watch with these are the condition of the rubber bushes at their mounting points, and where applicable the condition of rubber gaiters.

Clean up leaf springs with a wire brush and check along their edges to ensure there are no signs of fractured leaves. Use a spanner to ensure that all U-bolts and shackle bolts are tight (Figure 9.5). Watch out for signs of corrosion around the shackle mountings, or around the top mountings of suspension struts.

Gaiter/ball joint renewal

Again as suggested earlier, a damaged steering gaiter must be renewed, and fresh lubricant added. And since the work

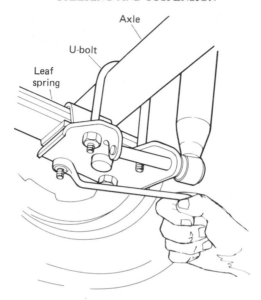

Figure 9.5. Check that leaf-spring U-bolts are tight

involved in fitting a new gaiter and in the renewal of a steering
ball joint is inter-related, it makes sense to cover both at the
same time.

Before a steering rack gaiter can be slid off, the track rod end
ball joint must be removed. Also, of course, the side of the car
must be jacked up and supported, and the appropriate road
wheel removed. The ball joint may be screwed on to or into the
rod. In some (non-rack) applications it may be integral with the
rod, so the expensive answer to a worn joint is renewal of rod
complete with joint. Where the joint is separate, it will be locked
to the rod with either a lock-nut or a bolted clamp. The nut or
clamp must be loosened off first, and with a nut the joint must be
held with a spanner on its flats, or by some form of wrench.

Note that screwing the joint in or out (it could have a left-hand
thread, incidentally) shortens or lengthens the rod, so altering
the steering toe-in or toe-out.

Although eventually the track will need resetting, it is as well now to maintain as near as possible the original setting. So some means of screwing on the old or replacement joint to the original position must be found. Methods include screwing back the loosened lock-nut to practically its original position, counting or painting the exposed threads, wrapping tape round the exposed threads, or counting the number of turns as the joint is screwed off. Once the car is back on the road, however, the track should be checked and re-set by a professional as soon as possible, or you risk rapid and expensive tyre wear. The ball joint has a taper pin which is secured to the steering arm by a nut on the threaded end. The nut may have a split pin, which must be removed, and renewed on reassembly.

Removing the ball joint

Some means must be found now of breaking the taper joint in the steering arm, a joint which can prove quite stubborn. How you do this is decided to some extent by whether the ball joint is to be renewed, or simply replaced. In days gone by the method used by professionals involved clouting opposite sides of the steering arm yoke simultaneously with medium hefty hammers to 'shock' the pin free. It was called 'impact hammering' and is a method that could still be used today. But space in which to swing the hammers can be limited, and there is a knack to the operation.

Fortunately, there are now easier ways, using one of today's relatively inexpensive 'special' tools. The simplest is a forked wedge you hammer between the joint and arm. But this does risk ruining the rubber boot on the joint. The best tool, which won't cost you a fortune, is a scissor-action ball joint breaker (Figure 9.6). To use this, undo the pin nut until it is flush with the end of the pin, and position the tool so its forked arm slides between joint and steering arm, and its other arm bears against the pin nut. Tightening the bolt at the opposite end of the tool closes the scissors, and forces the pin out of its seating. The ball joint can now be separated from the track rod.

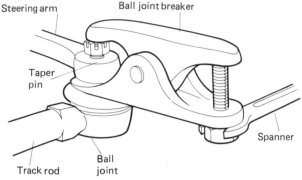

Figure 9.6. A scissor-action ball joint breaker shown in use

Removing the gaiter

If the ball joint was held by a clamp, this also (or the lock-nut) must be removed before the gaiter can be taken off (see Figure 9.7). Also clean any dirt off the rod, and have a receptacle handy beneath the gaiter to catch any remaining lubricant as it is withdrawn. Once its securing straps or clips have been slackened off, the gaiter can now be slid off the rod. But first note how the screw connections are positioned, and also exactly where each end of the gaiter reaches on the rod.

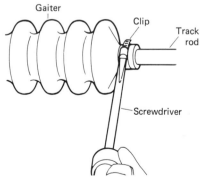

Figure 9.7. Note the positioning of the steering rack gaiter before slackening its clips and sliding it off the track rod

Reassembly

Provided no dirt has entered, and the inner joint looks sound, a new gaiter can be slid into place. Grease its inner ends slightly first to aid the operation. Your handbook or manual will tell you whether the internal lubricant is grease or oil, and also the type and quantity. If grease is required, pack the joint as well as the gaiter before reassembly. If oil is the lubricant, check first, by temporarily jacking the car to tilt it towards the open joint, that all the old oil has drained out. Then the new oil can be added before tightening the outer clip by pushing in the spout of a pump-type oil can. A combination of now jacking the car back the other way and holding the rod inclined upwards should ensure the oil runs the right way.

The operation might be helped by carefully turning the steering from lock to lock. However, this of course requires both road wheels either off the car, or at least clear of the ground. Afterwards, tighten the clips or wire securing the end of the gaiter. But note that neither clip should be so tight that it cuts right into the rubber. The ball joint can now be screwed back into (or onto) the rod, keeping to the measurement noted previously, but do not tighten the clamp or lock-nut yet. Enter the taper into the steering arm yoke and tighten its securing nut. Now check that the parts align correctly, turning the ball joint as required before locking it. Remember that the track alignment must be checked professionally as soon as possible.

Wheel bearings

Generally speaking, it is only the bearings of the non-driven wheels that have a regular service requirement. Your handbook may recommend that you check them for adjustment at normal service periods, and repack them with grease at long-service intervals – say, 35–40 000 miles.

As mentioned earlier, bearing slackness will show up as movement between drum and backplate, or disc and backplate when the road wheel is grasped top and bottom and rocked.

Barely perceptible movement is the usual rule-of-thumb recommendation.

Adjusting bearings

Should the movement seem excessive, it can generally be reduced by simply tightening the hub nut a little. Sometimes the correct adjustment is arrived at merely by 'feel', sometimes a torque setting for the hub nut will be given which should automatically achieve the correct adjustment. Check this data in your handbook or workshop manual.

Access to the hub nut requires removal of the dust or grease cap. You might also need to remove the road wheel. The cap may have a lip which allows it to be levered or tapped off, working evenly around its circumference. However, refer back to removing drum/hub units in the Braking System chapter for variations and suggested procedure here. Next, the hub nut. Here the arrangement can vary from car to car (see Figure 9.8). First, you may have to wipe away surrounding grease, so you can actually see what's there. Again cross-reference with the Braking

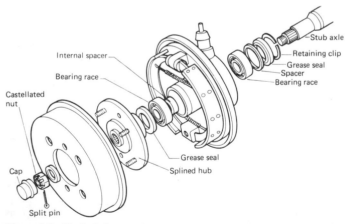

Figure 9.8. Exploded view of ball-race bearing hub assembly on a front wheel drive system

System chapter may help. Incidentally, examine the grease closely – if it appears to contain a lot of metallic swarf, the bearings are breaking up, and must be replaced. (If you wish to do this job yourself, a typical procedure is described later in this section, although in some instances you will need the precise instructions from the workshop manual for your car.).

Having wiped away the grease, you may see simply a castellated nut locked with a split pin, a castellated cap over a plain nut, the cap locked with a split pin, a plain nut peened into a groove in the stub axle, or (on some VWs) a clamp nut, locked with a through-bolt which may have a socket or hexagon head.

If the nut is peened, carefully chop away as much as possible of the peening with a small cold chisel. The leverage of the spanner on the nut will be sufficient to break away any remaining peening. Note that some nearside hubs will have left-hand thread nuts, also the peened type of nut must be renewed. Where a clamp nut is used with a socket-headed bolt, it is vital to ensure that the correct sized Allen key is used and that this fits firmly into the head. Where a split pin has to be removed, use a new pin afterwards.

Adjustment procedure

First, temporarily replace the road wheel, if this has been removed. Tighten its bolts just sufficiently to hold it. A typical procedure now is, while turning the wheel, to tighten the hub nut, either to the prescribed torque or until there is barely perceptible play, with the wheel still turning smoothly. Where a torque is specified, it may also be required that once the torque is reached, the nut should be turned back a specified amount. In other cases the nut may have to be first fully tightened, then backed off as specified. Check your car data to see what procedure applies to your vehicle.

When replacing a split pin, the castellated nut (or cap) may need fractional adjustment back or forth to align the pin holes. Use your own judgment as to which direction leaves you with the best bearing adjustment. Use a punch to lock the peened type of nut. Having achieved the correct adjustment, you should now check that the wheel still spins smoothly, with no 'grittiness' or undue noise that would indicate the bearings need renewal.

It is worth smearing a finger-full of fresh grease around the outer bearing, and sometimes it is recommended that the hub cap should be charged, maybe half-full, with grease before being replaced. Again, you need to check out this point with your car data, or local dealer for your make of vehicle.

Renewing bearings

Although details may vary from car to cary, a typical procedure would start with the removal of the wheel hub, as described previously for brake drum-hub removal. (The variations in hub nut set-ups have been covered in both the Braking System section and earlier in this section.) Note that with a disc brake hub you would have to first dismount the brake caliper unit and tie this securely out of the way (Figure 9.9). Also note that although some of the basic procedure will apply generally, we are really talking of the hub bearings in non-driven wheels. On, say, front wheel drive set-ups, the hub carrier has to be separated from both the drive shaft and the suspension mountings.

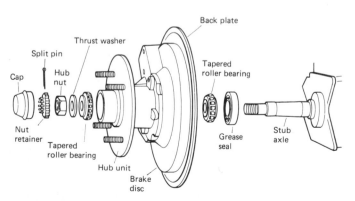

Figure 9.9. Taper roller bearing assembly on a disc brake unit

Having, then, withdrawn the hub – checking the position of thrust washers, etc. – the first thing to note is that the inner races of taper roller bearings will practically fall out as you pull the hub free, whereas parallel ball bearing races will usually remain firmly intact inside the hub. In fact, usually before the inner bearing can either fall out or be otherwise removed the grease seal at this end of the hub must be prised out. A new seal will be required, along with the bearings.

If the inner races of the bearings have remained intact inside the hub (e.g., ball bearing type) these must be removed next. Drive them out with a suitable drift, each in turn being drifted outwards from the centre of the hub.

Note the layout

Watch out for a tubular spacer fitted between the two bearings, and, if there is one, note which way round it fits as you withdraw it. It is also vitally important that replacement bearings are fitted the right way round in the hub. Starting with these inner races take note of any markings on them. On the outer races (i.e., the track only) which at the moment remain in the hub, a particular distinction will be a noticeable lip on one edge. Take note of which way it faces (usually this will be inwards, towards the centre of the hub).

Having now removed the inner races and any spacer fitted, it will help if the hub is washed out thoroughly with paraffin or petrol. This done it is easier to see both those outer races that must now be punched out, and also the cut-outs that often exist in the hub to allow access for the punch. Work from side to side evenly, so there is no danger of the race tipping and jamming. Again, work from the hub centre outwards.

It may be possible to use these discarded outer races to drift in the new ones, or maybe you can find a suitable sized socket. Remember there must be no risk of damage, such as might be caused if you attempted to punch in the new races in the same manner as you punched out the old. Don't forget to position the spacer, if there is one, *before* you fit the second bearing. Remember also that where, say, a ball-bearing unit is fitted as a whole unit, your tubular drift must bear only on the outer race.

Lubrication

Although the new bearings will probably be ready-greased to some extent, coat them yourself with fresh grease of a suitable type (Lithium-based may be recommended) working it in with your fingers. With the ball-bearing type this may have to be done before you fit them, whereas it is an easy job to coat the inner races of taper roller units before inserting them into their outer races. Some grease should also be packed in the space in the hub between the two bearings, although a typical recommendation would be to no more than half fill this space.

Don't forget to fit the new grease seal, using a hammer and block of wood to tap this in, with its lips facing into the hub. If necessary clean up any imperfections on the stub axle with fine emery cloth or wet-and-dry paper. Then smear the entire stub axle with grease. Now replace the hub unit, taking care that the threaded end of the stub does not displace the inner race of the outer bearing. If it is a parallel bearing, ball-race type, and a fairly tight fit, use a tubular drift carefully against the inner race of the outer bearing. With a taper roller bearing unit, you may prefer to fit the inner race of the outer bearing once the hub is in place.

Finally, replace washer and nut, and adjust and secure as appropriate, using a new split-pin where one is employed. Allow a hundred miles or so for bedding-in, then re-check the adjustment.

10

The electrics

The growing employment of 'maintenance-free' (or practically maintenance-free) car batteries these days has largely done away with what was one of the more frequent service requirements of the electrical system – that of checking and possibly topping up the battery's electrolyte level. Nevertheless, where the requirement still exists, it should be done meticulously, to the required level, and mopping up spillage, whether it be once a month or once a year.

While the need for battery maintenance fades, there seems to be a correspondingly increasing need for more widespread checking of headlamp beam alignment. It is a service that is relatively inexpensive at most tyre, battery and exhaust outlets (or your local garage) and you could do yourself a favour, as well as your fellow motorists, if you put more light on the road, rather than in the screens of approaching cars. Perhaps even worse are one-eyed monsters, so part of your as-and-when maintenance should be checking that all bulbs are working, and that lamp glasses are clean.

Other general maintenance requirements include checking that the battery terminals (and others) are clean, and that the generator drive belt is sound, and correctly adjusted. This belt is vital to your electrics, in that without it the generator can't keep the battery charged, so eventually you would run out of electricity. It may also be vital to your cooling system, for it most likely drives the water pump, if not the engine cooling fan as well. And running out of engine, which has become so hot that it's seized up, is rather more dire than running out of electricity. So always carry a spare belt, and the tools to fit it, in case one should break miles away from home. Incidentally, because at one time this belt usually also drove the mechanical cooling fan, it is often still referred to as a fan belt even when an electric cooling fan is fitted.

Apart from general maintenance, on high-mileage cars there might eventually be need for renewing generator or starter motor brushes, and these are some of the aspects we shall look at later. But first the basic service requirements:

Topping up the battery

Topping up the battery is simple enough (Figure 10.1) – except where access is tortuous. However, what you should avoid is spillage over the top of the battery, which encourages both dirt and the leakage of current. If spillage does occur, mop it up immediately. Note also that as the battery warms up the electrolyte will expand. This, of course, is particularly important where the battery is mounted in the engine compartment. So it is preferable to check the electrolyte level when the engine is

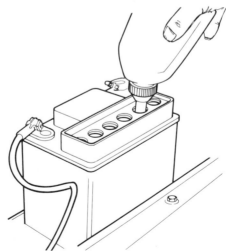

Figure 10.1. Use only distilled water or proprietary topping-up fluid for the battery

warm, after a run, so you avoid the over-filling that so often leads to overflow, dirt and corrosion.

Top up so that the level is just above the tops of the plates, or aligns with the level mark if there is one. Some batteries do, in fact, incorporate automatic level-finding, having a trough under one or more covers – as you pour the distilled water into the trough it will trickle into the cells until their level finders cut off the flow.

Don't be tempted to use ordinary tap water – the impurities this water may contain can cause internal deterioration that will drastically shorten the life of the battery. Considering the relative cheapness of the distilled water (or proprietary topping-up fluids) available in handy top-up bottles at accessory shops and garages, it's a chance just not worth taking.

Battery terminals

If corrosion already exists on the battery terminals, pouring hot water or a mixture of hot water and domestic soda, over the terminals and other corroded parts (e.g., the battery strap) is remarkably effective, but make sure you avoid spillage into the cells. This treatment should simply wash away the worst of the build-up. Then a wire brush and emery cloth will bring both connectors and battery posts back to shining brightness, while a knife blade or slim half-round file can be carefully used to clean out the insides of cup-type terminals. Be very careful to guard against shorts when working on the battery terminals. When reconnecting the terminals don't forget to reset the car's electric clock, if fitted.

A smear of petroleum jelly (such as Vaseline) or proprietary anti-corrosion preparation on the posts and terminals will guard against further corrosion and maintain good electrical connections. Screws or clamps on the terminal connections should be tight but not 'murdered'. A trick that will often overcome the problem of stripped screw threads in terminal posts is to feed a length of thin electrical solder into the threaded hole before inserting the screw. Finally, make sure the top and sides of the battery are clean and dry.

Checking the drive belt

As a rule of thumb, generator drive belt adjustment should be about right when there is no more than half-an-inch total deflection under moderate thumb pressure on the longest run of the belt. The belt shouldn't be overtight, since this can be harmful to generator and water pump bearings. That said, the adjustment for an alternator may have to be tighter than for a dynamo, since the alternator is harder to drive when under electrical load. Also check the belt's condition. Examine it for obvious wear, undue shininess, fraying or cracks.

Belt adjustment

A typical adjustment procedure involves slackening the pivot bolt(s) of the generator, and the strap bolts on engine and generator. The generator is then pivoted away from the engine until the belt is sufficiently tight, then all bolts are re-tightened. Should you find it difficult to hold the generator away from the engine to keep the belt taut while tightening the bolts, it is permissible to use a lever carefully between the engine and the drive end bracket of the generator.

A variation on some cars (e.g., VW Beetle) is that the generator has a split pulley and shim arrangement. Unbolting the two halves of the pulley and adding or subtracting shims widens or narrows the pulley, this having its effect on belt tension – e.g., narrowing the pulley forces the belt further out, thus tightening it. The spare shims are bolted to the outside of the pulley. See Figures 10.2 and 10.3.

Fitting a new belt

Fitting a replacement drive belt demands much the same procedure as for adjustment. But if it is tight, position it on one pulley, then feed it over the edge of the final pulley, turning this the while, rather as you used to fit a bicycle chain.

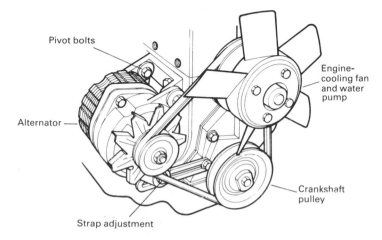

Pivot bolts

Engine-cooling fan and water pump

Alternator

Crankshaft pulley

Strap adjustment

Figure 10.2. The generator drive belt must be in sound condition and properly adjusted

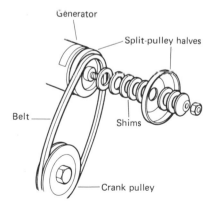

Generator

Split-pulley halves

Belt

Shims

Crank pulley

Figure 10.3. A split pulley arrangement allows for generator belt adjustment on air-cooled VWs

Flat battery

Cause and cure

Provided all connections are sound and the drive belt is properly adjusted (and you're sure the battery is otherwise in good condition) persistent 'flat battery' problems must be due to poor generator output. Mind you, this condition, or a complete lack of charge, should be indicated by persistant illumination of the generator warning light.

A basic check can be made with a multimeter, by switching this to volts and connecting it across the battery terminals, with the engine idling. Increasing the engine revs should register an increased voltage on the multimeter. If you haven't a multimeter, try switching on the headlamps then revving the engine – the lights should brighten. Or similarly a test-lamp connected across the battery should brighten.

If there is no positive reaction to these checks, there are some further tests you can make on a dynamo. Disconnect the 'D' and 'F' terminal leads from the end of the dynamo. The terminals should be of different sizes to avoid confusion, but if there is any doubt mark the leads for easy identification. Start the engine and let it idle at about 1000 rpm. Now connect the positive lead of your multimeter (switched to volts) to one of the dynamo terminals, and the negative lead to earth, at the same time bridging both dynamo terminals with, say, an electrical screwdriver blade. Should you now get a reading of about 14 volts on the scale, the dynamo is working. If you haven't a voltmeter (or multimeter) this test can be done using a 12 volt bulb, in which case the bulb should shine brightly if the dynamo is working. Either way, if the dynamo is proved to be in order, your low charge – or no charge – problem would seem to point to a faulty voltage regulator. And unless you're a competent auto electrician, a replacement unit is the only sure answer here.

If these tests fail to show a charge, however, there is a further check you can make provided you have a multimeter. With the multimeter switched to rpm, start the engine and run it up to about 2000 rpm. Now, with the multimeter switched back to volts, connect it between the 'D' terminal (the larger of the two) and earth. Hopefully, there will be at least some voltage reading, maybe only two or three volts, which might indicate that new brushes and/or a cleaned-up commutator will solve the problem. If the dynamo has seen long service it is in any case worth carrying out this work in the hope it will provide a cure – better than buying a new unit, particularly as some can be quite expensive.

But if you are thoroughly unsure of the problem, you can always take the car to an auto-electrician for more professional checking. And with an alternator anything further than those initial charge or brightness tests at the battery terminals might well require professional investigation. However, hoping that a low-charge problem with either unit simply requires brush renewal, we will follow with a typical procedure for both types of generator.

Brush renewal – dynamo

First remove the dynamo from the car, since it will be easier to work on when clamped in a bench vice (Figure 10.4). There may

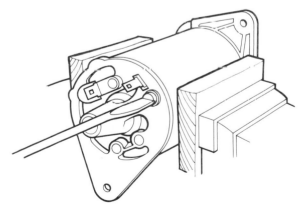

Figure 10.4. The dynamo is easier to work on when clamped in the padded jaws of a bench vice

well be windows in the brush end plate – or in the body, covered by a strap – through which the brushes can be inspected. To renew the brushes, this end plate must be removed. The plates are held by two long through-bolts, and a large screwdriver, firmly fitting in the screw slots, will be needed to shift them.

One of the terminals may pass through the brush end plate, insulated by a sleeve. Ease the plate away from the body casing, taking care not to lose the sleeve. The plates should have locating 'pips' on them, which mate with indents in the casing to ensure correct reassembly. Otherwise scribe alignment marks on plates and casing. Having lifted the brush plate away, the drive plate, pulley and armature can be withdrawn from the other end. Next, lift the ends of the coil springs from the old brushes, unscrew their leads and discard the brushes. Incidentally, before fitting the new brushes, thoroughly clean the end plate and brush holders. Then make sure the new brushes slide easily in the holders.

Now 'cock' the ends of the coil springs against the sides of the brushes, the latter withdrawn until their commutator ends are flush with the ends of the holders (Figure 10.5). This helps the brush slide over the commutator, rather than snag against it, when replacing the plate. But do not reassemble just yet. First

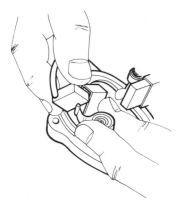

Figure 10.5. When reassembling cock the springs against the sides of the brushes

clean out the interior of the casing, using a brush or soft rag to avoid damage to the field coils and the insulation. Next, using some form of protective padding, carefully clamp the armature in the vice – tighten the jaws just enough to secure it. Now clean up the commutator, using a strip of fine glass-paper (not emery) looped round it and 'see-sawed' back and forth. Make sure this action is spread evenly around the entire circumference. Afterwards, check that there is still a depth of around 1 mm between the segments of the commutator. If not, the mica insulation can be carefully cut back to this depth using a fine hacksaw blade with its sides ground sufficiently slim. Use an electrical screwdriver blade to ensure all metallic swarf is cleaned from the grooves.

Smear some HMP grease in the shaft bush located in the brush plate, then reassemble, making sure the terminal sleeve is in place, and that any shims or washers at the commutator end are replaced. Locate the pips in the casing, then check the through-bolts pass behind the insulation and pick up cleanly in the drive end plate. Tighten them firmly. Now use a slim screwdriver poked through the inspection holes to carefully tease the ends of the coil springs off the sides of the brushes and onto their ends, so the brushes are pushed into firm contact against the commutator.

Brush renewal – alternator

Although the brushes of an alternator are generally smaller than those of a dynamo, they carry only the field current of around two or three amps, compared to the charging current of around 21 amps endured by dynamo brushes, and the slip ring that they ride on is far smoother than a dynamo's commutator. For these reasons they will normally last far longer than dynamo brushes. Generally speaking, too, alternator brushes are far easier to get at than those of a dynamo. The snag is that their location and renewal procedure varies, with the several makes of unit currently in use – more so than with a dynamo, and it is not possible in a book of this size to describe each type.

Starter motor

Starter motors currently in use fall into two basic types – the 'inertia' type and the 'pre-engaged' type (Figures 10.6 and 10.7). In the first example, the action of the motor spinning throws a pinion (part of what is called the 'Bendix' gear) down a screwed sleeve and into mesh with the toothed 'ring gear' on the flywheel. It's a design that has worked well for many years, but its somewhat brutal action invariably takes its toll eventually of both pinion and ring gear teeth.

More popular these days is the second type of starter motor. This has a solenoid integral with the motor. Turning the ignition key feeds power to the solenoid, which then operates a lever that in turn pushes the pinion into mesh with the ring gear – at this

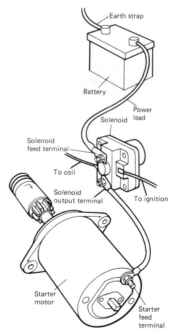

Figure 10.6. Inertia starter system

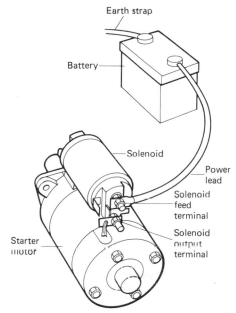

Figure 10.7 Pre-engaged starter system

point a secondary switch within the solenoid feeds power to the motor, so the latter cannot turn until the pinion is in mesh. Incidentally, the solenoid for the inertia starter will normally be found mounted on a wing or the bulkhead.

Starter faults

Starter motor faults can be electrical or mechanical. Should the starter fail to operate, an elementary initial electrical check is to switch on the headlights – if these do not light up, or if they merely glow, perhaps the fault is a flat battery. However, if the headlights do work, but dim when the ignition key is turned, it can be assumed that power is reaching the starter motor. The fault could still be electrical – maybe only worn out brushes – or there could be a mechanical problem, like the pinion jammed in mesh with the flywheel.

The latter possibility may be checked in one or two ways. On some units there will be a squared extension to the armature shaft protruding from the end plate – it may have a push-on cap over it. If you can reach this with a suitable spanner, turning it may free the pinion. Failing this, rocking the car back and forth (ignition off) in, say, second or third gear, might do the trick. Where an inertia type does operate, but merely spins furiously without turning the engine, the Bendix gear is failing to go into mesh, perhaps because of dirt on its screwed sleeve.

But if as the starter operates there is also a harsh metallic grating sound (and the engine doesn't turn) the trouble could be either a damaged Bendix pinion or damaged or missing teeth on the flywheel ring gear. If turning the engine manually, to present a different section of the ring gear, allows the starter to turn the engine, the ring gear is a major suspect. Unfortunately if that's the problem it means gearbox, clutch and flywheel removal, although removing the starter first will at least allow inspection of the ring gear.

Apart from worn or dirty brushes, electrical problems can be caused by faulty lead connections, or a breakdown in the solenoid. The earth return connections are particuarly important. Check the earth straps between the engine/transmission and the chassis (bodywork). Where these are poor, or missing, it is not unknown for the choke or throttle linkage back to the facia to get red hot (with attendant fire risk) when the starter is operated, and the return current seeks the easiest route back to earth.

Solenoid

Obviously the solenoid itself needs to receive power from an independent power source (i.e. the ignition switch) before it can operate and close its own switch to feed the direct battery power to the starter motor. Normally, when the ignition key is turned the solenoid should at least 'click', proving that power is getting this far. However, you can check by linking a test bulb between a sound earth and the (small) ignition feed on the solenoid – if there are two such feeds, try both (one feeds the coil) if you're not sure which is which. Turning the ignition key should light the bulb: if it doesn't, there's a fault in this lead, or the ignition switch itself.

Once you are sure the ignition switch is feeding power to the solenoid, you can move on to the next test. Connect your test lamp between the solenoid input terminal (the one connected directly to the battery) and a good earth point on the bodywork – if the lamp lights (as it should) the connections this far are sound. If the lamp does light, move the 'earth' connection to a point on the engine itself. If the lamp now *fails* to light, the earth connection between engine/transmission and bodywork is faulty. However, if the lamp lights in both instances, connect it next between the solenoid output terminal (the other large one) and earth, and have someone operate the ignition switch – if the bulb lights the solenoid is working, and the fault must be at the starter motor. If the bulb doesn't light, you need a new solenoid.

You can often confirm the solenoid is at fault (and obtain temporary starting) by bridging the solenoid's input and output terminals with the blade of a hefty and well insulated screwdriver. Do this carefully and watch out for sparks, but with luck the starter motor should now operate quite healthily. (Of course, the engine won't start unless the ignition is switched on.)

Whereas replacing the separately mounted solenoid of an inertia starter is straightforward, the procedure for a pre-engaged unit is different. Typically, you remove the lead connected between solenoid and motor, undo the two securing bolts and pull the unit away – you may have to tip it to unhook it from the pinion actuating lever, and, conversely, fiddle it back into engagement when replacing. Look out for an insulating 'buffer' between solenoid and motor body. If access is particularly difficult, the starter will have to be removed, as described next.

Starter removal

If there is an electrical or mechanical fault at the starter itself, the unit must be removed. The first job is to disconnect the battery earth lead, to guard against accidental shorts –

remember the main starter feed is permanently live. When removing the battery feed on the inertia type, be careful not to twist the terminal post – use one spanner on its lock nut, while undoing the lead securing nut with another.

Before removing the leads on the pre-engaged type, note where the secondary wiring attaches. Having disconnected the wiring, undo the two or three main bolts securing the starter motor to the engine, and withdraw the unit, making a note of the number and positioning of any shims that may be fitted.

Bendix gear

The Bendix gear of an inertia type starter motor can be examined, cleaned or dismantled as necessary, without any further dismantling of the starter motor (Figure 10.8). If it looks

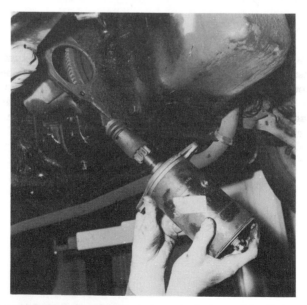

Figure 10.8. Note that when the starter motor is removed the ring gear can also be inspected. This is an inertia unit with Bendix gear

sound (no severe chipping of the pinion teeth, or breakage of the main buffer spring) but merely feels sluggish or gritty when turned on the shaft by hand, you may be able to clean it quite adequately without dismantling it. Do this by carefully dipping the gear in a cup of petrol and, with the aid of a brush, swill the gear thoroughly clean. Wipe away surplus petrol and allow the residue to dry thoroughly, remembering to take all usual precautions as far as handling petrol is concerned. Incidentally, don't oil the Bendix gear, since this attracts dirt, and causes an early return of the sticking problem.

Next, screw the pinion along its sleeve and let go. If it now moves easily and returns briskly, hopefully the problem is solved, and you can simply refit the motor. But first take the opportunity to check the ring gear teeth, turning the engine over to examine the entire circumference. If you need to actually dismantle the Bendix, either for renewal of damaged parts or for more extensive cleaning, you'll need to compress the buffer spring, so the jump ring that secures the assembly to the shaft can be removed.

There are relatively inexpensive compressors for this job sold by accessory shops. Or you can improvise with a valve spring compressor and distance tube, with a cut away in the tube so you can get in with a screwdriver blade and lever off the jump ring. (Earlier starters used a nut and split pin to secure the Bendix.) When using the compressor be careful not to let the parts fly all over the place, and when you dismantle note how the parts fit together. Before reassembling, with old or new components, check that the shaft is smooth, and that there are no chips or burrs on other parts. Cautious use of a fine file may clean up minor damage.

Pre-engaged pinion gear

On a pre-engaged starter motor, the very nature of the design should mean that the pinion assembly rarely gives trouble. In the rare event that it does, however, it's complicated to remove, you have to renew it as a complete assembly, and it's expensive.

If you have removed the motor to deal with an electrical fault, provided the pinion looks sound the best advice is probably to leave well alone. However, if renewal is a 'must', an outline procedure might be as follows:

Having removed the solenoid as already described and then the brush end plate as described in Brush Renewal, the drive end plate and armature can be withdrawn from the casing.

The next step is to separate the armature, pinion gear and engagement lever from the end bracket, the complete assembly being held in this bracket by the pivot pin through bracket and engagement lever.

This pivot pin may vary in type from a screwed design to simply a force fit plain pin which needs to be carefully punched out – 'carefully', because if parts are difficult to get you may need to re-use the pin. Note also that you may need to (again carefully) 'unpeen' one end of the pin first. See Figure 10.9.

As you then separate the units from the bracket, if there is any danger at this stage of the engagement lever becoming detached from the pinion gear, note which way round it faces. And, of course, bear this point in mind subsequently.

Your problem now is the withdrawal of the pinion gear from the shaft – on which it is most likely retained by a cup and snap

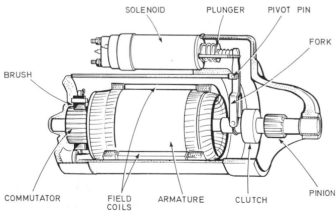

Figure 10.9. Cut-away view of pre-engaged pinion set-up

ring arrangement. A method the author has used successfully to deal with this device is first to support carefully the armature in the padded jaws of a vice. Then find an open-ended spanner whose jaws will just rest on the cup without touching the snap ring – cautious use of a hammer on the spanner close to the shaft should drift that cup down off the snap ring. Much patient juggling with screwdrivers will now be called for to persuade that snap ring out of its groove and off the shaft.

Reassembly is more or less a straight reversal of the procedure so far – but much grief will be caused should you neglect to fit that cup before re-installing that snap ring. For reassembly, clamp the spanner firmly in the vice, support the other side of the cup on the spanner jaws, then use a soft (copper) hammer on the shaft end to force the snap ring back into the cup.

Brush renewal

The mounting of the brush gear, and access to it, can vary so much from motor to motor that we can only generalise here (Figure 10.10). As on some dynamos, there may be a band clamped over 'windows' at the brush end, with generous access and all brush leads conveniently secured by screws, so you could virtually renew the brushes without even removing the starter. However, in many cases the brushes will be exposed only by removing the end plate. Sometimes the end plate (again, like the dynamo) will be secured by two long through-bolts, sometimes it will be held by separate bolts, usually about four smallish ones.

Before the end plate can be withdrawn, a spring clip may have to be eased off the end of the armature shaft, or a split pin removed. Watch out for washers on the shaft either side of the end plate, and note that the field brushes will have to be removed from their holders before the brush plate can be lifted away – note which brush goes where, and how their leads lie.

In some designs the brushes bear against a flat-ended commutator, rather than straddle its circumference. In these cases you'll find that replacing the plate and brushes is easier than normal, since the brushes do not have to be held in a 'cocked' position, and released once they are over the commutator.

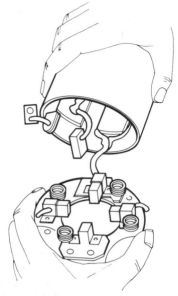

Figure 10.10. Typical starter motor brush gear

In the absence of specific recommendations, brushes much
under half an inch in length are probably due for renewal
anyway. One pair of brushes may come ready attached to the
unit's terminal post – in this case you may have to transfer the
insulating sleeve off the old post to the new. The field brushes
may come ready attached to just one length of lead. Note now
that the old brushes may be welded to the field terminal. There's
no way you can melt and re-solder this joint. So the answer is to
snip the old brushes off fairly close to the joint, snip the new lead
in two, corresponding to the old lead lengths, then use a
powerful soldering iron to solder the new leads to the tags of the
old. It's fiddly work, and you do need to end up with neat joints,
which should be carefully insulated with tape afterwards.

Clean the commutator as described for the dynamo earlier,
but do not under-cut the segments. If the brushes have to be held
half out (see earlier in this section) while replacing the end plate,

the procedure is as described for the dynamo. But where life can get awkward is where there are no inspection windows or apertures – it can then be very trying inserting some form of tool to hook the brush springs back over the brushes once these are over the commutator, and the end plate practically home.

There are some units having external screws through the end plate which secure the brush plate, where the problem can be solved by positioning first the brush plate, then the end plate, then replacing the brush screws. Anyway, a thorough examination of your starter motor beforehand should reveal what work is involved, and what procedures you're going to have to adopt.

Fuses

The fuses are there to protect the circuit and the electrical equipment should a fault, such as a short, or serious overload, occur. Should a fuse blow, it's sensible to look for the fault, rather than simply renew the fuse, or – worse – replace it with one of higher value. This merely invites not only damaged electrical equipment, but also a real danger of fire because of over heated wiring, melting insulation and bared cable causing further shorting and possibly sparks. Since the original fitment type of fuses may vary from car to car, it may help to know more of the types, and their possible faults.

Three types are now in common use. The glass tube fuse can suffer from corroded end caps and this can effectively stop power to any accessories on that fuse. Take the fuse out, clean the end caps and clean the fuse-holder fitting where the ends of the fuse make contact. Many a mysterious failure of lamps, wipers, indicators, horn or heater fan can be attributed to such a fault, which is not always obvious at first glance.

Continental type ceramic fuses have an exposed filament. Be careful when removing this type of fuse, because the filament can get hot enough to burn your fingers. The fuses can suffer with the same troubles as do the glass tube types – poor contacts on the end terminals. These should be scraped clean where this is evident.

The latest, and probably the most efficient, type of fuse is the plug in type. It is very easy to see if the filament has blown because the fuse is made of transparent plastic. The plug and socket fitting also ensures a more reliable constant contact.

Fuses have both 'continuous' and 'blow' ratings. Note that the 'blow' rating is twice the continuous rating. The continuous rating is the total current that the fuse will take on a steady load without overheating. The 'blow' rating is the actual current the fuse will take at the instant it blows. Perhaps this will explain why some fuses appear to have run hot but have not blown – they have been loaded with more than their continuous rating.

Circuit breakers

Circuit breakers are often fitted in place of the conventional fuse where the circuit can experience temporary overloads. Electric windows and door locks are an example, where temporary jamming can occur due to a sticking window channel or frozen-up door lock solenoid. In such a case, the circuit-breaker will trip out the supply, then restore it after a short period when the thermal bi-metal contact cools down and closes the circuit once more.

Part Two

Fault-finding and Repair

1

Introduction

Sooner or later almost every motor vehicle comes to an involuntary stop due to either an electrical or mechanical failure. Regular servicing can reduce the chances, but any machine as complex as the modern motor car can and probably will break down at some time regardless of how well it is maintained. The breakdown may occur in the relative safety of your driveway or in the hazardous conditions of a busy motorway, but in either event there are certain guidelines and common sense precautions you should be aware of before trying to rectify the failure or even discover the fault. The special procedures you should follow in a motorway or other road breakdown are given separately.

First of all avoid working on your car if you are wearing any loose clothing – this could include a tie, a scarf or even loose fitting sleeves, in fact anything that could possibly get caught up in moving parts on your engine such as the fan or pulleys.

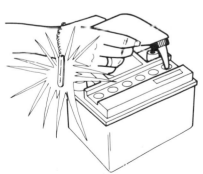

Figure 1.1. Do not wear metal jewellery when working on a car

157

Do not wear a wristwatch, particularly those with a metal strap – this could short out some electrical connection which besides damaging the car wiring system (and the watch) could cause a nasty burn. To some extent a ring or other form of jewellery could do the same or result in a cut finger if caught up anywhere (*Figure 1.1*).

If the engine has been running it may be very hot, particularly in the area of the exhaust manifold and could cause some painful burns if touched. In addition, on some cars with electric cooling fans at the radiator it is possible for the fan to start turning even though the ignition may be switched off.

Avoid removing the radiator cap or its equivalent on any expansion bottle in the engine cooling system when the engine is hot. The pressure retained in the system by the cap is all that keeps the coolant from boiling – release the pressure by removing the cap and the coolant can start to boil instantly and virtually blow out the radiator or expansion tank/bottle. This could cause severe scalding.

If you must remove the cap from a hot or even warm engine you would be wise to wear thick leather gloves or at least cover the cap in thick layers of cloth or newspaper, then turn the cap slowly until it can be turned no longer without downward pressure. Leave it in this position for a few minutes before attempting to turn it further.

Do not fill a warm or hot engine with cold water or conversely a cold engine with hot water. To do so could crack the engine block or cylinder head.

It is always advisable to remove the ignition keys before starting work, particularly if there are children in the car – you may also find it advantageous to disconnect the battery (or the horn) under these conditions. If the cause of breakdown is an electrical fault, it is usually a good idea to disconnect the battery anyway until the fault has been located.

Working under the car

As a general rule avoid working under the car unless it is firmly and adequately supported – the car jack alone is far to unsteady.

Ideally, axle stands should be used, although wooden blocks can be a satisfactory alternative. It is highly unlikely though that either would be available in a breakdown situation.

The most common reasons for car jack failure are:

1. Incorrect use;
2. Allowing the car to move when in the raised position.

If you are unsure of the type and location of the jacking points on your car or about how to operate the jack correctly, either ask a friend or your local dealer for advice and if possible go through a trial run. Most car jacks have a fairly small 'footprint' area, so not only can they sink into a soft surface (including newly-laid tarmac) but they will easily 'topple' over if the car moves. That is why some people carry in the car a piece of wood or old carpet to put under the jack on soft or slippery surfaces. Obviously, jacking a car up on a slope should be avoided at all times but even on the flat at least one of the wheels remaining on the ground should be chocked front and rear. In addition to this the handbrake should be applied and first gear selected.

On some vehicles the handbrake operates on the transmission and not on the rear wheels. With this arrangement jacking up one of the rear wheels will mean a complete loss of handbrake effort. Even having taken these precautions it would still be unsafe to venture underneath without some form of packing to take the weight of the car in the event of jack failure.

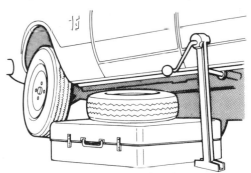

Figure 1.2. Do not rely on the car jack if working under the car – always use some form of packing

A packed suitcase with the spare wheel on top pushed under an axle or structural (box) member of the car body would be better than nothing (*Figure 1.2*). Alternatively, two wheels, one on top of the other may suffice. You may even find that sliding the spare under so that the wheel on the car 'sits' in the well of the spare may provide sufficient height.

Avoid shaking the car when it is jacked up – this often happens when trying to undo a particularly stubborn nut or bolt. Even when removing a wheel it is best to slacken off the clamping nuts/bolts before raising the car.

Breakdown procedures

It has been said that if breakdowns could be planned they would never happen when and where they do – usually during poor weather conditions and in a far from convenient, and often dangerous location.

There is not much we can do about the weather but with most breakdown situations we do have a limited control over the location, in that whichever component has failed, it will not prevent the car from being moved (pushed) or indeed prevent it from moving on under its own momentum (coasting). To some extent then the driver of a vehicle which has, for example, suffered an engine failure can either press the clutch or select neutral and then coast for some time before coming to a standstill. The object being, primarily to stop the car in a safe place and to avoid inconveniencing other road users – in other words to stop the breakdown becoming an accident.

In an ideal situation it should be possible to steer the casualty vehicle completely off the carriageway, failing that however, stop it in such a position that it is easily visible to oncoming drivers and causes the least obstruction to traffic flow.

Most modern cars are fitted with servo-assisted brakes in which the suction felt in the engine inlet manifold is used to reduce the pressure needed on the brake pedal. If the engine has stopped this suction will not exist, although a one-way valve between the servo and manifold prevents immediate loss of suction in the servo itself. This, however, will only be sufficient for one, possibly two applications of the brake, after which the pedal will have to be pressed much harder to achieve the same braking effect. Although less common, a number of cars are fitted with power-assisted steering, with these once the engine stops then the power assistance also stops and the steering will immediately become much 'heavier' and difficult to turn.

Although the situation prevailing at the time will often determine what action should be taken in the event of an electrical/mechanical failure, there are certain basic rules which should and in some cases must be followed depending upon where the breakdown occurs.

Motorway breakdowns

On any motorway it is vitally important to get your vehicle completely off the carriageway before coming to a stop. As soon as the vehicle develops a failure, use your indicators then coast over to the hard shoulder at the edge of the motorway and as far away from the traffic as possible. If the vehicle is in the outside lane when the failure occurs, beware of traffic approaching from behind in the slower lanes. Once parked on the hard shoulder switch on your hazard warning lights (four-way flashers). During the hours of darkness keep your side and tail lights on as well. If your car does not have hazard warning lights, switch on your side and tail lamps during daylight hours and if it is not raining, open your bonnet or boot so as to indicate that your car is stationary.

If you have a warning triangle, place it between the centre and outer edge of the hard shoulder about 150 yards (140 metres) behind the vehicle and in such a position that it can be seen easily by drivers of approaching vehicles.

Unless the broken down vehicle is likely to catch fire or is already ablaze, then in most instances the safest place for the driver and passengers is in the car – that is assuming it is well clear of other traffic. If it is necessary for any passenger to leave the vehicle, encourage them to do so through the near side – not on the motorway side. Take special care with children or animals (dogs) leaving the car. Under normal circumstances the only time the car should be left is when you need to summon assistance using one of the motorway telephones. In these cases ensure that the handbrake is applied firmly and the car is secure – all the doors and boot locked. Leave a note in the windscreen stating that you have gone to make the call.

Motorway telephones

Most motorways have emergency telephones on each carriageway sited at two-kilometre intervals. The nearest is shown by an arrow on the motorway distance marker posts, situated every 100 metres.

Never cross the carriageway to use the telephone on the other side, in fact if you value your life never walk on the carriageway at any time.

Lifting the handset on these telephones will put you into direct contact with the police at the motorway control centre – you cannot make any other call. Most of the telephones are also oneway only – the police cannot call you back; for this reason do not replace the handset until the police have all the information they require. After making the call return to your car. The police will obviously need to know where your car is – if you are unsure of the exact location give them the number of the telephone you are calling from, and approximate distance from your car and the direction. Additional information the police may require is the colour, make and model of your car, its year of manufacture and the registration number. It will also help if you can give some indication of the fault or the symptoms that led to the breakdown.

If you are a member of one of the motoring associations or a recovery organisation and you want their assistance, then inform the police when making the telephone call. Should the telephone be out of order return to your car and wait for a patrol car to stop. Usually when this kind of situation arises the police provide additional patrols.

Although there is no reason why you should not attempt to repair your car, remember that even on the hard shoulder a motorway is a dangerous place so only work either from the front of the car or from the near side. Ensure that should anyone stand at the rear of the car they do not obscure the lights. Any repair likely to take longer than about 30 minutes should not be attempted – the police may in any case decide to call out the emergency services.

Non-motorway breakdowns

Basically the same rules apply as with a breakdown on the motorway although it is unlikely that there will be any hard shoulder to stop on, or telephones at 2 km intervals.

Figure 1.3. Correct positioning of a warning triangle on a corner

It is still vitally important to cause the minimum obstruction to other traffic. If possible allow the vehicle to coast into a suitable parking spot, or very slowly onto the kerb. It may even be necessary to push the vehicle either backwards or forwards to a place of relative safety. Should all else fail, try coming to rest on a straight and level stretch of road where your car is readily visible to drivers approaching from either direction.

Unless in a parking area away from the carriageway, switch on your hazard warning lights and position any triangle in clear view at the side of the road at least 50 yeards (45 metres) behind the vehicle. If the breakdown has occurred on a curve or over the brow of a hill, position the triangle so that oncoming drivers can see it before entering the bend or reaching the top of the hill (*Figure 1.3*).

Emergency situations

Although any breakdown is potentially hazardous, some are much more so than others. With a simple engine failure, for example, the major problem will be avoiding or warning other traffic as the vehicle slows down. A failure in any of the vehicle control systems could cause additional and much more severe problems, and will almost inevitably end up in an accident unless the correct procedures are followed. A few examples of these and other emergency situations are:

Brake failure

If your brakes fail suddenly, quickly pump the pedal a few times to try and build up the pressure in the system – at the same time switch on your hazard warning lights. If the brakes still do not work try selecting a lower gear, but do not however overdo this as moving into a low gear at speed could induce a rear wheel skid. For example, in a typical family saloon travelling at over 50 mph select third gear, below that speed engage second.

Having changed gear operate the handbrake using a pumping action, do not hold it on as once again this could induce a rear wheel skid causing the car to spin out of control.

While all this is going on look for an escape route, into which you can turn. In an emergency such as on a steep downhill slope with either a crossroads or sharp bend at the bottom this technique may not be enough; in these cases it may be better to have what could be termed a 'controlled accident' rather than a big smash at the bottom. Pull your car over to the left of the road, scraping the bank or guard rail if necessary – do not do this too hard though or you could bounce back into the path of oncoming traffic. If you can, run into a field, even if it means smashing through a gate. It is preferable to run down small trees or bushes than collide with another vehicle. Remember that if a car travelling at 50 mph collides head on with another travelling at 30 mph, the result is much the same as running into a solid brick wall at 80 mph.

Tyre blowout

Resist the urge to slam on the brakes. Keep a firm hand on the steering wheel and try to keep the car going straight at the same time slow down by pumping the brake pedal gently. Switch on your hazard warning lights and where possible ease the car on to the hard shoulder or off the road.

Bonnet flies open

Quickly check in your mirror for any traffic approaching from the rear, slow down, switch on your hazard warning lights and pull over to the hard shoulder or side of the road. If you cannot immediately pull over to the side of the road, wind down the window so that you can put your head out just far enough to see what is ahead.

Windscreen breaks

If your car is fitted with a toughened windscreen the glass is designed to fragment into small and relatively safe chunks of glass when struck by a stone or other object. Some, termed 'zone toughened windscreens' will break, leaving slightly larger chunks of glass directly in front of the driver, through which the road ahead can still be seen. If you cannot see through the windscreen adopt the same procedure as that given for when the bonnet flies open, but in either case slow down and move over clear of the traffic.

Do not try and punch a hole in the windscreen while on the move – small fragments could break away and be blown back into your eyes. On the same theme never drive with a shattered windscreen of this type for it could collapse inwards, with once again the danger of fragments being blown into your eye. If you have the misfortune to get a splinter in your eye, do not rub the eye – seek medical attention immediately!

Some cars are fitted with laminated windscreens which crack, something like a normal house window pane but are designed to remain intact, providing some forward vision. If the impact on this type of screen is fairly heavy, you may find that some small but sharp fragments may have broken away. These should be cleared away from the dash and if you suspect any of having entered the heater intake, do not use the blower until they have been removed.

Normally it would be quite safe to carry on with a laminated windscreen that has cracked so long as forward vision is not restricted seriously but it would be wise, depending on the damage, to reduce speed.

Underbonnet fire

Pull over to the side of the road and stop the car switching off the engine as you do so (remember you may lose any power steering and brake servo action). Get everybody out of the car as soon as it stops.

If you have a fire extinguisher, raise the bonnet just sufficiently enough to locate the source of the fire and aim the extinguisher at the base of the flames. In some cases when the flames are relatively small, a wool blanket or jacket may smother them. Quite often the cause of the fire is an electrical short circuit, when a great deal of smoke may be produced by burning insulation. In such cases either cut the wires leading to the burning area or disconnect the battery.

Skidding

The best thing to know about a skid is how to avoid it. Watch out for wet leaves, mud or oil patches, deep pools of water, light rain after a long dry spell and the like and of course in winter beware of ice and snow. In all such conditions treat all the controls – steering, accelerator and brakes – gently.

In the event of a skid do not panic and press hard on the brake pedal – this will cause the wheels to lock making matters even worse. Equally, any sudden and violent movement of the steering or accelerator could have similar results. Try and relax – a tense driver will tend to jerk the controls and lose his 'feel' of the road. An expert rally driver once said, 'imagine there's a glass of beer on the bonnet and you don't want to spill any'.

Cars driven through the rear wheels will tend to skid rear first, whereas the now more common front-wheel drive cars will skid at the front first. The correction techniques differ considerably.

Rear-wheel skid: The feeling in this type of situation is that the car is trying to spin, which is exactly what it will do unless corrective action is taken. On a left-hand bend, for example, the rear of the car tends to break away to the right and in a right-hand bend it will break to the left (*Figure 1.4*).

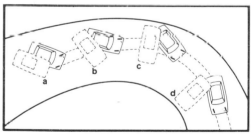

Figure 1.4. Rear-wheel skid
a. The start of the skid with the rear wheels sliding to the nearside. The driver steers the car in the same direction as the rear wheels are sliding – steering into the skid

b. The driver continues steering into the skid while at the same time decelerating and the car begins to straighten out. The dotted outline shows what would probably happen if no corrective action was taken

c. The car continues to straighten out; meanwhile the (dotted outline) car has started to spin and is now at right angles to the line of travel

d. With the car almost out of the skid situation the driver can think about driving on. The other (dotted) car though, is about to run off the road, completely out of control

The best way to overcome this is to let up on the accelerator and steer into the skid – that is if your rear wheels break away to the right, turn the front wheels to the right. Take care not to overcorrect and above all be calm. Once all four wheels are again in line, you can either drive on if the road is clear or lightly pump the brake pedal to slow down.

Front-wheel skid: In a front-wheel skid the car will tend to go straight on with a complete loss of steering control (*Figure 1.5*).

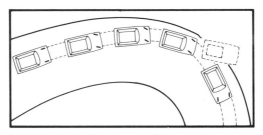

Figure 1.5. Front-wheel skid (front-wheel drive car). In this situation ease up on the accelerator and keep the front wheels pointing in the direction you wish to go. The dotted outline car shows what would probably happen if no action was taken or if the brakes were applied

The best way to correct this (with a front wheel drive car) is to let up completely on the accelerator and keep the wheels pointing in the direction you wish to go. As the car loses speed due to the steering effect of the front tyres on the road, steering control will be regained. Do not press the brake pedal until this happens and the car is travelling in a straight line; even then pump the pedal lightly.

Four-wheel skid: This can happen to both front and rear-wheel drive cars and is usually caused by sudden hard braking when all four wheels lock. It sometimes gives the feeling that the car is going faster than before the brakes were applied.

The obvious solution is to release the brake pedal allowing the wheels to roll again and then pump the pedal gently to reduce speed.

Towing a car

It is always a good idea to include a towrope in your emergency kit (as listed at the end of this chapter), but before using it you should be aware of the possible dangers involved and the legal requirements.

First, the registration number of the towed car should be covered over and replaced with a sign clearly showing the number of the towing vehicle. The maximum distance between the towing and towed vehicles must not exceed 5 metres (16½ ft) and if the rope is over 1.5 metres (5 ft) it should be made clearly visible to pedestrians – the best way to do this is to tie a piece of coloured rag on the rope at about the midway point (*Figure 1.6*). In most cases the suitable distance between two vehicles would be in the region of 2.5–3 metres (8 ft 6 in–10 ft).

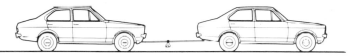

Figure 1.6. Making a towrope visible to pedestrians

Although the regulations provide for a maximum speed of 40 mph, it would be unwise to tow at that speed other than in ideal conditions and only then if both drivers were experienced in the art. In most cases it would be adviseable to limit the speed to around 25 mph.

Regardless of whether it is on tow or not any car used on public roads must be taxed and insured. It must also be roadworthy, with (where applicable) a current MoT Certificate. Obviously the drivers of both vehicles must have a valid driving licence and be covered by the vehicles insurance.

Attaching the towrope

Nearly all modern cars are equipped with towing eyes at both front and rear, the location of each should be shown in the car handbook. Where possible these should be used.

In cases where no towing eyes exists or is unusable, the rope can be tied around a chassis or subframe cross-member but preferably not in the centre; alternatively it can be often attached to a bumber mounting. Under no circumstances should you tie the rope around any steering or suspension component, the rear axle or the bumber itself. If the towing car is equipped with a towing hitch (for trailers), the rope should be attached to the ball-hook.

Driving the towing car

Before driving off, ensure that the steering lock on the towed car is disengaged (ignition key turned). Move off slowly to take up any slack in the rope without jerking, accelerate gently and change gear smoothly, feathering the clutch if necessary to avoid snatching. Switch on the cars headlamps to indicate to other drivers that there is something unusual about your car.

When negotiating corners, take the widest possible line (without crossing carriageways) and do not accelerate out of the bend until the towed car is through. Signal your intentions well in advance, including using hand signals to show when slowing down. Remember that the driver of the towed vehicle will have little time to react in any emergency. In addition his brake servo and power steering (if fitted) may be inoperative.

Driving the towed car

Although there is no legal requirement, an 'On Tow' sign at the rear of the car can be an aid to other drivers, but make sure it does not obscure rearward vision.

If the breakdown fault is such that it does not affect the operation of the engine, it may be a good idea to start it so as to power the brake servo and steering. If the engine is a non-runner disconnect the low-tension lead at the ignition coil and switch on the ignition so that the stop lights and indicators can be used – on some cars these will operate with the ignition off. In either event make sure that the steering lock is disengaged before moving off.

The main object when being towed is to keep the towrope taught. This will involve using the brake much more than normal, especially when travelling downhill. It may be advantageous at times to use the handbrake, but remember that if you do the stop lights will not function. Avoid the temptation of pulling out to see past the towing car unless you are sure that the road ahead is clear – always try to follow in the tracks of the towing vehicle.

If the broken down vehicle's battery is in good condition it may be a good idea to switch on the sidelights, but take care not to run the battery flat if there is a possibility that you may still be on the move after dark. It is always adviseable to work out some form of signalling with the driver of the towing car to cover such events as the need to slow down, pull off the road or stop as quickly as possible.

Towing automatics

Some automatics may be towed for short distances of up to 5 miles at low speeds of less than 10 mph. If this is so it should be stated in the car handbook. Where towing is not permitted it is adviseable to have the car transported, especially if it is a front-wheel drive vehicle. On rear-wheel drive cars it may be possible to disconnect the propshaft at the rear and securely support it from the underside of the body.

Pushing a car

Although it may seem obvious, avoid pushing a car unless an assistant familiar with the controls is sitting in the driver's seat and the steering column lock is disengaged. If the car is on a public road, the assistant would have to hold a current driving licence and be covered by the vehicle insurance.

It would be unwise to push a car on anything but a flat, level road unless you are trying to push-start the car on a slight downhill gradient. Ensure that when pushing, you are not obstructing any hazard warning or other lamps, especially during the hours of darkness. If possible, push the car by the nearside door or window frame rather than from the front or rear.

Overseas breakdowns

In general the procedure to adopt in a breakdown situation overseas would be much the same as in this country, although in some it is mandatory that a warning triangle is positioned behind the broken down vehicle together with a flashing lamp. Check with one of the motoring organisations before you go.

It would be wise, when planning your holiday route, to ask your local franchised dealer for a list of overseas dealers where repairs can be carried out and where spares are available, although this would hardly be necessary if, for example, you were taking a Volkswagen to Germany! In a number of foreign countries, repair agencies may be more specialised than in Britain; for example, one firm may deal only in radiators, another in vehicle electrics and yet another in brakes. Often it

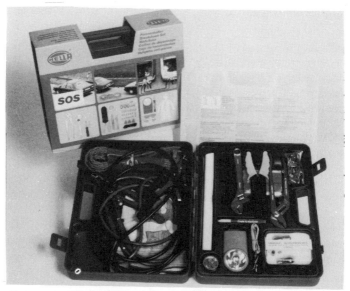

Figure 1.7. The Hella 16 piece breakdown kit, not only comprises the essential tools, but also includes a torch, plastic mac, work gloves, booster (slave) leads and, if all else fails, a strong nylon rope

can be cheaper and quicker to use one of these agencies rather than be towed some way to a listed dealer.

A form of breakdown insurance is available when travelling overseas; this includes assistance in obtaining spares and if necessary recovery back to the United Kingdom. Some may also include credit vouchers which may be used as payment for repairs or car hire; a full refund would have to be made on your return. This insurance is available through the motoring organisations, ferry operators or travel agents.

If you have a workshop manual for your car, take it with you on your overseas trip – it can be invaluable in pictorially identifying components and possibly for its wiring diagrams.

Emergency kit

It would be difficult to effect any kind of repair without tools of some sort; in addition you will often need some other equipment even if it is only a length of string.

Figure 1.8. The breakdown kit in the back of an RAC van has a larger selection of equipment than the owner-driver

The following list gives some idea of what to carry in the car. If it is packed well it should not take up too much space.

Tools

Open-ended spanners (7–21 mm or A/F equivalent)
Socket spanner set
Pliers
Self-grip wrench
Adjustable wrench
Pipe wrench
Screwdrivers (flat-blade, cross-head and electrical)
Hammer
Test lamp or multimeter

Other equipment

Fire extinguisher
First-aid kit
Torch
Hazard warning lamp
Warning triangle
Towrope
   (see page 13 on its use)
Insulating tape
String
Cable (electric)
Cable connectors

Soft wire
Silicone-based jointing compound
Fast-setting epoxy adhesive
Spare fan belt(s)
Spare set of bulbs
Spare coolant hoses
Aerosol water repellant/lubricant
Exhaust repair kit
Radiator sealer
Thick polythene sheeting

Overseas travel

When motoring on the Continent, it is also advisable to carry additional spares to those listed above, such as: set of sparking plugs; feeler gauge; set of points; sheet of sandpaper; distributor cap, rotor arm; leads; condenser; fuses. There is a scheme available where a spares pack for most popular cars can be hired for your holiday abroad. In addition to a small hire charge, you only pay for any of the parts used.

2

Warning signs

Although some breakdowns happen without warning, in a large number of cases there will be some indication of impending failure. This may be an unusual noise, a strange smell, a vibration, an erratic movement of the gauges on the instrument panel or a warning light that behaves in an odd fashion.

In other situations the signs of possible failure may be there but unintentionally ignored by the driver. Examples of this kind of problem could be wear in the steering ball joints or a slight but persistent pull to one side as the brakes are applied. In both cases it could take months for the defect to deteriorate to a dangerous level, and with no sudden or dramatic change in the car's behaviour the driver may well adjust his/her driving to suit. One solution to this kind of problem is to allow someone else to drive your car occasionally, or for you to drive a similar model in good condition. In either event check that you will be covered by insurance.

Whatever the indication is, it would be foolish not to carry out some investigative action before the breakdown occurs – if you do manage to locate the fault, it can often be rectified in relative comfort and possibly much cheaper than on a wet and cold evening at the side of the motorway! Some of the more common warning signs and their most likely causes are given in the following pages.

Unusual engine noises

Indication   *Likely causes*

Rattling noises from the   Worn timing chain.
front of the engine (*Figure*   Worn, defective or badly adjusted chain
2.1).   tensioner.
                                Loose fan assembly.
                                Loose generator pulley or cooling fan
                                pulley.
                                Generator mounting bolts loose.
                                Crankshaft pulley loose or key adrift.
                                Worn water-pump bearings.
                                Worn generator bearings.

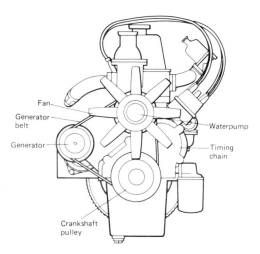

Figure 2.1. Noise areas at front of engine

Screeching sound from the   Generator belt slipping (slack or worn).
front of the engine.   Seized or frozen water pump.
                                Seized or dry generator bearings.
                                Slack or worn driving belt to power
                                steering pump or air conditioning
                                compressor.
                                Power-steering pump or air conditioning
                                compressor defective.

Unusual engine noises (*continued*)

Indication	*Likely causes*
High-pitched whine varying with engine speed.	Starter jammed in engagement with flywheel. Air leak at the inlet manifold or carburettor. Defective generator bearings. Defective water-pump bearings. Power-steering pump or air-conditioning compressor defective.
Rattling noise from the engine most evident when the car is cornering.	Low engine oil level (often accompanied by the oil warning light flickering). Exhaust pipe insecure. Engine mountings loose or defective. Air cleaner loose.
Light tapping noise, increasing with engine speed.	Excessive valve clearances. Rocker arms worn, pushrods bent (OHV engines). Cam follower worn. Camshaft worn. Defective valve or valve spring (often accompanied by a misfire).
Rumbling noise when the engine is under load or accelerating.	Worn crankshaft main bearings. Flywheel loose (this often also shows up as a clunking noise when changing gear). Loose crankshaft pulley or worn keyway.
Metallic tinkling noise when accelerating or climbing hills (pinking).	Ignition timing incorrect Use of low-grade petrol. Incorrect sparking plugs. Defective advance-retard mechanism in distributor. Engine requires top overhaul.
Heavy knocking noise at idle and as the engine is revved.	Connecting rod big-end bearings worn (both this and worn main bearings may be accompanied by low oil pressure – warning light flickering on and off).
Sudden whirring sound when idling with a hot engine.	Thermostatically-controlled electric fan coming into operation – this may not be a fault.

Unusual engine noises (*continued*)

Indication	*Likely causes*
Sharp slapping sound when starting the engine from cold.	Piston slap – some engines are more prone to this than others, but if the noise is also evident when accelerating with the engine warm, it could be a sign of excessive piston/cylinder bore clearance.
Rattling noise when starting the engine from cold.	Slow build up of oil pressure, possibly due to low oil level, worn crankshaft bearings, worn oil pump, defective pressure relief valve, incorrect oil filter or wrong grade of oil.
Hissing or whistling sound from around the carburettor.	Inlet manifold gasket leaking. Carburettor to manifold gasket leaking. Brake servo hose leaking. Emission control hose(s) leaking. Vacuum advance hose leaking. Carburettor throttle spindle worn. Air cleaner incorrectly fitted.
Bubbling noise when the engine is switched off.	Engine coolant boiling. Air locks in the cooling system or heater system.
Chuffing sound, most evident when accelerating.	Exhaust manifold gasket leaking. Manifold to exhaust pipe joint leaking. Exhaust pipe holed. Engine misfiring.

Unusual smells

Acidic smell.	Battery being over-charged. Battery leaking. Battery over-filled.
Petrol smell.	Fuel tank over-filled. Fuel tank filler cap missing. Fuel tank leaking. Fuel pipe connections leaking. Leaking fuel pump. Carburettor flooding due to defective needle valve. Fuel tank vent adrift.

Unusual smells (*continued*)

Indication	*Likely causes*
Smell of exhaust fumes inside car.	Exhaust system leaking. Rear door open or seals leaking – hatchback and estate cars. Heater fan on in slow-moving traffic queue.
Oily smell.	Engine oil filler cap missing. Valve cover gasket leaking (rocker cover). Emission control system blocked or leaking (pipe adrift). Excessive fumes from a worn engine.
Smell like burning rope.	Clutch slipping. Brakes binding. Bad driving habits – riding the clutch pedal or leaving the handbrake on.
Acrid burning smell.	Electrical short circuit – disconnect the battery and look for smoke. Electric cable (ignition) touching the exhaust.
General burning smell.	Old rag or something similar on the exhaust manifold or pipe. Cigarette or sweet papers smouldering in the ash tray. Discarded cigarette end burning the carpet or seat Heater fan drawing in fumes from outside the car.

Unusual transmission noises

Screeching noise when the clutch pedal is depressed.	Defective clutch release bearing (*Figure 2.2*). Defective spigot bearing in the flywheel.
Screeching noise as the clutch engages (pedal moves up).	Clutch plate worn down to the rivets.

Unusual transmission noises (*continued*)

Indication   *Likely causes*

Rattling noise as the clutch   Defective clutch pressure plate (broken
engages.   springs).
                                     Exhaust pipe insecure.
                                     Engine mountings broken or loose.
                                     Engine steady bar loose or adrift.

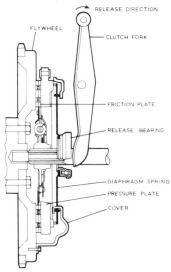

Figure 2.2. Diaphragm-type clutch assembly

Clanking or knocking   Propshaft loose.
sound as the car moves off.   Propshaft or drive-shaft joints badly
                                     worn.
                                     Engine steady bar loose or adrift.
                                     Defective rear axle mountings. Rear-
                                     wheel drive cars.
                                     Worn or loose propshaft centre bearing –
                                     when fitted.

Buzzing sound that stops   Gearbox constant mesh gears noisy.
when clutch pedal is   Gearbox bearings noisy.
pressed.   Gearbox oil level low.

Unusual transmission noises (*continued*)

Indication	*Likely causes*
Regular clicking noise, speed related and more evident when cornering.	Defective wheel bearing. Defective drive shaft – front-wheel drive vehicles.
Regular clicking noise, speed related.	Stone or other foreign object in tyre.

Other transmission warning signs

Clutch judder as the pedal is let up.	Worn clutch plate. Defective clutch pressure plate. Oil on clutch linings. Engine mountings broken or loose. Engine steady bar loose or adrift. Gearbox mounting(s) broken or loose. Rear axle mountings broken or loose. Propshaft bolts loose. Propshaft centre bearing loose.
Vibration felt throughout the car at certain speeds	Propshaft misaligned. Propshaft needs balancing. Road wheels need balancing.
Engine speed increases with no corresponding increase in road speed.	Clutch slip – possibly resulting from incorrect pedal free play adjustment, wear on the clutch plate or oil on the clutch plate.

Indicators of possible brake trouble

Squealing sound as the brakes are applied.	Anti-squeal shims missing or incorrectly fitted on disc brakes. Build up of brake dust in drum brakes. Use of incorrect brake pads or shoes. Worn pads or linings. Glazed pads or linings.
Squealing sound with the brakes off.	Brakes binding – possibly due to incorrect adjustment, sticking pistons or defective master cylinder.

Indicators of possible brake trouble (*continued*)

Indication	*Likely causes*
Grinding sound when the brakes are applied.	Brake pads or shoes badly worn. Stone or other foreign object trapped between disc and pad or caliper. Rust on disc or in the drums.
Grinding sound with brakes off.	Stone or other foreign object trapped between the disc and pad or caliper. Excessively slack or worn wheel bearing.
Brake fluid level falls.	A slow and progressive fall in the level as the brake pads wear is quite normal. Any untoward drop in the level would indicate a leak, possibly inside a wheel cylinder, or caliper – a potentially dangerous situation.
Brakes pull to one side.	Road camber. Incorrect tyre pressures. Odd or unevenly worn tyres. Incorrect brake adjustment. Contaminated pads or linings due to leaking seals in caliper or wheel cylinder. Brake pad seized in caliper. Piston seized in caliper or wheel cylinder. Air in hydraulic system.
Pedal 'spongy'.	Air in the hydraulic system. Flexible hose weak. Leak in the hydraulic system. Pedal mounting bracket flexing.

Indicators of possible steering trouble

Clicking or creaking noise heard and sometimes felt when steering wheel is turned.	Defective steering rack. Partially seized swivel bearings (kingpins). Partially seized column top bush.
Knocking noise on full steering lock.	Drive shaft constant velocity joint worn – front-wheel drive cars. Defective wheel bearing(s). Front tyres touching on bodywork or suspension member.

Indicators of possible steering trouble (*continued*)

Indication	*Likely causes*
Vibration felt through steering wheel at certain speeds.	Front wheel need balancing. Damaged wheel. Damaged, incorrectly fitted or out of round tyre. Wheel bearing slack. Wheel nuts loose.
Steering heavy.	Tyre pressures low. Partially seized swivel bearings (kingpins). Partially seized column top bush. Incorrect wheel alignment. Incorrect steering geometry (castor and camber angles). On power-assisted systems a broken or slack drive belt to the pump, low fluid level or a defective valve in the system could all result in a complete loss of assistance.

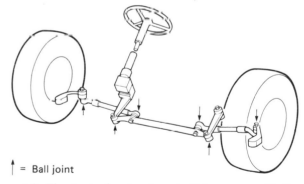

↑ = Ball joint

Figure 2.3. The steering box-type layout which uses several ball-joints

Excessive free play at the steering wheel.	Wear in the steering linkage (ball joints and idlers, when fitted. See *Figures 2.3 and 2.4.*

Indicators of possible steering trouble (*continued*)

Indication   *Likely causes*

Steering box or rack insecure.
Steering arm insecure on stub axle.
Wear in steering box or rack.
Wear in stub axle bearings.
Steering column joints worn or loose.
Steering wheel loose on splines.

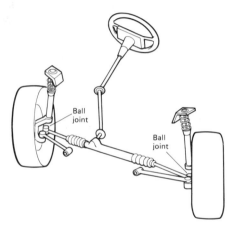

*Figure 2.4. The rack and pinion steering gear layout which uses only two
ball-joints*

Steering vague or wanders.   Incorrect wheel alignment.
                                Wear in the steering linkage.
                                Wear in the steering box or rack.
                                Steering box or rack insecure.
                                Steering arm loose on stub axle.
                                Wear in stub axle bearings.
                                Steering column joints worn or loose.
                                Steering wheel loose on splines.
                                Incorrect tyre pressures.
                                Ineffective suspension dampers.

Indicators of potential electrical troubles

Indication	*Likely causes*
Loud grating noise as starter is used.	Loose starter motor.
	Loose starter motor body bolts.
	Flywheel or pinion teeth damaged.
	Sticking pinion.
	Misaligned starter motor.
Sluggish starter motor action.	Battery defective.
	Battery in a low state of charge – possible charging system fault.
	Loose connection at battery or solenoid.
	Poor earth connection between engine and car body or from car body to battery.
	Loose starter motor.
	Loose starter motor body bolts.
	Internal fault in starter motor.
Burning smell as starter is used.	Loose starter motor.
	Loose starter motor body bolts.
	Starter in use for long periods.
	Internal fault in starter motor.
	Partially siezed engine.
Lights flicker when going over bumps or pot holes in the road.	Loose connection in circuit to the lamp.
	Loose bulb.
	Poor earth connection.
Battery splashed with acid.	Charging rate too high.
	Battery overfilled.
	Battery filler caps loose.
Both fuel and temperature gauges show above normal readings.	Instrument voltage-stabiliser unit faulty – usually located behind the instrument panel.
Water gauge reading higher than normal, then drops back.	Initially engine overheating, followed by loss of coolant.
	A similar problem could result in the heater fan suddenly blowing cold air.

Indicators of potential electrical troubles (*continued*)

Indication	*Likely causes*
Oil warning light staying on a long time.	Low oil level. Low oil pressure due to worn crankshaft bearings, worn oil pump, defective pressure relief valve, incorrect oil filter or incorrect grade of oil. Faulty oil pressure warning light sender unit on engine.
Oil warning light flickers when cornering.	Low engine oil level. Sender unit wiring loose and shorting to earth.
Ignition warning light staying on a long time.	Faulty regulator (cut-out with dynamo systems). Loose or slipping fan belt. Internal fault in generator.

3

Non-starters

In some breakdown situations, locating the source of the trouble is straightforward – a flat tyre for instance should be immediately obvious as would a broken windscreen. In other cases tracing the fault may be a little more difficult, but even then there is usually some indication of where to start looking – an engine that spluttered, picked up again and then hesitated before stopping is most likely suffering from some sort of fuel problem, whereas one that cut out suddenly probably has a fault in the ignition system. Checking procedures for these are given in the appropriate chapters.

Quite often though there may be no indication whatsoever in that an engine may have been running perfectly until switched off, after which it refuses to start. The checks given in this chapter cover the various possibilities causing a non-start situation. It may be, of course, that the fault is somewhere in the ignition or fuel systems – this is pointed out at the appropriate stage in the checking procedure.

Starter motor will not turn the engine over

The easiest way to locate that fault is to follow the step-by-step procedure given in the chart (*Figure 3.1*), accompanied by the following more detailed explanation of each stage. The box numbers in the chart correspond with those in the text.

1. Switch on the headlamps and operate the starter. If you cannot see whether the lamps dim as the starter is operated, switch on the interior light and watch that. Do not operate the

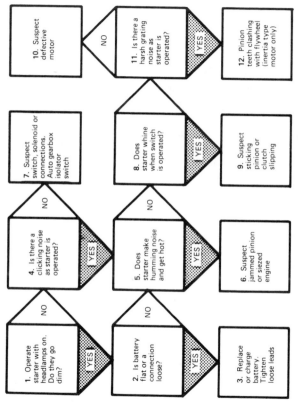

Figure 3.1. Fault tracing chart for non-starters

starter in these conditions for periods longer than about 5 seconds with at least a 10 second interval between attempts.

2. If the lights dim as the starter is operated, the most likely cause is a flat battery. This may be due to a fault in the charging system or a defective battery (see Chapter 10). Alternatively, the problem may be due to a loose or dirty connection somewhere in the battery-solenoid-starter circuit (*Figure 3.2*) or in the earth return between the engine-car body-battery line. Quite often a fault in the earth return line could result in the strange phenomenon of the choke cable getting hot as the starter is operated.

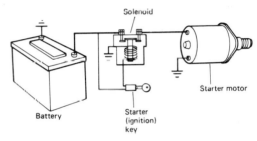

Figure 3.2. Basic starter circuit

3. Unless there is a short circuit somewhere or a light has been left on, it is unlikely that a battery would be so flat that it would not power the ignition. Quite often then a car in this condition can be pushed or tow started – a further alternative which can work with a battery in an even worse condition is to 'jump' or slave start it from another vehicle – the correct procedure for this is given on page 277.

4. A rapid clicking noise from the solenoid as the starter switch is operated could indicate a flat battery, a defective battery or a poor connection in the circuit.

5. A single click as the starter switch is operated, often accompanied by a humming noise from the starter motor often means that there is some mechanical reason for the starter failing to turn. Prolonged use of the starter switch in this condition

could cause the motor to overheat, particularly in the commutator area.

6. In addition to a jammed pinion or seized engine, the following defects could also be responsible for the starter failing to turn the engine; starter defective, starter motor loose, seized (frozen) water pump, seized alternator (dynamo), seized power steering pump or air conditioning compressor.

Some starter motors have a squared-off section at the end of the armature shaft. This can be turned with a spanner to release a jammed pinion (anti-clockwise on most engines) – see *Figure 3.3*. Alternatively, third gear should be engaged, the handbrake released and the car rocked backwards and forwards – with the ignition switched off. If neither of these measures work, the only thing left is to remove the starter motor from the engine.

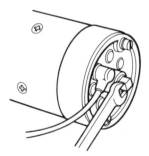

Figure 3.3. Freeing a jammed starter motor pinion by turning the squared end of the armature shaft

7. No clicking noise from the solenoid as the switch is operated would indicate either a faulty solenoid or a problem in the battery-switch-solenoid circuit, including of course a defective switch.

With most inertia starters the starter switch can be by-passed by making a temporary connection between the large terminal (from the battery) and the small terminal (from the switch) at the solenoid. Alternatively, in an emergency both the switch and the solenoid can be by-passed by making a temporary connection between the two large terminals of the solenoid. This connection must be made quickly and firmly, even then there will be

considerable arcing and burning between the connector and
terminals, so for this reason use a substantial connector to bridge
the two. A large screwdriver or pair of pliers can be used, but
they may become pitted with the arcing (*Figure 3.4*).

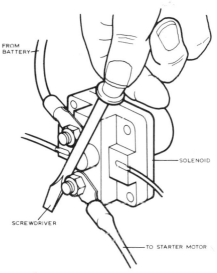

FROM
BATTERY

SOLENOID

SCREWDRIVER

TO STARTER MOTOR

Figure 3.4. Bridging starter solenoid terminals

Some older solenoids have a button (usually black or red)
which provides for manual operation of the solenoid. If so the
starter can usually be operated by pressing the button. On
pre-engaged starters where the solenoid is attached to the
starter, it may be necessary to make a further connection to the
small terminal in addition to bridging the two larger ones. Adopt
these measures only as a last resort after checking all other
possible reasons for failure. Be aware of the hazards involved,
including possible reaction to the sparking.

Cars fitted with automatic transmission are so wired that the
starter can only be operated with the gear selector in N (neutral)
or P (park) positions. It is possible that the inhibitor switch

incorporated into this circuit may be sticking or faulty – move the selector through the gears a couple of times and try again.

8. A whining or whirring noise as the starter switch is operated indicates that the starter motor is turning but the pinion is not engaging with the flywheel.

9. Basically there are two types of starter motor fitted to cars in this country – the inertia and the pre-engaged types. With the former a sticking pinion (most likely due to dirt on the splines) can result in it not engaging with the flywheel. The only longterm answer to this situation is to remove the starter from the engine and clean the splines/thread on which the pinion moves – in an emergency, however, it can sometimes be freed by tapping the motor housing while an assistant operates the starter switch; take care though for the engine could start.

With the pre-engaged type of starter motor a sticking pinion is unlikely, but many of them incorporate a type of clutch, which if defective can produce a similar result. Any defective clutch will probably need replacing. Although it is a rare occurrence it is possible that the teeth on the flywheel are broken (this would probably have been preceded by the harsh grating noise as in No. 11). If so turning the engine over by hand (with the ignition switched off) or by pushing the car with the gear engaged, should move the flywheel sufficiently for the pinion to engage with undamaged teeth.

10. The most common cause of motor failure is the brush/commutator contact being poor. This may be due to a number of reasons but generally results from wear (see Chapter 10). Although this and other minor problems such as a broken connection in the brush lead can be repaired, nearly all other faults – burnt field winding or damaged armature would, in most cases be solved more cheaply by fitting a replacement unit. Most high street motor accessory shops sell them on an exchange basis fairly cheaply.

11. As is the case with broken flywheel teeth (9) it may be that where only the flywheel teeth are damaged turning the engine so that the pinion engages at another spot around the flywheel will enable the starter to turn the engine.

12. A harsh grating noise as the starter is operated generally

means that the leading edges of either the pinion or flywheel teeth (or both) are damaged preventing engagement of the pinion. Prolonged operation of the starter in these conditions will only make things worse. This fault is unlikely to occur with a pre-engaged motor.

Starter turns the engine very slowly

Many of the faults that prevented the starter from turning the engine could, if they were slightly less serious, result in it turning the engine over slowly. Briefly these can be summarised as:
Battery low on power.
Loose or dirty connection in the starter circuit – including earth return.
Starter motor commutator/brushes dirty or worn.
Defective starter motor.
Starter motor loose.
Engine partially seized.
Partially seized accessory (water-pump, alternator etc).

Cold weather slows down the chemical process within the battery so reducing its power output. At the same time low temperatures make the engine more difficult to turn. In effect then the battery produces less, yet the starter demands more power – hence the increase in battery/starter problems during the winter months.

Starter turns the engine briskly but it will not fire

This means there must be either a fuel/ignition fault or a mechanical problem which prevents the engine from starting – see the initial test in the ignition fault finding sequence on page 201.

Engine fires but always stops again when the starter switch is released

This would indicate a faulty ballast resistor in the starter circuit – *see* page 210.

4

Poor runners

Just because an engine starts does not mean that it runs as it should. For instance, there could be a misfire, the engine could overheat or it could produce a metallic tinkling sound known as 'pinking', when accelerating or climbing hills. Many of these defects could result from a number of different faults, some in fact could be due to a fault in either the ignition or fuel systems or even with the mechanical condition of the engine.

Tracing the fault in these situations is usually a matter of elimination – for example, with a regular misfire it would be normal to check out the ignition before considering other possibilities.

In this chapter a number of these problems are given, together with a list of possible causes – these are of necessity brief but most are covered in more detail in the appropriate section – ignition, fuel system and mechanical condition.

Poor-running engines – symptoms and causes

Problem	Possible causes
Engine stalls at idling speed but is otherwise in order.	Cold engine – fast idle adjustment incorrect.
	Warm engine – slow running and/or mixture control incorrectly set.
	Carburettor slow running circuit blocked.
	Carburettor float or needle valve defective.
	Fuel contaminated with dirt or water.
	Throttle spindle badly worn.
	Poor compression(s).
	Air leak at inlet manifold, or any attached pipework.
	Contact points require attention.
	Faulty distributor vacuum advance.
	Ignition timing incorrect.

Poor running engines – symptoms and causes (*continued*)

Problem   *Possible causes*

Irregular idle.   Idle speed too low.
                                 Mixture control incorrectly set.
                                 Carburettor slow running circuit
                                 restricted.
                                 Carburettor float or needle valve
                                 defective.
                                 Air valve or damper sticking (Ford VV,
                                 SU and Stromberg carburettors).
                                 Air leak at inlet manifold or any attached
                                 pipework.
                                 Faulty distributor advance mechanism.
                                 Faulty distributor vacuum advance.
                                 Incorrect ignition timing.
                                 Poor compression(s).
                                 Contact points require attention.

Hesitation on accelerating.   Cold engine.
                                 Faulty diaphragm (Ford VV, SU and
                                 Stromberg).
                                 Damper oil incorrect (SU and
                                 Stromberg).
                                 Air valve/damper sticking (SU and
                                 Stromberg).
                                 Air valve sticking (Ford VV).
                                 Faulty accelerator pump or circuit (where
                                 fitted).
                                 Defective second choke – twin-choke
                                 carburettors.
                                 Faulty distributor vacuum advance.
                                 Faulty distributor mechanical advance.
                                 Sparking plugs dirty, worn or gaps
                                 incorrectly set.
                                 Contact points require attention.

Pinking noise when   Ignition timing incorrect.
accelerating or climbing   Faulty distributor vacuum advance.
hills.   Use of incorrect grade fuel.
                                 Engine requires top overhaul (de-coke).
                                 Contact points require attention.
                                 Engine overheating.
                                 Hot-spot in combustion chamber.
                                 Use of incorrect grade sparking plugs.
                                 Carburettor mixture strength weak.

Poor running engines – symptoms and causes (*continued*)

Problem	*Possible causes*
Regular misfire.	Defective sparking plug. Defective or dislodged sparking plug lead. Tracking at sparking plug. Tracking in distributor cap. Air leak at inlet manifold. Poor compression.
Irregular misfire.	Tracking in distributor cap or at coil. Contact points require attention. Loose connection in ignition LT circuit. Partial blockage in fuel supply system. Dirt in the carburettor. Water in the fuel. Carburettor float level incorrect.
High speed misfire.	Incorrectly set or dirty sparking plugs. Incorrectly set or dirty contact points. Weak contact point spring. Faulty condenser in distributor. Faulty coil. Weak valve springs. Partial fuel blockage in carburettor or in supply line. Defective fuel pump. Carburettor mixture strength incorrect. Dirty carburettor air cleaner.
Engine overheats.	Low coolant level. Fan belt slack or broken. Thermostat sticking closed. Thermostatically-controlled electric fan inoperative. Air flow through radiator restricted. Faulty radiator/expansion bottle sealing cap. Carburettor mixture strength incorrect. Ignition timing incorrect. Coolant passages in engine block and/or radiator clogged with scale. Radiator frozen (winter only). Air lock in cooling system.

Poor running engines – symptoms and causes (*continued*)

Problem	*Possible causes*
Engine runs on after being switched off.	Engine overheating. Engine requires top overhaul (de-coke). Use of incorrect grade of sparking plug. Hot-spot in combustion chamber. Idle speed too high. Carburettor mixture control incorrect (weak). Ignition timing incorrect (retarded). Bad driving habits – switching a fast running engine off.
Engine backfires through inlet manifold.	Carburettor mixture control incorrect (weak). Fuel contaminated with water. Defective inlet valve or seat. Incorrectly set valve clearances. Tracking in distributor cap.
Explosion in the exhaust – commonly called a backfire.	Ignition timing incorrect (retarded). Defective exhaust valve or seat. Defective exhaust valve spring. Any ignition fault which prevents the plug from firing the mixture. If the fault occurs at high speeds only, suspect contact breaker spring or other possible causes of high speed misfire.

5

Ignition

More cars break down or refuse to start due to a fault in the ignition system (*Figure 5.1*) than for any other single cause. Furthermore, a high percentage of these result from a lack of maintenance and care. On the low-tension (LT) side of the system for instance, it is the contact breaker which causes most trouble – either dirty and pitted or incorrectly gapped, or sometimes both. This results in a weak or non-existent spark, particuarly on starting and in the higher speed ranges.

Dirt is also a factor in the most common type of problem with the high-tension (HT) circuit – dirt coupled with damp conditions will form an excellent alternative path for the high

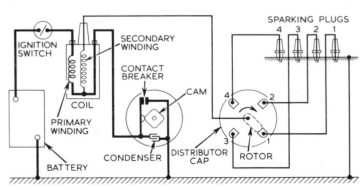

Figure 5.1. Typical coil-ignition system. The diagram shows the two circuits in the system – the primary (or low-tension) circuit and the secondary (or high-tension) circuit. The low-tension circuit is indicated by the thicker line. Note the 1,3,4,2 firing order of the sparking plugs. The contact-breaker lead must always be connected to the ignition-coil terminal bearing the polarity sign of the battery earth post

voltage (15–20,000 volts) current. When this happens at either the top of the coil or at the rotor arm, it would normally mean no spark whatsoever. If it were just the distributor cap that is affected, the result could be the same or possibly a misfire on one or more cylinders with some backfiring through the inlet manifold. It is also possible for the HT current to leak down the side of a dirty and damp sparking plug – this would result in a misfire at the affected cylinder.

Most non-start situations on a cold and misty morning are entirely due to this combination of dirt and damp and can in some cases be rectified by the simple expediant of spraying the affected areas with a water displacing spray such as WD 40 or similar. Once the engine has started, the build up of heat will also assist in drying out the system. A well maintained and clean ignition system is unlikely to suffer from either of these problems. This, however, is no guarantee that nothing else will go wrong – it may do, but by adopting a set pattern in tracing the fault, ignition problems are generally easier to sort out than those in other areas.

An engine failure or a refusal to start does not automatically mean that there is an ignition fault – there could be something wrong with the fuel supply or a mechanical failure. Unless the fault is self evident such as a connecting rod through the side of the block, the first check in every case should be for a spark at the plug – usually that at the front cylinder, although it could be at any.

The procedure from then on is as shown in the fault finding chart on page 44. Follow this through the simple Yes/No stages shown on the chart, relating each with the more detailed explanation given in the accompanying text. The numbers at each stage correspond with those in the text. Before even attempting the first of these checks though, remember that the high-tension circuit employs very high voltages. With only a small current being passed these voltages are unlikely to harm most people should they receive a shock. However, the reaction to any shock could.

Therefore, it is wise to take precautions – avoid touching any part of the HT system with your bare hands unless the ignition is

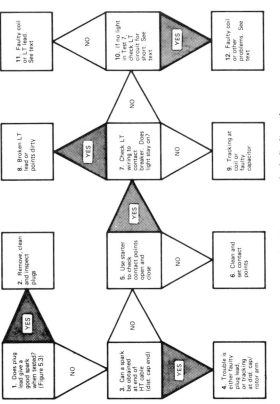

Figure 5.2. Ignition system fault-finding chart

switched off. Use insulated pliers, a pair of rubber gloves, a dry
rag or something of that nature. This is even more important for
someone suffering from a heart condition, and also on any car
fitted with electronic ignition.

Normal safety precautions apply when dealing with electrical
equipment – see Chapter 10.

Fault finding sequence (*Figure 5.2*)

1. This check involves removing a plug lead from the sparking
plug and holding the end of it about ⅛ in (3 mm) away from a
metal part of the engine while an assistant operates the starter. If
everything is in order, you will see a spark jump from the lead to
the engine.

*Figure 5.3. When testing a sparking-
plug lead with a recessed insulator, use
a nail, screw or something similar in
recess*

Do not remove the plug lead by pulling on the cable – pull on
the insulator instead. On some with recessed insulators it may
not be possible to hold the end of the lead that close to the
engine, in which case insert a nail, bolt or something similar in
the end of the insulator (*Figure 5.3*).

Do not hold the end of the lead against the carburettor for
obvious reasons, perhaps less obvious is that the rocker cover

may be full of explosive gases so do not use that as an earth either.

It should not be necessary to disconnect any more than one plug lead but if you do, ensure that each goes back onto its original plug, or at least to the same cylinder if you have also removed the plugs. Do not mix the leads up – it may be best to number them in some way – the little tags that some bakers use to fasten the wrappers on their loaves make ideal markers for plug leads.

2. If the test showed a good 'fat' spark at the plug lead, the next step should be to remove the plugs and check them for condition. Plugs with their electrodes soaked in petrol could mean that the engine has been overchoked – this may be coupled with a problem in the ignition system which results in a poor spark, especially under cranking conditions. This situation is often made worse by the driver pumping the accelerator pedal, so forcing even more fuel into the engine.

The immediate remedy is to remove the plugs and dry them – preferably in an oven and try again. If on the next attempt the plugs again become wet it is possible that the carburettor is delivering an excess of fuel – *see* the fuel system fault finding chart on page 237. A plug wet with water probably means a defective cylinder-head gasket or a cracked cylinder head. Either of these faults could result in serious engine damage if a cylinder were to become even partially filled with water (coolant) and the engine was cranked – even worse if it fired on one of the other cylinders.

3. If test No. 1 resulted in a 'no spark' situation, the next stage is to check for power (a spark) at the distributor end of the main HT cable from the coil. This is done by disconnecting the cable from the distributor cap (usually the central cable) and then holding it, as before, about ⅛ in (3 mm) away from some metallic part of the engine while an assistant operates the starter (with the ignition on when equipped with a separate switch). The sparks produced in this test should be much more frequent than those from a plug lead. If there is no assistant available, the same test can be carried out by first removing the distributor cap and then, with the ignition switched on, flicking the contact points

open and closed. Every time the points open a spark should
jump across the gap between the end of the main HT lead and
the engine.

Should the engine have stopped in such a position that the
points are in the open position, use a screwdriver to bridge the
gap, in effect shorting the two points together. In this case every
time the screwdriver is withdrawn a spark should be produced.
4. If test No. 3 proved satisfactory – that is it produced a spark
but there still was not one at the plug, the fault could be in the
lead itself (to the plug), or, more likely, tracking at either the
rotor arm or distributor cap.

Tracking is where the HT current finds its own path or track
over an insulated surface (the distributor cap, rotor arm, coil top
or sparking plug) – see *Figure 5.4*. When this occurs the tracks

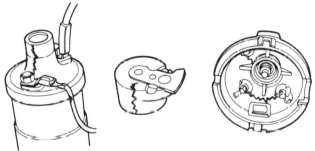

*Figure 5.4. Typical areas where tracking may occur on the coil HT tower
(left), rotor arm (centre) and inside distributor cap (right)*

can sometimes be seen as thin greyish-black lines. On the
distributor cap for instance these lines may extend from the
central terminal area to one of the plug lead towers or segments,
in which case the engine may only fire on one cylinder. In some
case, however, the tracking may be between two segments
resulting in a misfire. Both problems could also cause backfiring
through the inlet manifold (see page 197).

If the tracking is taking place on the outer surface of the
distributor cap, it can often be seen at night as a thin streak of
lightning over the cap. It can be difficult to check a distributor

cap for tracking because the area most likely to be faulty, around the main HT cable tower, would have been disturbed when carrying out test No. 3. Probably the best solution is to remove the cap and inspect it thoroughly for signs of tracking on both the inner and outer surfaces. Any cracks or scratches emanating from a tower or segment area should be treated as suspect. Also ensure that the cap is perfectly clean before it is replaced.

The rotor arm can be checked for serviceability by carrying out the same kind of operation as in test No. 3, but instead of holding the end of the cable about ⅛ inch away from a metallic part of the engine, hold it the same distance away from the centre electrode of the rotor (with the rotor arm fitted in its normal place) (*Figure 5.5*). If a spark jumps from the cable to the

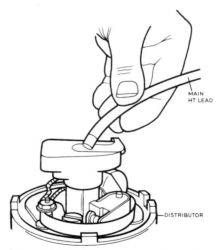

Figure 5.5. Testing a rotor arm for tracking

electrode, then the rotor arm is faulty. If the cause of tracking is dirt or dampness over the insulated surface, and it is detected in its early stages, then a thorough clean with a petrol soaked rag may clear it.

In more extreme cases where the tracking follows a minor scratch or crack, or has formed a definite path, it may be possible to clean the track out and fill it with a hard setting, non-conductive adhesive – most two-pack epoxy resins come into this category. An alternative is to scratch a deeper track across the existing one and then fill the new track with adhesive, in effect creating a barrier across the path of the leaking current. A hole drilled in through the existing track would produce a similar barrier.

In an emergency, instead of adhesive a thin smear of clean engine oil or a coating of nail varnish may solve the problem. Although unlikely to happen in normal use, it could be that the carbon brush located in the distributor cap and meant to be in spring-loaded contact with the rotor arm, has either disintegrated, stuck or fallen out. In this case the large gap between the cap electrode and that on the rotor arm would be so great that there will be no current flow whatsoever or that the likelihood that tracking will occur is increased.

In an emergency a short length of metallic foil, such as a milk bottle cap, can be cut off, rolled and fitted in the hole in place of the carbon brush (*Figure 5.6*). If the reason for lack of a spark at

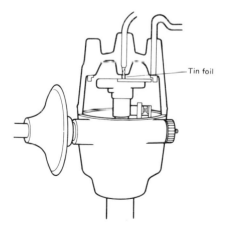

Figure 5.6. An emergency repair. Where the spring-loaded carbon brush in the distributor cap is not in contact with the rotor arm (or is missing), a piece of tin foil (milk bottle cap) inserted in its place will provide a temporary solution

the plug was a faulty lead or if the main HT lead itself was defective, it could, as a temporary measure be replaced by a length of ordinary cable. This would need to be tied with string in such a way that it was well away from the engine or it could be insulated by sheathing it in plastic tubing – windscreen washer tubing is ideal for this purpose. If there is no cable available a length of bare wire, suitably insulated, may be used instead.

5. For this test the distributor cap and in many cases the rotor arm should be removed. Then with an assistant operating the starter check that the contact points open and close.

6. If the engine is to run with maximum efficiency the contact points setting (and condition) is critical. Not only does the gap size regulate the energy build up or storage time of the coil but it also effects the ignition timing, whereas dirty points even if correctly set will reduce spark energy. In an emergency, if no measuring equipment (feeler gauges or dwell meter) is available, a less accurate setting may suffice. The average credit card, for instance, could be used as a feeler gauge if a calculated guess proved wildly inaccurate. However, it is important to set the points correctly at the first opportunity.

The method of adjusting the contact-breaker gap can vary in detail according to the make and model of distributor; some can be adjusted from the outside of the distributor; however, the general procedure for most will follow a similar pattern. With the distributor cap and rotor arm removed turn the engine until the points are at their widest setting, that is with the highest part of the cam directly against the moving contacts fibre heel. The gap should now correspond to the manufacturer's specification.

If the setting is incorrect, adjustment is usually effected by slackening off the fixed-contact retaining screw(s) and then moving the plate – and with it the contact – to close or widen the gap (*Figure 5.7*). The retaining screw should only be slackened sufficiently so that it still 'pinches' the contact plate slightly, preventing unwanted movement. If using a feeler gauge as a measure, insert it between the two points. When the setting is correct the gauge should be a free sliding fit without lifting the moving contact. Take care not to insert the feeler gauge at an angle as this will give a false reading.

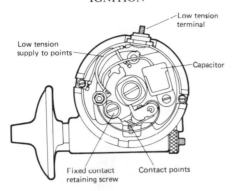

Figure 5.7. A typical Lucas distributor with the cover and rotor arm removed

In use the points become not only dirty but also pitted, that is with a small pit in one contact and a corresponding dimple on the other. Any adjustment with the contacts in this condition is sure to result in an inaccurate setting for the feeler gauge will 'ride' on top of the dimple and the gap will be too wide. Cleaning a set of contact points removes both the dirt and the dimple but the pit remains. In addition, cleaning invariably upsets the relationship between one contact area and the other, in other words the contact area may be reduced. Cleaning contact points should then only be considered a temporary measure. For full efficiency a new set should be fitted.

Some distributors feature what are termed 'sliding points'. As their name suggests these points slide against one another as the contact faces meet, giving them a self-cleaning action.

7. In this check the test lamp is connected between the low tension (LT) terminal at the distributor and earth. If there is no suitable connection at the distributor the lamp can be connected to the CB or − terminal at the coil – in other words at either end of the thinner cable connecting the coil and distributor. In neither case disconnect the existing cable. Now when the engine is cranked (with the ignition on), the lamp should normally go on and off as the points open and close. To prevent the engine from starting, disconnect the main high tension (HT) lead at the coil.

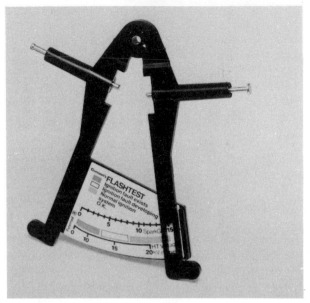

Figure 5.8. If the major purpose of the ignition system is to produce a satisfactory spark, then one way of testing the systems efficiency is to check the quality of the spark. This Flash Test device from Gunsons helps you to do just that

8. The lamp goes out when the points close, that is when the circuit through the points to earth is complete. If the lamp stays on, there must be a break in the circuit. The first possible cause of this is that the points are not closing; although they may have appeared to do so in the visual test, it is possible that they may be prevented from closing by a small particle of dirt lodged between them; alternatively, they may be so dirty themselves that no electrical contact is made. A simple check is to bridge the two contact points with a screwdriver; if the test lamp then goes out, the fault lies with the points. If, however, the lamp still remains on, it means there is a break somewhere in the circuit between the lamp connection and the contact-breaker points, possibly in the small feed cable to the moving contact within the distributor.

9. If in the previous test the lamp flashed on and off in time with the contact points but there was still no HT output from the coil, it could be due to a fault in the capacitor or coil, although faults with either may also result in a low HT output and a poor spark. It could, of course, be that there is in fact an output from the HT but it is 'tracking' to earth, probably at the top of the coil.

The only practical method of testing a capacitor is by substitution. However, as one of the reasons for its existence is to reduce arcing at the contact points, an inspection of these as the engine is cranked over should give some idea of the capacitors serviceability. It is possible for the capacitor to develop an internal short which could earth the LT current. In this case the test lamp at the distributor LT connection would not come on at all.

The coil is similar to the capacitor in that the most practical way of testing it is by changing it for another. It can happen that the coil will fail when it is hot but show no sign of any defect when it has cooled down again. This could result, for example, in an engine running satisfactorily for some time and then stopping, only to start again after perhaps half an hour has elapsed.

10. If in check No. 7 the test lamp failed to come on at all, the first thing to do is to check the lamp itself by connecting it across the battery. Assuming then that the lamp is in order, the reason for it not lighting up could be either a short to earth somewhere between the lamp connection and the contact breakers or a fault further back in the circuit. To isolate one from the other disconnect the LT lead at the distributor and wire the test lamp between the end of the lead and earth. If the lamp then lights up, the fault is somewhere between the terminal on the distributor and the contact breaker, most likely at the small connecting cable between the two. On a number of distributors incorrect assembly of the moving contact terminal post will result in a short to earth.

Where the test lamp failed to light in this test, connect it between the other LT terminal at the coil (often marked SW or +) and earth, then switch the ignition on again.

11. If the test lamp shows power to the SW terminal of the coil, but none at the distributor LT connection (Check No. 7) it

indicates either a faulty coil or a defective lead between the coil and distributor. To isolate one from the other check for power at the coil CB or − terminal. If the test lamp then lights up (with the ignition switched on) it means that the lead is faulty, whereas no light would indicate a break in the primary circuit of the coil.

12. A no light situation at the coil SW terminal could be due to a number of reasons – from a defective coil to a problem further back in the circuit to the switch and battery. To isolate these possibilities disconnect the cable at the SW terminal and check with the test lamp between the end of the cable and earth (with the ignition switched on). If in this check the lamp comes on, then the fault is in the coil or it could be a short to earth in any radio interference suppressor fitted to the coil and wired to the SW terminal. This can be eliminated easily by disconnecting it from the SW terminal and repeating the checks with the test lamp.

No power at the end of SW feed cable would mean a fault further back in the circuit such as a loose connection, a defective ballast resistor (if fitted), a faulty ignition switch or even with some layouts a blown fuse – if this is the case it would be wise to ascertain why the fuse blew before replacing it. Tracing a fault in the circuit from the coil back to the battery is identical to fault finding in any electrical circuit and is covered in the chapter on Electrics.

Ballast resistor

This is a resistor wired into the ignition system so that a more powerful spark can be provided when starting. The resistor may be in the form of a small block often attached to the coil or it may be a resistive lead somewhere between the ignition switch and coil. Under normal running conditions, with the resistor in the circuit, the voltage drop across it is in the region of 4 volts, meaning that the coil is supplied with only about 8 volts ($12 - 4 = 8$). The coil used in these systems is designed to function at these lower voltages.

When the starter motor is in use, the ballast resistor is by-passed and the full battery potential of a little over 12 volts is

applied to the coil (*Figure 5.9*). This in a sense can be said to
supercharge the coil, so producing a better spark. In practice,
however, with the starter drain on the battery its output at such
times is unlikely to exceed 10 or 11 volts. A less popular method
of achieving the same object is similar but uses a heat-sensitive
resistor, in which the resistance (and therefore the voltage drop)
increases as the resistor wire heats up. The maximum voltage
drop using this method is again designed to be in the region of 4
volts. As the resistor is by-passed when the starter is used, a
defective one will often mean that the engine will only fire when
being turned by the starter. Immediately the ignition switch is
released from the 'start' position the engine will stop.

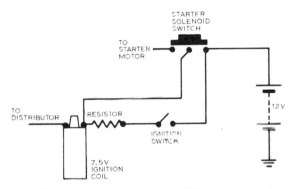

*Figure 5.9. Ballast resistor ignition system. With this system, the ignition
coil is designed to operate on about 7.5 volts during normal running and is
then connected to the ignition switch through a resistor lead. When starting
the engine, the resistor lead to the coil is shorted out by the starting lead;
this applies full battery voltage to the coil.*

Using the starter motor to crank the engine in the tests for a
spark at the plug or coil HT output will not show up a failed
ballast resistor; the tests in fact will appear to indicate that
nothing is wrong. Carrying out the same coil HT test, but flicking
the points open and closed instead of using the starter will,
however, show it up with no spark being produced. To check a
suspect resistor connect up a test lamp from earth to each end of
the resistor in turn. If the unit is defective, the lamp should light

up when connected to the supply side but will not at the other end. With a good ballast resistor you can expect the light to be brighter at the supply terminal than it is at the end connected to the coil. Lack of a light at either end indicates a fault in the supply side, possibly the ignition switch or intervening connections/junctions. If so, the fault may sometimes be by-passed as in any standard system, but ensure that any 12-volt supply will only go to the input side of the resistor, never to the coil side or to the coil itself – this at best would burn the coil out, at worst it could start a fire. If a replacement ballast resistor is unavailable, the only answer is to fit a normal 12-volt coil connected to the resistor supply cable and disconnect the starter operated by-pass system – this is normally at the starter solenoid.

Tracing the cause of a misfire

A regular misfire is usually caused by a defective sparking plug, a problem in the HT supply to one plug or a poor compression on one cylinder. To isolate the defective cylinder short out each plug in turn or, alternatively pull off and replace the plug leads one by one. A change in engine note will be evident every time a good plug is disconnected, but not when the defective one is. Having located the non-firing cylinder, check to see if there is a spark from the end of the plug lead in the same way as the first check in the ignition fault-finding sequence. Lack of a spark could be due to a defective plug lead or tracking from that particular segment or tower in the distributor cap. A good spark on the other hand could mean a defective sparking plug, tracking down the outside of the plug or a poor compression in that cylinder.

   If the plug appears to be in order but the misfire remains, try swapping the plug with that from another cylinder and repeat the test. If the misfire is now at the same cylinder as the suspect plug then the plug is faulty. If however, the misfire remains at the original cylinder then it is probably due to poor compression. A simple test for compression can be made by first removing the sparking plug and then sealing off the vacant hole with your thumb, while an assistant operates the starter; remove the main

HT lead before this test to prevent the engine from starting. Compare the pressure on the suspect cylinder with that from another.

An intermittent misfire can be due to a number of causes, many not associated with the ignition system – see page 40.

Sparking plug condition

The general condition of the plugs offers some useful guidance to the state of the engine, as illustrated in *Figure 5.10*. A sparking plug from an engine in good condition and in a good state of tune will be coated with a greyish-brown deposit over that area exposed to combustion (*a*). Wet black oily deposits (*b*) are caused by lubricant reaching the combustion chamber, either through leaking valve seals, worn valve guides or worn bores or rings – see Chapter 8 for how to check for these faults. A dry sooty appearance on the plug (*c*) is an indication that the car is running on a rich mixture – too much petrol, whereas a weak

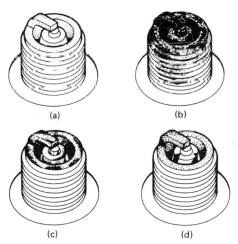

Figure 5.10. Sparking plug condition. The condition of the firing end of plugs provides evidence of the state of the engine in which they have been running, as explained in the text. a. Normal condition, b. Oil fouling, c. Carbon fouling, d. Points burned

mixture will show up with the plug taking on a burned appearance with a dead white insulator (*d*).

The best time to inspect the plugs for this kind of check is immediately after the engine has been running for some time on a fairly fast run – say after a 10 mile or more trip on the motorway. The engine should not be left to idle but switched off immediately; otherwise much of the colour evidence may be lost.

Ignition timing

In modern petrol engines the spark at the plug is timed to occur just before the piston reaches the top of its stroke (top dead centre ot TDC). This allows a period of time (measured in milli-seconds) for the fuel to burn and the mixture to expand, before it begins pushing the piston down on the power stroke. If the spark is early (advanced), the whole combustion process together with some expansion takes place before the piston reaches TDC, and so tries to push it back down in the reverse direction. This reverse thrust due to an over-advanced ignition is usually evident when the starter is used, making the engine kick back against the starter. An over-advanced ignition can also result in loss of power, overheating, pinking on acceleration or when climbing hills, a 'lumpy' engine especially at tickover and in extreme cases severe engine damage.

If the spark is late (retarded) the piston will be on its way down the cylinder as the burning gases expand, the pressure felt on the piston will therefore be less than it should be. This obviously results in loss of power and overheating with often a flat spot on acceleration, a backfire in the exhaust and a slow idle.

Automatic ignition advance and retard

The burn time of the fuel-air mixture within the combustion chamber is, for any given mixture strength, constant. As the engine speed increases, however, the time allowed for it decreases. Therefore it is necessary to make the spark occur

earlier as the engine goes faster. This is achieved in nearly all
ignition systems by a couple of weights within the distributor
which are pivoted at one end and which fly outwards under
centrifugal force, this outward movement being controlled by
springs (*Figure 5.11a*). In moving outwards the weights move the
cam round slightly in its normal direction of rotation. The cam
lobes therefore operate the contact breaker earlier, so advancing
the ignition.

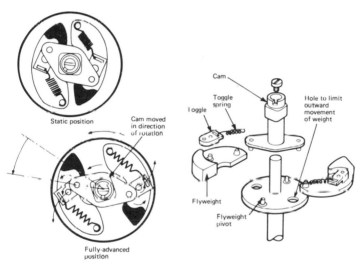

Static position

Cam moved
in direction
of rotation

Cam

Toggle
spring

Toggle

Hole to limit
outward
movement
of weight

Flyweight

Flyweight
pivot

Fully-advanced
position

*Figure 5.11a. Exploded view of mechanical automatic advance
mechanism*

Most of the problems associated with the centrifugal advance
mechanism are due to either sticking weights or weak or broken
springs.

Checking that the mechanism is operating correctly requires
the use of a stroboscopic gun (strobe) and a rev-counter. With
the strobe connected up first disconnect the vacuum advance
pipe and then ensure that the ignition timing is correct. Next
increase the engine speed in graduated steps, during which, if the

mechanism is working correctly, the moving timing marks will be seen to advance steadily around the scale.

The start of centrifugal advance is usually above the fast-idle position and in many cases advance is complete at around 2,750 rpm. The actual design advance characteristics (the advance curve) is usually given in the manufacturer's workshop manual; see *Figure 5.11b*.

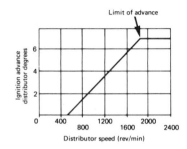

Figure 5.11b. Typical mechanical advance curve

Most manufacturers also use what is known as vacuum advance – this takes the form of a capsule containing a diaphragm mounted on the side of the distributor (*Figure 5.12*).

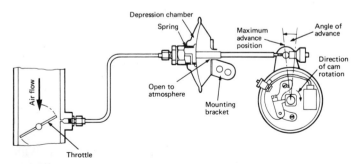

Figure 5.12. Vacuum timing control is achieved by the use of a spring-loaded flexible diaphragm which is subject to the changes of vacuum in the inlet manifold

One side of the diaphragm is connected to the base plate of the distributor so that as the diaphragm flexes it moves the base plate and therefore the contact breakers in relation to the cam. The other side of the diaphragm is subject to manifold pressure, so that at light load when the throttle is only partly open full vacuum advance is achieved, but at full load and at idle there is no vacuum advance.

The most common fault with vacuum advance is a leaking diaphragm although in some layouts the base plate of the distributor may stick. To check whether the unit is functioning is easy both with and without a strobe. When using a strobe make sure the vacuum pipe is connected and then with the engine running open the throttle quickly with the strobe directed at the timing marks. These should be seen to advance quickly and then return to a more retarded position. An alternative check is to remove the vacuum pipe at the carburettor and suck on it; if the unit is functioning the base plate should be seen to move (distributor cap off).

On some distributors the vacuum capsule is remote from the distributor body and the link between the capsule and base plate can be seen to move when the engine is accelerated quickly.

Electronic ignition

For practical purposes and discounting the method of generating the spark, there are two types of electronic ignition – those that retain the contact points (contact assisted or TAC) and those that do not (contactless). Only contactless systems are fitted as original equipment by car manufacturers. The basic layout for both types is shown in *Figure 5.13*.

Many of the contact-assisted systems are fitted with a changeover switch from electronic ignition to conventional. If for some reason the engine stops or will not start in the electronic mode, switch over to standard and try again. Basic fault finding in this position will be more or less identical to that given in the chart on page 200.

With contactless systems, other than the very few without a

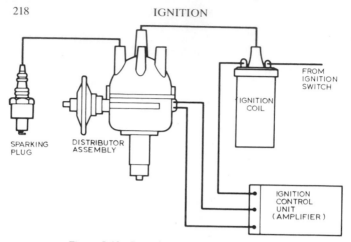

Figure 5.13. Basic layout of electronic ignition

distributor, checking the HT side of the system is identical to that shown for the standard ignition system, but with the higher voltages generated greater care should be taken to avoid a shock. In addition, some systems may be damaged if run with HT leads disconnected – if so it should be stated in the driver's handbook. Checking the low-tension side of contactless ignition systems is generally limited to testing for a supply to the amplifier unit, although on some it may also be possible to check

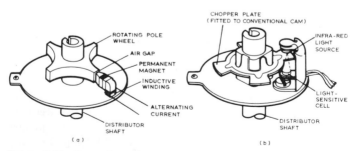

Figure 5.14. Contactless electronic ignition triggering systems: (a) magnetic; (b) optical

at the pick-up in the distributor as well. Also check the condition and security of any earth lead at the amplifier unit.

The pick-up or trigger mechanism in the distributor is invariably either magnetic or optical; see *Figure 5.14.* In magnetic layouts the air gap must be correct; however, as there is no reason why the gap should alter, any discrepancy is very unusual. Should the chopper plate or rotating pole wheel be disturbed at any time, ensure it is free to rotate with the drive shaft without fouling any other part or cable in the distributor.

6

Fuel

The fuel system on a modern motor car comprises a storage tank, pump to deliver fuel from the tank to the engine and a device which mixes the fuel with air to form a combustible mixture, all interconnected with the necessary plumbing. Many systems also incorporate one or more filters. In the most common arrangement, the fuel tank is for safety reasons fitted at the opposite end of the car to the engine; with many modern cars it is enclosed within the passenger 'non-crush' zone, so that in the event of an accident it is unlikely to be damaged.

The fuel pump can be either electrically or mechanically operated (*Figure 6.1*). If electric the pump is usually mounted at

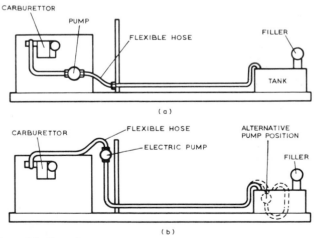

Figure 6.1. Basic layout of fuel system. Fuel flow from tank to carburettor controlled by: (a) engine-driven mechanical pump; (b) electric pump

the back end with the fuel tank; in some layouts it may be encapsulated within the tank. A mechanically-operated pump is mounted on the engine and is usually driven from the camshaft. Either type of pump is designed to deliver much more fuel than the engine can use, but most incorporate some type of 'idle' mechanism, whereby output ceases once the demand has been satisfied.

On most petrol burning cars a carburettor is used to mix the air and fuel, although a growing number of manufacturers are using fuel injection, albeit at the present only on the top or sporting models in their range. Fault finding on fuel injected cars is covered in a separate chapter. In addition to mixing the air with the fuel, a carburettor also regulates the amount of fuel going into the engine or rather the amount supplied by the pump. This is achieved by the use of a float within a (float) chamber, which rises and falls with the level of fuel in the chamber; as it rises it lifts a needle valve cutting off the supply. When the float drops the needle valve opens again and the supply is restored.

Working hazards

There is always an element of risk when working on a car and the greatest danger when doing anything to the fuel system is that of fire. It is almost inevitable that some spillage will occur whenever a union is disconnected, or it could be that the fault is in fact a leak – in such case take extra care, try to soak up the leaking fuel with a rag and avoid doing anything that could cause a spark.

Never smoke when working on a fuel system – in general do not smoke when working on your car at any time. Never use naked lights and keep any lead-lamps away from spilt fuel. Unless it is needed for test purposes, disconnect the battery so as to reduce the possibility of a spark igniting any fuel.

Besides the fire hazard, fuel systems can cause problems in other ways; for instance care should be taken when dismantling components and in particular the carburettor. If done *in situ* on the manifold it is quite easy to inadvertantly drop small parts (washers, nuts, etc) into the manifold, where they could be drawn into the engine causing extensive damage. In addition avoid dismantling any component unless you are sure how to put it together again – make a special note of which way valves are fitted for instance or how the needle valve lever is positioned in the float chamber – if in doubt make a sketch beforehand and lay each separate item down in strip order on a clean surface.

Cleanliness is vitally important, in fact many fuel system faults are caused by dirt. Water can also be a problem, so make sure any strip-down procedure is carried out in as clean and dry conditions as possible.

Fault diagnosis

Usually when a car breaks down with a fuel related problem the engine will splutter, pick-up again and then hesitate before finally stopping. An ignition fault on the other hand will generally (but not always) cause the engine to cut-out immediately. This then should give some indication of what to look for – in any fuel suspect situation, the first check should obviously be for petrol in the tank. Do not automatically rely upon the fuel gauge particularly in a strange car. If this check proves satisfactory, then go on to the basic fault finding procedure shown in *Figure 6.2*. The box numbers on the chart correspond with those in the text, where each stage is explained in more detail.

In some cases, of course, the fault may be self-evident; for example, a leak could well be fairly obvious once the bonnet has been opened. Petrol issuing from the carburettor vent holes or from around the top of the float chamber, or even possibly from any manifold drain tubes would be indicative of a flooded carburettor – see check No. 5 in the fault-finding chart.

However, it does not necessarily follow that a fault in the fuel system will cause an engine to stop or refuse to start. Fuel system faults could produce any number of different engine troubles from a misfire and poor acceleration to overheating. These possibilities are covered in Chapter 4 – Poor runners.

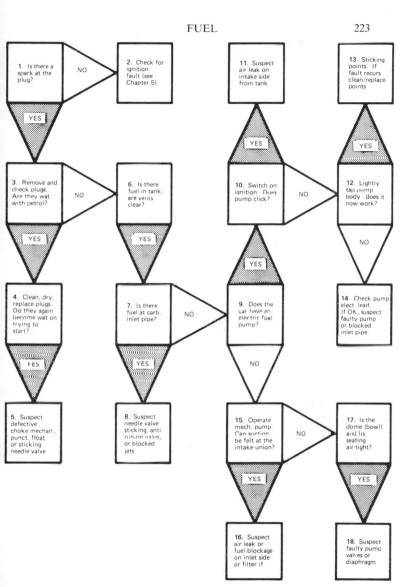

1. Is there a spark at the plug? — NO → 2. Check for ignition fault (see Chapter 5)

YES

3. Remove and check plugs. Are they wet with petrol? — NO → 6. Is there fuel in tank; are vents clear?

YES

4. Clean, dry, replace plugs. Do they again become wet on trying to start?

YES

5. Suspect defective choke mechan., punct. float or sticking needle valve

6. Is there fuel in tank; are vents clear?

YES

7. Is there fuel at carb. inlet pipe? — NO → 9. Does the car have an electric fuel pump?

YES

8. Suspect needle valve sticking, anti-run-on valve, or blocked jets

11. Suspect air leak on intake side from tank

YES

10. Switch on ignition. Does pump click? — NO → 12. Lightly tap pump body — does it now work?

YES

9. Does the car have an electric fuel pump?

NO

15. Operate mech. pump. Can suction be felt at the intake union? — NO → 17. Is the dome (bowl) and its seating air-tight?

YES

16. Suspect air leak or fuel blockage on inlet side or filter if

13. Sticking points. If fault recurs clean/replace points

YES

12. Lightly tap pump body — does it now work?

NO

14. Check pump elect. lead. If OK, suspect faulty pump or blocked inlet pipe

17. Is the dome (bowl) and its seating air-tight?

YES

18. Suspect faulty pump valves or diaphragm

Figure 6.2. Fuel system fault-finding sequence

Fuel system fault-finding sequence

1. If your engine stops or will not start, unless it is due to an obvious mechanical failure (seizure for example) or battery related problems, the first check should be for a spark at the plug. The procedure for this is detailed as the first check in the ignition fault-finding sequence on page 201.

2. Lack of a spark at the plug means an ignition fault.

3. If the engine will not start and you find that one plug is wet with petrol, then the odds are that they all will be unless one or possibly two cylinders have been firing. If so remove all the plugs and dry them, preferably in an oven – failing that use a match or cigarette lighter (well away from the engine). Check also the gaps and cleanliness of the plugs.

   One of the most likely causes of this problem is that the engine has been over-choked, perhaps compounded by an ignition/electrical problem resulting in a poor spark at cranking speeds. This situation is also very often made worse by the driver pumping the accelerator pedal, so forcing more fuel into the engine. In such cases it may be possible to start the engine by first slowly pressing the accelerator pedal to the floor, then with the choke in the 'off' position crank the engine on the starter motor. This gives maximum air flow through the engine, which is sometimes sufficient to dry the plugs out. Do not begin pumping the accelerator pedal once the engine fires and do not attempt this procedure if you suspect a faulty needle valve or float – see check No. 5.

4. With the plugs clean, dry and if necessary gaps reset try and start the engine again, using less choke or none at all at least for the first few seconds – there could be an excess of fuel still in the inlet manifold which coupled with choke operation could again 'flood' the engine.

5. If in check No. 4 the plugs again became wet with petrol, the reason could be a problem in the choke operating mechanism or fuel enrichment device, a punctured float or one that is sticking/jammed in its chamber, or it could be due to the needle valve sticking open. The easiest way to check if the choke is operating correctly on most fixed-jet carburettors is to remove

the air filter, when generally the choke flap valve in the carburettor can be seen. On manually operated versions this should be seen to move from the open to the fully closed position as the control is operated – ensure that it returns to the open position when the control is pushed in.

With some carburettors the flap valve or strangler may not appear to be fully closed or indeed fully open; for the purposes of this check, however, it is sufficient that it is moving from one position to the other. On those cars with automatic chokes the flap valve should only be closed when the engine is cold. With some it may be necessary to fully depress the accelerator pedal for the valve to move to the closed position.

Variable choke carburettors (such as SU, Stromberg, Ford VV) are not fitted with the flap valve/strangler type of choke but use a fuel enrichment arrangement for cold starting. This generally takes the form of a linkage which will lower the jet in relation to the needle and/or lift the air valve slightly. On the Ford carburettor an auxiliary miniature carburettor is used to supplement the mixture provided by the main system.

Usually in cases of a punctured float or where the needle valve sticks open, the carburettor will flood and leak petrol externally, particularly from around the float chamber flange. In most cases it will be necessary to remove the float chamber or the float chamber cover to inspect the float, although some carburettors have a window in the chamber wall. If the float is punctured, it will generally be sitting on the base of the chamber well below the level of the fuel. The float itself will be found to contain petrol; this can be heard if the float is shaken in the hand.

Temporary repairs can be made to a punctured float but first it must be emptied of fuel. It is unlikely that any hole in the float will be large enough to let the contents run or even drip out and the best course is to allow the petrol to evaporate – this process can be speeded up by dipping the float in very hot water. Do not try heating the float with a naked flame and if the float is made of plastic take care if dipping it in hot water. Once the float is empty it can be sealed using an epoxy resin (two-pack) adhesive (*Figure 6.3*), or if a metal float it can be soldered. Use only the minimum amount of repair material, ensuring that it does not prevent the float from moving freely in its housing. Excess material may also affect the float weight and therefore the fuel level.

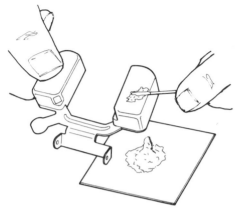

Figure 6.3. Repairing a float with petrol-proof adhesive such as a two-pack epoxy resin

Unfortunately, without removing the float chamber there is no way of checking if the float is punctured or if the needle valve is sticking (other than on those carburettors with a window). A sticking needle valve (see stage No. 8) can sometimes be freed by giving its housing a sharp but not heavy blow, say with a handle of a medium screwdriver – it may be advantageous to try this before starting to dismantle the carburettor.

6. It is bad practice to continually run low on fuel, not only from the inconvenience of running out completely but also that at low levels any dirt in the tank is less dispersed and so is more likely to be drawn up into the intake pipe, causing trouble later on. With a blocked vent(s) the engine will continue to run until the depression in the tank formed by the falling fuel level equals that produced by the fuel pump; at this stage no more fuel will flow. This will be evident by the inrush of air when the fuel tank cap is removed. It has been known for the fuel tank to collapse inwards under conditions of this nature. At times this may not be harmful

other than reducing tank capacity and producing incorrect reading at the contents gauge, on occasions though it can result in the tank splitting.

If the suspected cause of a breakdown is blocked vents, try starting the engine with the tank filler cap removed. If this is successful, make an emergency repair by tying a piece of clean rag over the filler neck in place of the cap so as to prevent dust getting into the fuel. The rag must, of course, be porous and allow the passage of air or it too may get drawn into the tank. In some countries this emergency repair may contravene local regulations.

The most common causes for this kind of problem are an incorrect filler cap having been fitted (a non-vented cap where a vented one should be used), an under vehicle vent blocked by underbody sealant or heavy dried mud and on some cars where the pipe is unprotected it can be crushed by luggage/heavy equipment in the boot.

7. The procedure for checking if fuel is being delivered to the carburettor depends to some extent on the type of fuel pump – either electrical or mechanical. In both cases, however, the first operation is to slacken off or disconnect the fuel inlet pipe at the carburettor. On some layouts with what is commonly called a 'weir' system, there may be two fuel pipes at the carburettor, one of which is the return to the tank. The inlet pipe can be identified by tracing it back to the pump.

The next stage is to operate the pump. On those cars with a mechanical pump this will involve cranking the engine over   the ignition HT lead at the coil or the LT lead should be disconnected to prevent the engine from starting. On most electrical pump systems the pump will operate when the ignition is switched on. Take care when carrying out this test, for if the fuel system is in order petrol will be discharged from the pipe. With most electrical pumps this will be in a fairly rapid series of jerks or pulses, whereas with mechanical pumps it will be much slower. If possible use some form of container to catch the fuel, or soak it up with a piece of rag. Always ensure that any spilt fuel is 'mopped' up before attempting to start the engine or carry out any ignition/electrical checks.

8. If check No. 7 proved positive in that fuel was being delivered to the carburettor, then the fault must be within the carburettor itself, most probably a sticking needle valve. In some cases the valve may be sticking because small particles of grit or dirt prevent it from either closing or opening; alternatively, the valve may be partially gummed up or slightly off-set in its housing. Often the problem can be rectified by the application of a sharp but not too heavy blow on the carburettor in the region of the valve. If this fails then the only option is to remove the valve and physically free it – in most cases this will involve first removing the float chamber. If this is found to contain sufficient petrol for the float to lift the valve, then the fault is unlikely to be at the valve.

Some carburettors are fitted with an electrically-operated valve which is used to cut the fuel supply between the float chamber and carburettor venturi, usually in the idling system. Switching on the ignition energises the valve, holding it in the open position. Immediately the ignition is switched off the valve closes under spring pressure, cutting the fuel supply and so preventing the engine from running on or 'dieseling'. These valves may be called anti-run-on devices, anti-diesel or fuel cut-off valves and as they are electrically opened it follows that any failure in the electrical circuit to the valve would result in it staying closed. Probably the easiest way of locating one of these valves is to check for any electrical cables at the carburettor, often the only one (if any) will be to the valve (*Figure 6.4*), although some carburettors may be equipped with an electrically-operated choke. If the anti-diesel valve is working, it can often be heard to click as the ignition is switched on.

Figure 6.4. One type of anti-run-on valve. Also known as anti-diesel valve

If the valve is suspect, first check its power supply (12 volts) using either a test lamp or voltmeter – see Chapter 10. Alternatively, remove the valve and with its power cable connected and the valve body earthed (hold it on the manifold or cylinder head) when it should be seen to operate as the ignition is switched on and off.

A fault in the power supply to the valve should be fairly easy to rectify or if not the fault can be by-passed if necessary by re-wiring the valve directly from the battery – preferably with an in-line fuse in the circuit. If wired direct, do not forget to disconnect the valve when the ignition is switched off. If the valve itself is faulty it should be possible with most to first remove it from the carburettor (unscrew it), then cut off the head of the valve and refit the body back into the carburettor – this however, should only be carried out as a temporary measure.

An alternative but less common type of anti-run-on valve is connected to the inlet manifold. This type opens when the ignition is switched off allowing an excess of air into the manifold, so weakening the mixture that running-on is prevented. If this type of valve fails for any reason, it is usually a fairly easy operation to block off the air intake to the valve.

Partly due to the better storage and handling of fuel and partly because of better filters in a car's fuel system the problem of blocked jets is a fairly infrequent event, which is just as well for with most modern carburettors the jets are inaccessible without a more or less complete strip of the unit. On some older carburettors the jets can be removed externally or possibly by just removing the float chamber. It would be unwise to strip down a modern carburettor without a workshop manual or some other form of detailed instruction and drawing – it may also require the use of special tools and an exhaust gas analyser to correctly set up on reassembly. Jets can generally be cleaned by blowing through them in a reverse direction. If this does not remove the obstruction, try dislodging it with a bristle from a fairly stiff brush (or something similar). Avoid using a metal prod such as a length of wire or a pin.

9. If it is not stated in the car's handbook, the easiest way to

determine the type of fuel pump fitted is to follow the fuel supply
pipe back from the carburettor. Mechanical fuel pumps are
invariably driven from the camshaft, so the pump is mounted on
the engine. Electrical fuel pumps are usually mounted near the
fuel tank or actually within the tank; in either case the fuel
supply pipe to the carburettor runs under the floor of the car and
can be seen to do so from under the bonnet. Do not confuse the
fuel supply pipe with any return pipe used in 'weir' systems, see
page 227.

10. Most electrical fuel pumps are of the solenoid-operated
diaphragm type, in which an electromagnet is used to draw a
diaphragm down against the pressure of a spring. Current for the
electromagnet is switched on and off by a set of contacts
operated through a toggle mechanism by a pushrod attached to
the diaphragm (*Figure 6.5*). With this type of pump every time
the toggle mechanism operates it produces an audible click – this
corresponds with the stroke of the pushrod/diaphragm and
therefore output pulses from the pump. An alternative type of

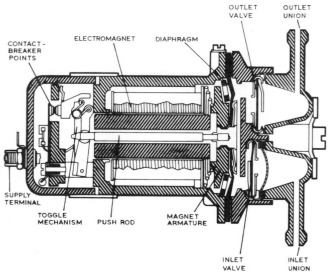

Figure 6.5. Section through diaphragm-type electric fuel pump

pump, used mostly in fuel injection systems, features some form of rotor attached to the shaft of a DC motor. This should produce a 'humming' noise when in use.

Regardless of the type of pump, there are various means of wiring them into the electrical circuit of a car. On some more recent cars this circuit may include some form of safety device to cut power to the pump in the event of an accident or when the engine stops. These safety devices may take the form of an inertia switch, a pressure switch coupled into the engines lubrication switch or a switch activated by the pulses produced in the ignition circuit. With the latter two types it may be necessary to crank the engine to make the pump work.

11. Normally the pump will click about once every few seconds at engine tickover speeds. It may click once or twice when the ignition is switched on and the engine stationary; if it is heard to click at a much more rapid rate, it generally indicates that the pump is drawing in air instead of fuel on its inlet side. This may be due to a leaking union or pipe, or simply because of a low level in the tank. See page 233 on how to check for a leak.

Other possible reasons for the pump to click rapidly and yet give no output could be a sticking valve or damaged (holed) diaphragm. Methods of overcoming both these problems on a temporary basis is given in No. 18 of this fault-finding sequence – this relates to problems with a mechanical pump but the same principles apply here. To isolate defects within the pump from those external to it, remove the inlet pipe at the pump and seal the pump intake with your finger. Now operate the pump; if you feel a slight suction and the pump clicks a couple of times and then stops, there is an air leak in the supply (or no fuel in the tank). If, however, the pump continues clicking, assuming your 'finger seal' is satisfactory, the fault is inside the pump – most probably a sticking valve.

12. In a large number of cases when an electrical fuel pump becomes inoperative, the fault lies with the contact points or their operating (toggle) mechanism. This can often be rectified by giving the pump body a sharp tap with, for example, the handle of a large screwdriver. Take care not to hit the plastic cover sometimes fitted over the toggle mechanism. Leave the

ignition switched on and if necessary crank the engine when
carrying out this operation.

13. If after tapping the pump body the pump works, the
problem is sure to have been with the points or their operating
mechanism and could well recur. Therefore, it would be wise to
inspect and clean/replace them at the first opportunity. If on
tapping the pump body the pump just clicks once or twice, then
again the trouble lies with the points. On many pumps of this
type access to the points is fairly simple, necessitating the release
of two nuts and removal of a plastic cover. Access to the pump
itself though is often restricted and could involve removing the
fuel tank.

14. Depending upon its location, it may sometimes be easier to
check for a power supply to the pump earlier than this. Use
either a test lamp or voltmeter to carry out this test – do not try
'flashing' the supply cable to earth. If a satisfactory (12-volt)
supply is provided at the pump terminal, either the earth return
is suspect (this may be through the pump mounting or an extra
earth-return strap) or the pump is defective in some way – it may
only need cleaning. With some faults the pump body may get
warm; if so switch off the ignition. It can happen that if either the
inlet or outlet of the pump were blocked or a valve stuck closed
then the pump will not operate; this, however, would be
unusual.

   Do not forget when checking for a 12-volt supply that in those
layouts incorporating a safety switch, it may be necessary to
crank the engine. Where there is no electrical supply to the
pump and the reason cannot be found (the method of checking a
circuit is given in the Electrical section), it should be a fairly
simple operation to add an extra cable, preferably from an
ignition-controlled fuse. If the new wiring is taken from a
permanently live source (battery), it should be fitted with an
in-line fuse and be disconnected whenever the engine is switched
off for periods exceeding two minutes.

15. Mechanical pumps (*Figure 6.6*) are invariably driven from
the camshaft and in most cases the only way to operate it is to
crank the engine on the starter motor. Some pumps, however,
are fitted with a priming lever whereby the pump can be

manually operated. On those pumps with a priming lever, if the engine has stopped in such a position that the diaphragm is being held down by the pump operating lever and cam, the priming lever will just 'idle'. In order to manually operate the pump the engine should be turned one complete revolution.

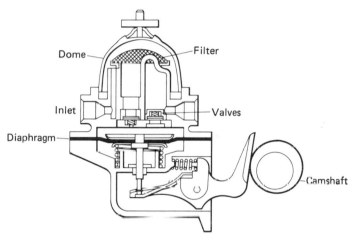

Figure 6.6. Section through mechanical-type fuel pump

16. A positive result in test No. 15 (suction felt on your finger) would indicate that the pump is in order and that the reason for it not producing any fuel is either an air leak or blockage in the fuel line back to the tank. It does not necessarily follow that where air is leaking into the system fuel will leak out. However, an inspection of the pipe back to the tank should be the first check, paying particular attention to any unions, joints or flexible hose connections. If fuel can be seen to have been leaking in the past, this is probably where air is now leaking in. Where there are no signs of a leak, the only alternative is to suck or blow on the feed pipe (use a tight-fitting length of plastic hose over the end of the pipe) and have an assistant check along the system back to the tank.

Note that if the fuel level in the tank is low and the vehicle parked on an incline, it is possible that the intake pipe could be uncovered. This would produce symptoms similar to an air leak.

In most cases where an air (or fuel) leak exists it should be fairly simple to effect a repair. For example, if the leak is at a threaded union then merely tightening the two halves together may be enough; alternatively, a thin smear of jointing compound over the two mating surfaces may help. Small pin-prick holes in a metal pipe can be sealed with a thin smear of hard-setting jointing compound or silicone-based material covered over with plastic insulating tape. A more permanent repair would be to solder the pipe, but this would probably mean that it has to be removed from the vehicle, in which case it would be better to replace it. A cracked or otherwise damaged pipe can often be replaced (in part) by a petrol-proof rubber or plastic hose.

The easiest way to remove a blockage in the pipe is usually to blow it back into the tank, using once again a length of plastic tubing on the pump end of the pipe. The major disadvantage with this, however, is that the same problem could (and probably would) occur again, especially if the fuel level in the tank is low. The only longterm answer is to drain and clean out the tank, which often means that it has to be removed from the vehicle.
17. If no suction is felt in test No. 15, it is possible that the pump is still drawing in air through a defective filter bowl gasket or because the filter bowl is loose/distorted or damaged. With a defective gasket it may be possible to make a temporary repair simply by turning the gasket upside down and re-fitting the bowl. An alternative is to cut out a replacement gasket from a sheet of rubber or similar plastic material (old wellington boot or plastic football for example). A further alternative is to form an 'O' ring of the correct size using a tube of silicone-based RTV (room temperature vulcanising) gasket jointing material. Once the ring has cured (set), it can be inserted in place of the gasket.

A cracked dome can often be repaired by solder if it is made from metal or by using an epoxy resin over the crack. Depending upon the dome shape, it can sometimes be replaced by using the cap (preferably metal) from a suitably sized aerosol can – hairspray, deodorant and paintspray cans are a few examples.

Care should be taken when clamping down the replacement, particularly if it is plastic. Ensure also that it is petrol proof.

18. If the dome and its sealing are in order and the pump is not creating any suction at the inlet union, then the fault is most probably a leaking valve or damaged diaphragm. A failure in the pump operating mechanism is not unknown but happens very infrequently and even then this is often due to incorrect assembly. The valves in mechanical fuel pumps are usually simple spring-loaded discs fitted above the diaphragm in the body of the pump and are very reliable. In most cases any failure can be attributed to dirt between the disc and its seat.

At one time these valves could be replaced, being held into position by a screw and clamp. The modern trend is to 'stake' the valves in position, making their removal almost impossible without damaging the pump – neither are replacements available. Some pumps are in fact sealed units, so you cannot even get to the valves. Sometimes dirt between the valve and its seat can be removed simply by blowing through the pump inlet union. If not, the pump will have to be dismantled (sealed type excepted) when it may be possible to clear any obstruction by physically moving the valve disc in its housing. This is best done with the pump immersed in a bath of petrol and moved from side to side so as to help dislodge any debris.

A leaking diaphragm may only reduce pump output, It may even go unnoticed except that in most cases the leaking fuel ends up in the engine sump, considerably reducing the lubricity of the engine oil and increasing the risk of fire. If for no apparent reason the engine oil level appears to get higher, suspect the fuel pump diaphragm. Some pumps have a drain hole at the base of the lower chamber. With these, any fuel seeping from the drain hole will be due to a defective diaphragm.

Depending on the condition of the diaphragm it is often possible to carry out an emergency (get-you-home) repair. If the diaphragm is punctured, it may be possible to seal the hole with some form of rubber solution or silicone based RTV gasket cement. Do not use any hard setting material, which would probably crack as the diaphragm flexed. A split or porous diaphragm can sometimes be patched using a sheet of thin rubber or plastic (polythene bags have been used in this role). It is usually best to cut any 'patch' so that it fits completely over the existing diaphragm (*Figure 6.7*). The two can then be joined at the centre with a suitable adhesive (petrol proof) and around the circumference by the pump body screws. The patch virtually becomes a second diaphragm.

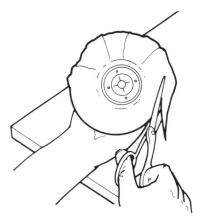

Figure 6.7. Cutting out a temporary replacement fuel-pump diaphragm from a sheet of polythene

Carburettors

The major role of the carburettor is to supply the engine with the fuel it needs, fully mixed with the correct proportion of air. The ratio of fuel to air changes according to the operating condition of the engine. How the different types of carburettor achieve this is beyond the scope of this book, except to state that all carburettors can be divided into two distinct groups – those with fixed jets and chokes (venturis), and those where the effective sizes of both the jet and venturi changes according to the engine speed, load and position of the throttle.

Some carburettor faults apply to all types, including problems associated with the float and needle valve, incorrect adjustment of the controls and wear, mainly at the throttle spindle. Although the only permanent solution in the case of a worn throttle spindle is to drill and re-bush the housing, one method of preventing air leaking into the carburettor is to seal the ends of the spindle and housing with some RTV silicone-based jointing compound. It is advisable to make up a small disc of thin metal or plastic, which can be located over the end of the housing and held in place by the compound, this reduces the possibility of any jointing compound finding its way between the spindle and housing.

There are some faults, however, which are peculiar to, or at least more prevalent on one type of carburettor. This is not to say that one type of instrument is more reliable than another, but rather that each has its own particular trouble areas.

Fixed-jet carburettors (Figure 6.8)

Although there are several makes and types of fixed-jet carburettor, they are all more prone to the problem of blocked jets than the variable-jet type. In the first place they use smaller size jets and secondly they use more of them – at least two in each carburettor. In some cases for instance a separate slow-running jet is used – obviously if this becomes blocked the engine will not idle. See page 194 for other faults that could cause this condition. It is sometimes possible to clear blocked jets by connecting an air line or foot pump to the carburettor fuel inlet union and pressurising the float chamber sufficiently to clear the blockage at the jet. It often helps if you can seal off the float chamber breather with your finger; this is not possible on many modern carburettors which have an enclosed breather circuit to comply with emission regulations. Should this prove ineffective, the only alternative is to remove the jets and clean them as explained on page 229.

Fixed-jet carburettors and some variable-jet designs use a form of pump to provide an extra 'squirt' of fuel when the throttle is opened quickly such as when accelerating hard. There are both plunger and diaphragm versions of these accelerator pumps in use and failure of either will usually result in a 'flat-spot' when accelerating possibly accompanied by some backfiring. The most common fault with the plunger version is that the plunger or piston is sticking in the bore, often being gummed up. Generally, it will have to be removed for cleaning although in some cases a squirt of penetrating oil or proprietary carburettor cleaning fluid will free it.

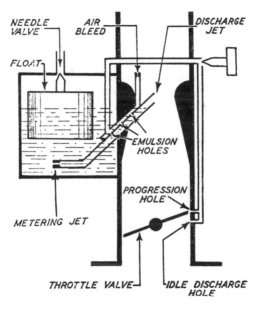

Figure 6.8. Principle of fixed-choke or open-choke downdraught carburettor, that gives a variable air supply working in conjunction with fixed-size air and petrol metering jets. In this idling system, the quality of the idling mixture is adjusted by the amount of air permitted to pass the cone of the air-regulating screw into the channel connecting the idling jet and the idle-discharge hole

Diaphragm-type accelerator pumps suffer mainly from a leaking diaphragm (split or holed); these can be temporarily repaired in much the same way as those in fuel pumps (page 235). With most carburettors, once the air filter is removed, the pump can be checked by looking into the carburettor intake while an assistant presses the accelerator a couple of times. There should be a short injection of fuel into the inlet manifold which can be either seen or heard – if the engine is hot the fuel may instantly vaporize. The engine should not be running for this test. If the accelerator pump does not appear to be working, the first check should be on its operating mechanism/linkage, followed by further checks on any jets or oneway (ball and spring) valves in its fuel circuit.

Variable-jet carburettors

Variable-jet carburettors are also known as constant vacuum or variable venturi carburettors. The three main types – Ford VV, Stromberg CD and SU (*Figures 6.9, 6.10* and *6.11*) – although differing in construction, work on the principle of a tapered needle moving inside a jet and controlled by the volume of air passing through the instrument.

Some problems common to all types of variable-jet units are: a sticking piston or slide (air valve), a bent or offset needle or in older units a worn needle. Other faults are peculiar to the different makes. For example, an SU carburettor can suffer from a fuel leak at the float chamber to jet tube connection, a sticking excess fuel device and poor damping of the piston. The Stromberg and Ford VV are diaphragm-controlled and can therefore suffer from a punctured or split diaphragm. The Stromberg, like the SU, can be poorly damped, whereas the Ford unit, being the only one fitted with an accelerator pump can experience troubles in that area.

A sticking piston can produce a number of symptoms depending upon where and when it is sticking. Among the more common problems which can be attributed to this fault are:

1. Engine will not (or is reluctant to) start.
2. Engine starts but will not accelerate.
3. Engine stalls during normal running.
4. Engine refuses to idle.
5. Engine performance down and fuel consumption up.

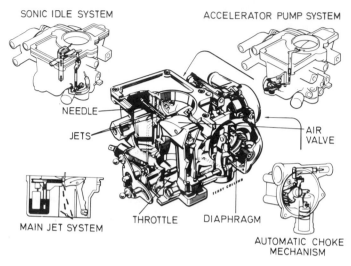

Figure 6.9. Ford Variable Venturi (VV) carburettor. The amount of fuel passed into the engine is controlled by a tapered metering rod, attached to the venturi valve, which slides through the main jet. As the engine's fuel demand is increased the tapered rod is pulled outwards through the main jet. This enlarges the main jet size and therefore allows more fuel to be fed through the system.

Fuel is drawn through the main jet system at low engine speeds and loads becuase the vacuum at the main jet outlet is high, due to the air valve reducing the venturi size and thereby increasing the air velocity

Some SU and Stromberg carburettors incorporate a piston/slide lifting pin under the air chamber housing. If this is pressed and then quickly released, the piston should be heard to fall back on its stop – this however only checks the piston over part of its range. If no pin is fitted, the easiest method of checking piston movement is to remove the air filter and then physically lift the piston with your finger or small screwdriver, ensuring there are no tight spots and that it falls freely to its stop. If the piston is found to be sticking it could be due to any of the following causes:

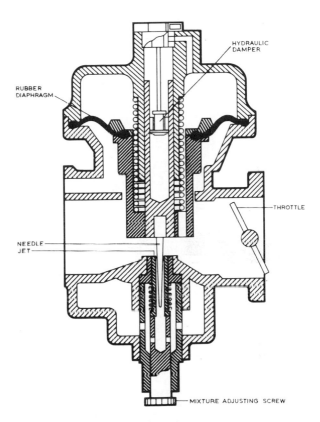

Figure 6.10. Section through Stromberg CD (constant depression) carburettor. The principle of operation is similar to the Ford VV unit. The size of the air passage is automatically varied by a sliding air-valve piston under the control of a diaphragm which responds to varying manifold depression. As a result, constant air speed is maintained through the carburettor under all operating conditions. The effective size of the single petrol jet is correspondingly regulated by the tapered metering needle

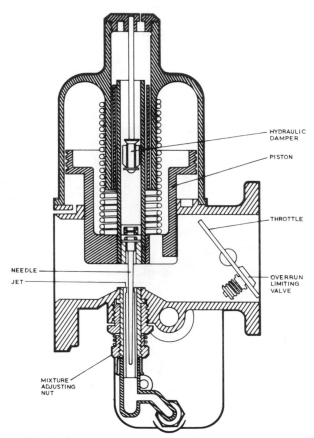

Figure 6.11. Section through SU constant depression carburettor. In this type of variable-choke unit, the air-valve piston operates with an extremely fine clearance in the suction chamber. The hydraulic damper in the piston guide prevents sudden rising of the piston when the throttle is opened quickly for acceleration, thus allowing the temporary enrichment of the mixture needed during acceleration

1. Gummy deposits on the piston or slide.
2. High spots/abrasions on the piston/slide or housing.
3. Bent needle.
4. Bent damper rod (where fitted).

Gummy deposits or abrasions can be cleaned off whereas the only satisfactory solution to the bent needle or damper rod is replacement. Depending upon its condition, a defective diaphragm in bith the Ford and Stromberg carburettors can produce symptoms similar to a sticking piston. A temporary repair such as that given on page 235 may be possible where this fault exists.

Poor damping on the SU and Stromberg units can produce:

1. Irregular idling with the engine hunting.
2. Hesitation or stalling on acceleration.
3. Engine surging (kangarooing) during normal running.

In most cases poor damping will be due to either a low oil level or the use of an incorrect oil in the carburettor dashpot (damper).

7

Fuel injection

Although there are a number of different types and makes of fuel-injection equipment on cars today, Bosch equipment is the most widely used and the procedures in this chapter are mainly based on their K-Jetronic system (*Figure 7.1*). Having said that some of the checks will apply to other systems as well.

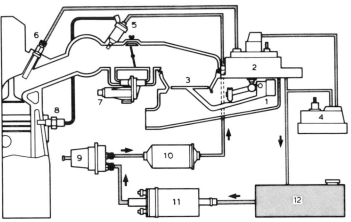

Figure 7.1. Bosch K-Jetronic mechanical petrol-injection system. (1) Mixture control unit. (2) Fuel distributor. (3) Air flow sensor. (4) Warm-up regulator. (5) Cold start valve. (6) Injector (one per cylinder). (7) Auxiliary air valve. (8) Thermo-time switch. (9) Fuel accumulator. (10) Fuel filter. (11) Fuel pump. (12) Fuel tank

In nearly all injection systems a pressure is maintained within the circuit even though the engine is switched off. Some spillage is therefore inevitable when making a disconnection. To reduce the fire risk it is advisable to disconnect the battery before commencing with any checks. Other points to note are:

1. Never make a disconnection, or even slacken off a joint when the engine is running.

2. Cleanliness is much more important in a fuel-injection system than in a carburettor layout, so ensure that the exterior of any joint is clean before making a disconnection.

3. Where possible, always use new jointing washers or seals on reassembly.

Fault diagnosis

The most probable reasons for any particular problem are shown in the accompanying fault-finding chart. Where possible DIY checks are given for diagnosing individual faults with the numbers in the text corresponding to those in the chart. If no such check is given, then it can be assumed that special equipment is needed for that particular test. Many of these checks, however, involve some dismantling and require a degree of skill on the part of the operator. As the system can be easily and expensively damaged by unskilled or clumsy handling, unless you are sure of your ability it might be best to leave it alone.

Nearly all fuel-injection systems are wired into the vehicles electrical system in such a way that the pump (and often certain other components) will only work when the engine is being cranked on the starter or is actually running. Many of the tests require that this safety circuit be bridged or by-passed. With some earlier Bosch systems this involved nothing more than removing the plug from the air-flow sensor. With many later versions there is no electrical connection at the sensor. These can be bridged by using a link (preferably fused) between the two contact terminals (30 and 87) of the pump relay. The location of this relay and the terminal numbers may vary from model to model.

Fault-finding procedures

1. Air leaks at the intake system can be traced in much the same way as on a carburettor engine. There may be a whistling sound

Fuel-injection fault-finding chart

Fault	Procedure									
	1	2	3	4	5	6	7	8	9	10
Engine will not start or is difficult to start when cold	●	●	●		●	●	●			
Engine will not start or is difficult to start when hot	●	●			●		●	●	●	
Poor idle during warm-up	●		●			●	●		●	●
Poor idle when warm	●	●				●	●		●	●
Engine misfires under load	●						●		●	
Engine runs on after being switched off		●				●			●	
Flat spot when accelerating	●	●					●			●
Idle speed cannot be adjusted (too high)				●						
Engine starts but then immediately stops						●	●			

Procedure cause
(*see relevant number in text*)

1. Intake system leaking (after sensor plate)
2. Sensor lever and/or control plunger sticking
3. Auxiliary air device does not open
4. Auxiliary air device does not close
5. Fuel pump inoperative
6. Cold start valve leaking or system defective
7. Control pressure incorrect
8. Fuel system internal leak (accumulator or pump)
9. Injector valves leaking
10. Unequal fuel delivery

which changes pitch or stops altogether if the leak is covered with a finger or rag. Alternatively, cover any suspect points with a penetrating fluid (WD 40 equivalent) and watch for where it may be sucked in.

2. Sensor plate travel should be checked with the engine warm (above 20°C). Access to the sensor plate will vary on different

model cars – in most up-draught layouts where the air intake is below the plate it will involve removing the dome above the sensor, whereas in downdraught systems it will be necessary to remove the air filter. Once access is achieved, switch on the ignition for about 10 seconds with the safety circuit bridged. Then with the ignition off, move the sensor plate (lift in up-draught layouts, depress in down-draught) systems – see *Figure 7.2*. The resistance felt throughout the entire sensor plate movement should be equal. Check also that the sensor plate returns freely. Lift or depress the plate to its full deflection and then release it – the plate should snap back to its normal rest position, then bounce once or twice on its spring-loaded stop.

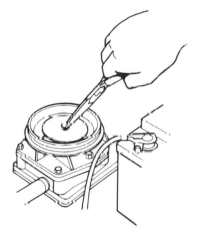

Figure 7.2. Checking for movement of sensor plate

Should the sensor plate become stiff or tight at any point through its normal range of travel, do not attempt to force it.

The easiest way to check the control plunger movement is to first of all carry out the previous test for sensor plate movement and then, after lifting or pressing the plate to its limit of travel, move it back quickly to a point just before its rest position. The

control plunger will follow this rapid movement of the sensor plate much more slowly and will therefore lose contact with the secondary lever. Under normal circumstances it will be possible to feel, at the sensor plate, when the plunger again makes contact. If this is so, it can be assumed that the plunger is free.
3 and 4. Check the auxiliary air device with the engine cold. First disconnect the electrical connections to the air device and warm up regulator, then remove the hoses from either side of the unit. It should now be possible with the aid of a mirror, to see right through the air inlet and outlet ports (*Figure 7.3*).

Figure 7.3. Auxiliary air device (removed from system)

Next remake the electrical connections, bridge the safety circuit and switch on the ignition. After about 10 minutes, the valve should be fully closed blocking off the view between the two ports.
5. Usually, the pump can be heard operating when the safety circuit is bridged and the ignition switched on. If it does not operate, check the electrical supply to the pump – this should be a minimum of 11.5 volts. A lower voltage may result in the pump running but failing to deliver its full output.

If the electrical supply to the pump is in order, ensure that it is earthed satisfactorily (usually through its mounting). If this is in order, then the pump is probably faulty. Other than removing and replacing the oneway valve (see 7 and 8) any defect within the pump will necessitate its renewal. Do not at any time run the pump dry – this will ruin the roller to housing seals within the pump, rendering it unserviceable.

6. Check the cold start valve with the engine cold. First of all remove the valve, leaving the fuel hose connected – on those cars with steel tubing it may be necessary to link the two with a length of hose. Disconnect the electrical plug from the valve and reconnect the valve to earth on one side and an ignition-controlled supply to the other. Now direct the nozzle of the valve into a suitable container (a jam jar) and, with the safety circuit bridged, have an assistant switch on the ignition. The cold start valve should now spray fuel and continue to do so until the ignition is switched off. Restrict the duration of this test to less than 30 seconds and take care with the electrical connections – a stray spark could start a fire.

Besides the other faults shown in the chart, a leaking valve could result in excessive fuel consumption and a black exhaust. 7 and 8. Special equipment is needed to check the pressures within the system and to test the pump output. An internal leak at the pump would be through the oneway valve – this can be removed and checked.

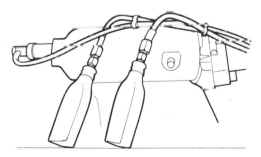

Figure 7.4. Check spray from fuel injectors in glass bottles

9 and 10. Testing the fuel injectors normally calls for special equipment. However, an indication of their performance can be gauged by using a similar procedure to that for the cold start valve, except that the engine should be warm.

First remove all the injectors from the engine and direct each into a separate container, leaving their fuel pipes attached (*Figure 7.4*). Next bridge the safety circuit and switch on the ignition – nothing should happen until the sensor plate is moved from its rest position, when the injectors should begin spraying. The spray formation should be straight, even and more or less central. Check also that the quantity of fuel in each container after the test is about the same.

If the engine is warm, the cold start valve should not spray fuel; however, if in doubt it would be wise to disconnect it electrically before carrying out this test.

Finally beware of the fire risk when carrying out this test – ensure that all the containers are stable and the injectors located so that they cannot fall out. Removal of the injectors from the engine in most cases will involve first slackening off the hose union and then prising the injectors out of their housing with a screwdriver. Do not forget to retighten the hose unions before carrying out the test.

8

Engine mechanical

The mechanical condition of an engine is a factor to be considered when trying to trace the cause of a misfire or refusal to start. A low compression on one cylinder, for instance, will usually result in a regular misfire, whereas low compression on two or more cylinders in an average four-cylinder engine could well result in it not starting.

Poor compression in all, or most cylinders in an engine would most likely be due to general wear of the bores, piston rings and valves – often this will be accompanied by pressurisation of the crankcase and in some case oil fumes being blown out of the crankcase breather system. The engine will also probably be burning oil and issuing clouds of blue smoke from the exhaust. Poor compressions in one or possibly two cylinders would in most cases be due to a mechanical fault – this could be due to any one (or more) of the following:

1. Incorrect valve clearances
2. Weak or broken valve spring
3. Poor valve seating
4. Burnt or otherwise defective valve
5. Cylinder-head gasket leaking
6. Piston ring(s) broken, worn or sticking

Where a regular misfire is evident, the first action should be to isolate which cylinder is at fault. This can be done quite easily by running the engine at idling speed and either shorting out or disconnecting each sparking plug in turn. As the plug on each good cylinder is shorted out the engine will run even rougher, or it may even stall. Shorting the plug on the defective cylinder, however, will make no (or very little) difference. It does not

251

necessarily follow that a regular misfire is due to poor compression at the cylinder concerned – a defective sparking plug or plug lead could be among a number of other possibilities causing the same problem. The only accurate method of checking compression pressures is with a compression tester used in accordance with the manufacturer's instructions.

An indication of poor compression on one or two cylinders can, however, be gained by disconnecting the main HT lead at the coil and then spinning the engine on the starter. If one (or two) compressions are greatly different from the others, it will be apparent by the sound and operation of the starter motor.

To check for loss of compression on individual cylinders, first remove all the sparking plugs, then with an assistant operating the starter, seal off each plug hole in turn with your thumb. Take care when carrying out this check; in the first place it would be wise to disconnect the ignition at the coil to prevent any sparking; secondly watch out for any moving parts such as the fan, and finally either wear goggles or keep your eyes as far away from the area of the plug hole as you can. If your car is equipped with a starting handle, the compressions can normally be felt as the engine is turned over. The number felt in two revolutions of the handle should correspond with the number of cylinders.

Incorrect valve clearances

A specified clearance is provided somewhere within the valve operating mechanism (see *Figures 8.1* and *8.2*) to allow for expansion of components due to heat. If the actual clearance at any one valve is smaller than that specified, it can result in the valve not seating when the engine reaches its normal working temperature. This would not only cause a loss of compression at the cylinder concerned, but would also result in a rapid deterioration of both the valve and seat.

Although somewhat less serious, a clearance smaller than that specified but still large enough to allow the valve to seat will nevertheless result in a partial loss of compression and therefore performance. This is due to the valve opening earlier and closing

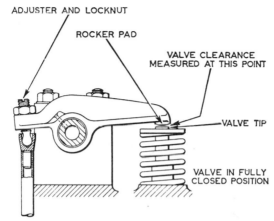

Figure 8.1. Typical pushrod overhead-valve clearance adjustment

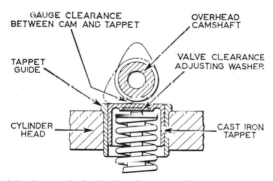

Figure 8.2. One method of valve clearance adjustment when the valve is operated through a tappet. Another arrangement uses a special screw in each bucket tappet so that adjustment can be carried out without having to remove the camshaft in order to change the shims

later than it should. Other than when there is a complete loss of compression, a defect of this nature may go unnoticed for there will be no noise. This is not the case when the clearances are larger than specified when, depending upon the degree there will be a distinct 'tapping' noise, becoming more of a rattle if more than one valve is affected. Besides once again affecting the period when the valve is open, a large clearance can sometimes result in the valve snapping back on its seat harder than it would normally do. In extreme cases this may cause the valve head to break off, with the consequent probability of severe engine damage.

In overhead valve and some indirect acting overhead cam layouts it is possible for an indentation to be formed in that part of the rocker face which contacts the valve stem. When setting the valve clearances the feeler gauge will bridge this indentation, resulting in an incorrect (oversize) gap and a continued tapping noise. This problem can be isolated by inserting a thinner than specified feeler in the gap while the engine is running – this will usually result in indentations being punched into the feeler rendering it unserviceable for future use. It is possible to remove the defective rocker and 'stone' down the face taking care not to alter its profile. The only alternative is to fit a new rocker.

Other defects which can give all the indications of a larger than specified valve clearance is a bent pushrod, a defective cam-follower and a broken valve spring. A bent pushrod can usually be seen to oscillate as the engine is running, a defective cam-follower can only be diagnosed by a visual inspection and should therefore only be considered when all other possible causes have been eliminated.

Weak or broken valve spring

A weak or broken valve spring will usually show up when checking the valve clearances by being noisy in operation, even when a feeler gauge is interposed between the valve and its operating mechanism. In some cases a broken valve spring will be instantly obvious, once the rocker/cam cover is removed. An alternative method of checking for this kind of defect is to press down on the top of each spring when the valve is fully closed. Both weak and broken springs can be pushed down much easier than good ones.

It is always a sound idea to check all the valve springs whenever the head and valves are removed for any purpose such as a top overhaul. All that is needed is one new or known to be good valve spring of the same type, a small metal plate and a vice. Mount the good spring and one for test, end-to-end in the vice with the metal plate between the two springs. Next compress the springs by winding in the jaws of the vice. If the test spring is weak, it will be compressed much more than the good one and will be seen to be shorter. Weak valve springs should be replaced.

It is sometimes possible to replace a broken (or weak) valve spring without taking the cylinder head off, but it will be necessary to use some method of preventing the valve from falling into the cylinder. With some layouts a slightly curved bar of about ⅜ inch (10 mm) diameter inserted through the plug hole and in contact with the valve head will do. The bar can be held in place by turning the engine carefully until the rising piston touches the bar – the engine must of course be turned backwards to release the bar.

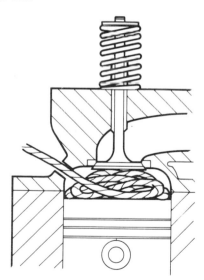

Figure 8.3. The string (clothes line) method of retaining a valve in position when renewing a weak or broken valve spring

Another possibility is to turn the engine until the piston in the problem cylinder is at the bottom of its stroke. Next remove the sparking plug and through the vacant plug hole feed a length of thick string or thin rope into the cylinder (*Figure 8.3*) – sometimes a thin washing line would be suitable. Keep hold of or tie up one end of the rope, then turn the engine until the rising piston compresses the rope in the combustion chamber, so holding the valve in place. Turn the engine backwards to withdraw the rope.

Avoid running the engine with a weak or broken valve spring as in some cases it could result in the valve striking the ascending piston and causing considerable damage to the engine – see *Figure 8.4.*

Poor valve seating

Cleaner fuels, superior oils and improved materials have resulted in nearly all engines being capable of at least 50,000 miles before requiring any work on the valves. Modern engines, however, run hotter and with higher compression pressures than those of a few years ago, so good valve seating is even more important. Weak valve springs, incorrect valve clearances and incorrect fuel/air mixtures are among the factors that can, over a period, result in erosion and wear at the valve seat. Once this condition exists continued running of the engine will result in it becoming even worse. The only answer is to reface or in extreme cases replace the valve seat and regrind the valve.

Burnt or otherwise defective valve

Poor valve seating will allow the hot burning gases to escape through the narrow gap (or passage) between the valve and its seat. In a very short time this will result in the valve being burnt and possibly breaking up, causing extensive engine damage. Any defect with the valve itself or with its operating mechanism which resulted in the valve not seating correctly will produce a similar effect. It is inadviseable to run an engine in this condition.

Figure 8.4. This engine was run with a broken valve spring. The two collets securing the valve to the spring cap jumped out, allowing the valve to drop into the cylinder and causing extensive damage

Cylinder-head gasket leaking

When a leaking cylinder-head gasket results in loss of compression, it invariably does so on two cylinders. This is when the narrow section of gasket between two adjacent cylinders fails – in most cases this will be where two exhaust valves are close together, making that particular area one of the hottest in the engine. With many in-line four-cylinder engines this is between the two middle cylinders.

If a compression test shows a lack of pressure on two adjacent cylinders, the cause is almost certainly a defective head gasket.

A fault such as this, if detected early enough, would normally require just a new gasket. Prolonged running with a defective gasket, however, could cause the hot gases to pass through the break in the gasket, and damage both the cylinder head and block.

A defective cylinder-head gasket should always be replaced; do not tighten the cylinder-head bolts/nuts down further in an attempt to stop the leak.

Piston ring(s) broken, worn or sticking

A straightforward compression test would only show a lack of pressure at any faulty cylinder; it would not give any indication of what the fault is. To determine if the problem lies with the piston to bore sealing or with the cylinder head (valves or gasket), a further test is necessary after squirting about a tablespoonful of clean engine oil into the cylinder. If on this second (wet) compression test the readings were a considerable improvement over the first (dry) test, it would mean that the piston/bore seal was poor. No appreciable improvement on the other hand would indicate that the fault lay with the cylinder head.

A poor piston/bore seal on all (or most) cylinders is an indication of wear, requiring a rebore and new pistons, or in some cases special piston rings may prove suitable. If, however, the tests showed the majority of cylinders to be in order and the fault limited to one or at the most two cylinders, then the problem could be broken or sticking rings. In some cases use of an upper-cylinder lubricant may free sticking piston rings, but generally a fault such as this would require the engine to be dismantled. Broken rings can score the cylinder walls; a rebore and new pistons would be required in such instances.

A poor piston/bore seal for any reason will often result in an excessive oil consumption, pressurisation of the crankcase with oil fumes being blown out of the dipstick hole and any oil-filler cap breathers, and blue smoke issuing from the exhaust pipe.

Oil pressure

With most cars the first indication that there may be a problem with the engine oil pressure is that the oil warning light comes on, or fails to go out when it should. When this occurs the engine should be switched off and the reason investigated. Any of the following faults can cause this condition:

1. Defective oil-pressure switch
2. Wiring fault
3. Oil level very low
4. Oil too thin
5. Low oil pressure

At times these faults may be related; for example, a low oil pressure may be due to the oil being too thin, which in turn may be due to it being too hot because the oil level is very low.

Defective oil-pressure switch

In most cases the oil warning lamp is earthed through the pressure switch, which normally fails in the 'open' position; this means that the oil warning light will not light up when it should. With this type of switch a simple check is to disconnect the lead at the switch; with the ignition switched on the oil warning light should be out. Now touch the end of the lead to a good earth (the engine block) and the light should come on. Other than carrying out this test, the only practical method of checking the oil-pressure switch is by substitution.

Wiring fault

If in the last test the oil warning lamp stayed on when the feed cable to the pressure switch was disconnected, or failed to light up when earthed, the fault is probably in the wiring circuit and should be investigated as explained in Chapter 10.

Low oil level

Usually a low oil level will result in the warning lamp coming on intermittently, particularly when cornering, long before it drops to such a level that the lamp comes on permanently. There are only two possible reasons for a low oil level – either the oil is being burnt, which will produce clouds of blue smoke from the exhaust or it is leaking out of the system.

An oil leak can occur from many places where oil is present, and the more likely areas can vary depending upon the make of engine. In general, however, the following items should be checked:

1. The rocker valve or cam cover gasket
2. The oil filter seal
3. The sump gasket and drain plug
4. The timing chain cover (where fitted)
5. The front and rear main bearing seals

In some cases simply tightening the securing nuts/screws around the covers or housings will stop a leak, whereas in others, such as the front or rear main bearing seals, a considerable amount of dismantling may be required.

Take care if tightening down securing bolts or screws not to distort the cover – this may be the reason for the leak in the first place. Where distortion has occurred it may be possible to use two gaskets, one on top of the other. An alternative remedy is to make up a supplementary gasket with one of the RTV (room temperature vulcanising) silicone-based jointing compounds. This material can also often be used in place of a gasket. There is a natural tendency when using this type of jointing compound to apply it too thickly. This means that when the two surfaces of the joint are brought together, the excess compound is forced out on either side of the joint area. The surplus on the outside is no great problem, for it can be wiped or cut away, but the compound that oozes from the inner face cannot. Now when the engine is started some of this excess material will be washed away by the oil in the form of little balls of silicone rubber, which can find their way easily into the oil channels, thus causing a blockage and loss of oil pressure.

Oil too thin

Assuming the correct grade of oil is being used, it can be diluted with petrol, either through excessive and prolonged use of the choke or by a defective fuel pump diaphragm (see Chapter 6). The oil can also become diluted with coolant water (often giving it a milky colour) as a result of some defect in the cooling system – possibly a leaking head gasket. Any oil becomes thinner when hot, but not normally to the extent that it causes the oil warning lamp to stay on.

Low oil pressure

One of the most common reasons for low oil pressure is wear, particularly at the crankshaft main bearings and at the pump itself. However, this is normally a slow process and is usually accompanied by other signs of general engine wear.

A sudden loss of oil pressure could be due to one of the following causes: severe oil leak; oil pump failure or blocked inlet; collapse of a main bearing; defective pressure relief valve (*Figure 8.5*). The most probable cause of sudden loss or pressure is due to the relief valve not fully closing – often because of dirt between the ball and its seat. On some engines the valve is accessible and can be removed for cleaning; in others, however,

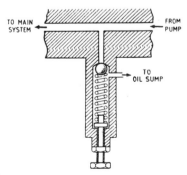

Figure 8.5. Oil pressure relief valve. Oil pressure acts against the spring pressure. In the type of valve shown, the operating pressure is adjustable by a screw

it is located near the pump and the only way to get to it is to remove the sump.

As already stated it does not necessarily follow that just because the oil warning light did not do what it should that there was a lack of pressure. Obviously, the first check is the level of oil in the sump; if that is correct and no other fault self-evident, it is often possible to get some idea of whether the oil is circulating by looking down through the oil filler cap/breather orifice with the engine running at idling speed. With most engines the oil can be seen oozing out, over the valve operating mechanism (camshaft or rocker shaft); if so the oil is circulating and although the pressure may be low, it should be sufficient to drive the car, gently, to the nearest garage.

Exhaust troubles

A broken or leaking exhaust system is not only noisy and a possible fire risk, but is also dangerous because fumes can be drawn into the car. Most accessory shops sell both exhaust bandage kits and exhaust putty. When using these, follow closely the instruction provided. If the material is correctly applied, the repair can last a considerable time and satisfy an MoT examiner so long as the structural soundness of the system is not affected. If an exhaust pipe breaks in two, it can sometimes be repaired temporarily by using a metal 'bandage' wrapped around the broken area and secured with soft wire or hose clips. Ideally, exhaust putty should be used to help seal the repair. The metal bandage may be made up by using a beer or soft drinks can.

In cases such as this a permanent repair should be carried out at the first opportunity – remember that fumes from a leaking exhaust can enter the car both when standing still or when moving fast.

Exhaust pipes are invariably mounted on, or hang from some form of rubber strap. If one of these breaks or is missing it puts a considerable strain on the pipe and could result in it breaking. In most cases a temporary repair can be made with a length of soft wire.

9

Cooling system

Everything considered, the ideal operating temperature for a modern liquid cooled engine is in the region of 90°C. This means that in some localised hot spots around the combustion chamber areas the temperatures can rise to over 100°C, with the consequent danger that the coolant (anti-freeze solution) surrounding these areas can boil. To overcome this modern cooling systems are pressurised, which has the effect of raising the boiling temperature of the coolant.

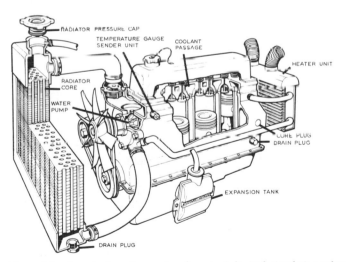

Figure 9.1. A typical cooling system layout. A limited circulation takes place on the engine side of the thermostat through a by-pass passage when the thermostat valve is closed

If the radiator or filler cap is removed when the engine is hot, the pressure will drop and the coolant can immediately start boiling and shoot out of the filler neck with scalding results. For this reason never take the radiator cap off when the engine is hot; always allows a cooling-off period of about 15 minutes and even then take care – initially just turn the cap to its first stop then pause a second or two before pressing it down and turning it further to release it. Always wear heavy gloves or protect your hand with a thick cloth (old jacket or overalls) when removing the cap from anything other than a cold engine.

Never pour cold water into (or over) a hot engine or conversely hot water into a cold engine. Should this happen, the resulting expansion/contraction stresses in the metal could result in a fracture of the head or block.

When an engine is switched off the coolant stops circulating and the engine temperature temporarily increases by a few degrees. This is sometimes sufficient to 'trigger' the thermostatically-controlled switch operating the electric fan on some cars. Therefore, do not work in the area of this type of fan until the engine has cooled down.

Cooling system faults

The inevitable result of any fault in the cooling system is that the engine overheats. Overheating, however, is not only due to faults in the cooling system; other external factors such as binding brakes, a low engine oil level, an excessive load in the car or even a sheet of plastic or something similar thrown up from the road and blocking the radiator air intake can all result in the engine getting hotter than it should. If when on a journey overheating is a problem and the cause difficult to identify, it will sometimes help if the heater controls are set in the hot position and the fan switched on its highest speed, then open the car windows if it gets too hot.

Obviously, if the cause of overheating is dangerous in itself, the car should not be driven. Examples of this are low coolant or oil levels, defective cylinder-head gasket or binding brakes.

Even if no danger is apparent, a close watch should be kept on engine temperature – if necessary stopping every few miles to allow the engine to cool. The more common causes of overheating are:

1. Slack or broken fan belt
2. Low coolant level
3. Cooling systems sludged up
4. Faulty pressure cap
5. Radiator air passaged blocked
6. Defective thermostat
7. Water pump inoperative
8. Expansion tank pipe faulty
9. Electric fan not switching on
10. Incorrect ignition timing
11. Incorrect fuel mixture

Slack or broken fan belt

A slack fan belt can slip at high speeds or when a heavy electrical load is put on the generator. Often it will produce squealing sounds as it slips, although other factors such as misalignment can also cause the belt to squeal. Considerable wear takes place as the belt slips making the condition even worse.

Although manufacturers may quote all kinds of different settings and even sometimes state that special tools are required for measuring fan belt tension, a satisfactory test can be carried out using just thumb pressure. Select a part midway between the two most widely spaced pulleys or in other words in the middle of the longest straight stretch of the belt and apply moderate pressure with your thumb (*Figure 9.2*). If correctly tensioned, the belt should deflect about half an inch (13 mm). Moderate pressure can be defined as sufficient to force away the blood from the tip of your thumb. An overtightened belt may not make a noise but it could ruin the bearings in both the generator and water pump. Check also that the belt is not 'bottoming' on the base of the Vee in the pulley – the sides of the belt should grip the sides of the Vee.

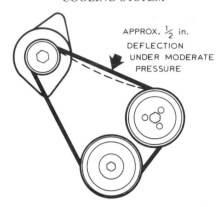

APPROX. $\frac{1}{2}$ in.
DEFLECTION
UNDER MODERATE
PRESSURE

Figure 9.2. Fan belt layout, showing where to check for belt tension

Although many cars are now equipped with an electric fan, most people still refer to the belt driving the water pump and generator as the fan belt. Probably the first indication of a broken fan belt will be that the ignition warning lamp comes on; although in some cases the fan belt may get thrown off, making a noise as it does so. As for a large part of the year, cars fitted with fixed-blade belt-driven fans are overcooled, loss of the fan belt may not immediately lead to an overheating situation. In the winter months it may make no difference whatsoever to the engine temperature, but because the generator will not be charging the battery the lack of a fan belt cannot be ignored. It is always advisable to carry a spare fan belt, especially if a long journey is anticipated. Although many filling stations carry a limited stock they may not hold your particular one and the nearest stockist may be some way off.

Many accessory shops sell an emergency belt which can be cut to length and re-joined; however, as these are generally more expensive than the genuine article, buying one would seem a false economy. A nylon stocking, knotted together and stretched tightly over the crankshaft and water pump pulleys, often works as a temporary substitute, but in most cases will slip badly and burn if stretched over the generator pulley as well. Ensure that any loose ends are cut off.

Low coolant level

If the coolant level is low, it means that what remains is carrying away proportionally more heat; therefore, in its early stages a low coolant level will show up on the gauge (if fitted) as a higher than average temperature. However, once the level drops below the gauge sender unit or transmitter in the engine block, the gauge may well show a lower than average reading, possibly dropping to zero. A further indication of a falling coolant level could be if the heater began blowing cold air even though the controls were in the 'hot' position. In addition, as the engine gets hotter there will be a marked inclination for it to 'pink' (see page 177) when accelerating or climbing hills.

A falling coolant level obviously means there must be a leak somewhere in the system, probably due to one of the following defects:

1. Faulty hoses, including those to and from the heater
2. Defective radiator cap
3. Holed radiator or heater element
4. Drain tap or plug leaking
5. Gasket leak at thermostat or pump
6. Pump spindle seal leaking
7. Faulty cylinder-head gasket
8. Defective core plug in the cylinder head or block
9. Cracked cylinder head or block

In many cases the location of the leak will be fairly obvious, although a core plug leaking at the back of the engine or under the manifolds may be difficult to trace. Look for signs of red rust on the engine block.

Faulty hoses

All hoses deteriorate with age – some may become hard and brittle yet others get soft and weak and many are cut by the hose clips securing them to the engine or radiator. It is wise to check all coolant hoses occasionally and especially before a long (holiday) journey. Inspect them for cracks, splits and signs of bulging along their complete length; pinch them between finger and thumb to check for cracks and condition (*Figure 9.3*). Check the hose clips for tightness and that they have not damaged (cut into) the hose.

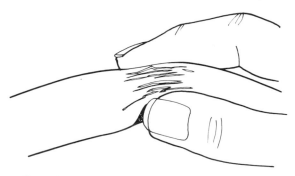

Figure 9.3. Pinching coolant hose to check for cracks

In an emergency it is often possible to carry out a temporary repair to a defective hose depending upon the severity of the problem. A small hole or split in a hose can be taped up, although it be best first of all to clean and then seal it with a silicone jointing compound, before binding it up. Ordinary insulating tape will do but most accessory shops sell special hose bandage kits.

An alternative temporary repair that can sometimes be carried out is to cut out the damaged section of the hose and replace it with a length of suitable diameter metal or plastic tube. Plastic tubing must be capable of withstanding the temperatures in the system and any tubing must be firm enough to withstand the pressure. The following items are representative of what can be used in this emergency: box spanner; grease gun section; certain medical pill containers; old (cheap) torch body; aluminium cigar tube; rigid plastic waste piping. Use a length of soft wire to secure the hose to the tube; where none is available, use thin electric cable or even string wound in tourniquet fashion.

If the defective hose is one of the two for the heater, it may be possible to remove it completely at both the heater and engine

connections. The second hose can then be disconnected at the
heater end and doubled back to the now vacant connection on
the engine, thus forming a loop. This puts the heater out of
action but solves he hose problem. An alternative is to block off
or clamp (with a self-grip wrench) any defective heater hose.

Defective radiator cap

The initial check on a suspect cap (*Figure 9.4*) should be an
examination of the seals; if these appear to be in order but the
cap still thought to be defective, look for signs of dampness or
drips at the end of the overflow pipe. In some cases the cap will
only leak when the engine is hot and the system pressurised. A

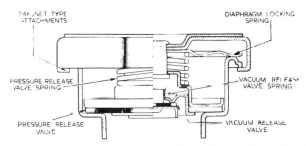

*Figure 9.4. AC radiator pressure cap. The rubber sealing gasket is an
integral part of the cap. It should be examined for wear whenever the cap
is checked*

simple test for this is to tie a plastic bag over the end of the
overflow pipe; if this fills with coolant the cap is leaking. In those
systems without some form of expansion tank it is essential to
leave an air pocket in the radiator header tank to allow for
coolant expansion; this is normally achieved automatically by
extending the filler neck down into the radiator.

Most garages can pressure test a radiator cap. It is important
to ensure that any replacement cap is of the correct type and
pressure rating.

Holed radiator or heater element

Depending upon the size of the hole there are a number of ways of making temporary repairs to a leaking radiator. Most accessory shops sell various types of radiator sealer, sometimes as liquid in a can, sometimes as a powder stick. In most cases the sealant is either inserted or poured into the radiator, while the engine is running at idling speed; if the cooland level is low, it should be topped up. For best results the engine should be at normal working temperature with the thermostat open. Beware of taking the radiator cap off when the engine is hot. It normally takes 10 minutes or even longer before the sealant actually seals the hole; during this period it is advisable to let the engine continue running at idling speed with the radiator cap off; this prevents any build up of pressure forcing the sealant out.

If proprietary brands of sealant are unavailable, a couple of teaspoonfuls of mustard powder or even the yolks from a couple of hard boiled eggs, used in the same way will often seal minor leaks, such as small pin-prick holes – these temporary 'additives' will not cure a strong leak. Some bad leaks can often be stopped by the application of an epoxy (two-pack) adhesive, after first ensuring that the area is clean and dry. The disadvantage of this, however, is that it can make any subsequent permanent repair more difficult.

In some cases it may be possible to have the radiator soldered as a permanent repair. With the growing use of aluminium and plastic in the construction of radiators, however, this may not be possible. The only satisfactory solution then will probably be a replacement radiator.

Drain tap or plug leaking

Sometimes merely tightening the plug or tap will stop the leak or perhaps a replacement gasket/washer is all that is needed. A leak from around the thread housing can sometimes be cured by using similar methods to that for a holed radiator, whereas leaks past the threads themselves can often be prevented by the use of plumber's PTFE tape. If a drain tap is defective and cannot be repaired, it may be possible to remove it and fit an alternative form of plug. Should this not be possible, remove the tap and block its drillings with some form of adhesive or sealant.

Gasket leak at thermostat housing or pump

Sometimes merely tightening the clamping bolts or nuts will cure the leak, only take care not to overdo this for it could result in a broken stud or bolt, or even worse a fractured housing. If this does not work, the correct solution is to remove the pump or thermostat housing and renew the gasket after first cleaning off all traces of the old one from the two mating faces. Where no replacement gasket is available it may sometimes be possible to make up one using cardboard from a breakfast cereal packet, or even thick paper.

A further alternative is to use a silicone-based (RTV) sealant as a gasket; simply clean off the two mating surfaces then apply a thin bead of sealant to one and clamp the two together. It may sometimes be advantageous to smear both surfaces completely with the sealant; first apply a thin bead and then spread it out using a wet finger.

Pump spindle seal leaking

On some older cars it is possible to strip down a water pump and replace the seal. Nowadays, it is general practice to manufacture pumps as sealed units which cannot be dismantled; in any case replacement seals are no longer generally available. The only solution with a leaking pump is to renew it. In an emergency loss of coolant through the pump spindle seal can be minimised by keeping the system depressurised. Do this by trapping a short length of match or something similar between the seal of the radiator cap and its opposing surface in the radiator itself. Keep a close watch on engine temperature and frequently stop and check the coolant level in these conditions.

Faulty cylinder-head gasket

If the gasket is leaking externally, it may be possible to cure it by tightening the cylinder-head bolts or nuts. This, however, should be done only in the sequence recommended by the manufacturer over the whole head and only to the specified torque. In all other cases the cylinder-head gasket should be replaced as a matter of urgency.

Defective core plug in cylinder head or block

In most instances core plugs leak due to a small pin-prick rust hole. Often as a temporary measure it is possible to block this hole with a small self-tapping screw. On rare occasions the leak may be from around the periphery of the core plug. By tapping the plug in further with a hammer and if necessary a punch will normally effect a cure. Take care, however, not to hit the plug too hard or the punch could either penetrate the plug or make it concave.

Cracked cylinder head or block

Although it is possible to repair cracked heads or blocks, in most cases the cost of repair will be more than that of a replacement unit. Depending upon the location and size of the crack it may sometimes be possible to effect a temporary repair, using a suitable adhesive/sealer. However, this should only be used as a very short-time repair. In all cases it would be wise to determine the cause of the failure before any repair/replacement operation.

Cooling system sludged up

This condition is most likely to occur at the radiator purely because the coolant channels elsewhere are larger. In some cases simply draining and refilling will be sufficient, although ideally the radiator should be back-flushed — that is to wash it through with water in the reverse direction to the normal coolant flow. If removal of the radiator is relatively easy, it is often better to wash it through away from the vehicle. Most accessory shops sell radiator/cooling system cleaning agents, many of which are claimed to remove scale as well as sludge or dirt.

If neither of these methods work the radiator can sometimes be cleaned by one of the firms specialising in this field; if not, the only answer is a replacement.

Radiator air passages blocked

This problem usually occurs towards the end of summer when the radiator air passages are clogged with dead insects and leaf debris. Either use a vacuum cleaner or try and force the foreign bodies out the way they came in by using a water hose with strong pressure. Do not attempt to dislodge any obstruction with a metal tool such as a screwdriver, otherwise you will probably penetrate the radiator.

Defective thermostat

There are two types of thermostat in use: in the older unit (*Figure 9.5a*) alcohol is contained within a bellows which boils at a lower temperature than water. This action forces the bellows to expand, so opening the valve and allowing the passage of coolant. In the wax-type (*Figure 9.5b*), which has practically replaced the bellows version, except where still retained on older cars, a wax pellet expands as it is heated, thereby causing the valve to open. Wax-type thermostats are said to be less susceptible to variations in cooling system pressure than the bellows versions.

A bellows-type thermostat invariably fails in the open position. Although this would result in the engine taking longer to get warm, it would not cause overheating. The wax version, however, generally fails in the closed position, restricting coolant

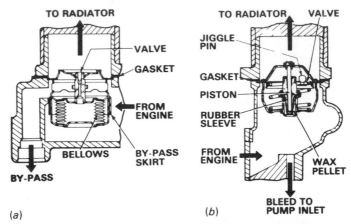

(a)   (b)

Figure 9.5a. One type of by-pass recirculating cooling system where a bellows thermostat controls both the coolant flow to the radiator and to the by-pass back to the pump. When the thermostat valve reaches the fully open position, the by-pass passage is closed by the by-pass skirt on the thermostat. The metal bellows of the thermostat contains a volatile liquid, which evaporates when heated, causing the bellows to expand and lift the valve off its seat

Figure 9.5b. In this cooling system a permanent bleed is maintained to the water pump inlet. In the wax-type thermostat shown, the valve is opened by the expansion effect of heated wax. The jiggle pin, situated in a small bleed hole in the thermostat, provides an additional bleed in the event of a stalled pump. Under normal running conditions, water pump pressure forces up the jiggle pin which closes the bleed hole

flow and causing the engine to overheat. As a temporary measure it is usually possible to remove a defective thermostat fairly easily and then to run the engine without it.

To test a suspect thermostat immerse it in water and then heat the water noting the temperature when the valve begins to open; this should roughly compare with the recommended opening temperature – usually stamped on the unit. A simple method of determining when the valve begins to open is to suspend it in the water on a length of string. If one end of the string is trapped between the valve and its seating, as the valve opens the thermostat will drop.

Water pump inoperative

This is not a common problem and is due to the impeller turning on its shaft. The only remedy is to replace the pump. In an emergency, the car can be driven but a close watch kept on the engine temperature and frequent stops made to allow the engine to cool.

A squealing water pump can be due to a dry bush or seal; this can sometimes be rectified by adding a proprietary water-pump lubricant to the coolant. If this is not available, use about an egg-cup full of soluable oil – or in an emergency a low or non-foaming liquid soap or shampoo. There should be no perceptible play felt in the water pump bushes or bearings.

Expansion tank pipe faulty

A soft pipe between the radiator and expansion tank while allowing any excess coolant in the radiator to pass to the expansion tank, could collapse when the engine cooled and the subsequent depression in the radiator tries to draw back some of this excess coolant. This would eventually result in a permanent low coolant level with consequent overheating. The only remedy is to replace the faulty pipe.

Electric fan not switching on

In most installations the electric fan is thermostatically controlled; failure is much more likely to be at this control or in the wiring circuit than in the fan motor itself. If this is the case, the fan can be connected either direct to the battery (through an in line fuse) or preferably to some ignition-controlled supply as a temporary measure. Where the control switch is accessible, it may be possible to by-pass it with a link wire from one switch terminal to the other. Obviously, this is only of any use if the control is in fact defective.

Incorrect ignition timing

Both advanced and retarded ignition can result in the engine overheating – the first, however, would normally be accompanied by 'pinking' (*see* page 21) and the second by a flat spot on acceleration and low power output. Further to this any fault which upsets the mechanical or vacuum advance can cause the engine to overheat.

Incorrect fuel mixture

A weak mixture will cause overheating and can result in excessively high temperatures in the combustion chamber, with possible damage to the pistons and valves.

10

Electrical system

Working on a car's electrical system can be hazardous in that if a power cable or terminal is accidently shorted to earth, it could result in the cable overheating and a possible fire. Therefore, it is always advisable to disconnect the battery before starting work. The only exception to this would be when a power supply is needed for test purposes.

Do not wear a metal bracelet, watchstrap or ring when working on the electrics. It is advisable to remove your watch in any case.

Do not smoke or strike a match in the vicinity of the battery and avoid any condition which could cause a spark in that area.

If a fuse has blown, do not wrap it in foil and re-insert it. Where no replacement is available, wind a length of domestic fuse wire (of the same value) around the fuse cartridge and then re-insert it into its holder. When disconnecting the battery always remove the earth lead first; on most modern cars this will be the negative terminal at the battery. This way, if you inadvertently touch any metallic part of the car with the spanner when making the disconnection, it will not matter. Reverse the procedure when connecting the battery.

Slave starting a car with a flat battery

Sometimes called 'boost' or 'jump starting', this is a method of starting a car with a flat battery by connecting it (temporarily) to the battery of another vehicle, by the use of jump leads.

First position the donor car so that the two battery compartments can be reached easily by the jump leads. Do not allow the two cars to touch, especially if the polarity of one is different from the other, that is if one has a negative earth and the other positive. With the red jump lead (if they are coloured) connect the positive (+) terminals of the two batteries, then with the black lead join the two negative (−) terminals. In each case it is better to make the donor battery connections last, and if possible make the very last connection (that to the donor negative) to the earth strap or earthing point, rather than to the battery itself.

Next start the donor car and with it running at a fast idle try to start the casualty. If the engine starts, allow the donor car to idle (tickover) and with the casualty running at a fast idle (with its ignition warning light extinguished), disconnect the leads, reversing the connection sequence. Only operate the starter of the faulty car for periods of about 10 seconds with up to a minute's pause between attempts. If the engine does not start after about three attempts, check the fuel, ignition and starter systems as explained in the relative chapters.

Some cars equipped with electronic ignition and/or fuel injection systems may be damaged if the car is slave started in this way. If so, it should be stated in the car's handbook. The alternative in these cases is to remove the battery from the faulty car, then connect the jump leads as before and run the donor car at a fast idle for about 20 minutes. This should charge the battery enough to start the car. Remember at all times – regardless of car polarity, the connections must be from positive to positive and negative to negative. A false connection could ruin the alternators and batteries of both vehicles.

Charging system faults

There are two basic types of charging system in use – those that use a DC (direct current) generator called a dynamo and those that use an AC (alternating current) machine known as an alternator. Nearly all cars less than about 10 years old are fitted with alternators. The electronic components used in alternator systems are easily damaged. Never connect or disconnect any charging circuit leads while the engine is running – this includes the battery leads. Some older alternators could also be damaged if a battery charger is used – if in doubt, disconnect the battery before using the charger.

In most cases the first indication that something is wrong with any charging system is that the ignition warning lamp does not do what it should. Some examples of this and the most probable causes are given in the accompanying table.

Ignition warning light – determination of faults

Indication	*Possible causes*
Ignition warning light remains on when the engine is running.	Generator drive belt broken or slipping. Generator seized or drive pulley slipping on shaft. Regulator defective (both alternator and dynamo systems). Fault in alternator. Fault in dynamo, including dirty or defective brush or commutator.
Ignition warning light gets brighter with increased engine speed.	Poor earth at control box – dynamo systems. Dirty cut-out points – dynamo systems. Fault in cut-out windings – dynamo systems. Fault in rectifier (diode defective) – alternator systems; this does not necessarily mean that the alternator is not charging.
Ignition warning light flickers when the engine is running.	Generator drive belt slipping. Faulty voltage regulator. Dirty or faulty brushes and slip-rings – alternator systems. Dirty or faulty brushes and commutator – dynamo systems.

Indication warning light – determination of faults (*continued*)

Problem	*Possible causes*
Ignition warning light does not come on at all.	Warning light bulb blown. Flat battery (fully exhausted). Ignition switch faulty. Circuit fault – battery, solenoid, ignition switch. Blown fuse in ignition circuit (where fitted). Dirty or faulty brushes and slip-rings – alternator systems.
Ignition warning light remains on when the key is turned to the OFF position.	On a dynamo system this probably means that the cut-out points have failed to separate. This is potentially a dangerous situation in that the control box, dynamo and circuit wiring could burn out. If the warning light should stay on, immediately disconnect the battery, then physically separate the points and investigate the reason for them sticking. In an alternator system it could mean a fault in the alternator unit itself. Although this is a far less serious situation it can effect the charging rate and should be attended to. Disconnect the battery if leaving the car for more than a few minutes.

Overcharging

One charging system fault that would not show up at the ignition warning light is overcharging. It would, however, result in the battery needing to be topped up more frequently than usual and in serious cases will cause the battery to overheat, giving off acidic fumes and possibly bubbling of the electrolyte. Further indications of overcharging are unusually bright headlamps and faster operation of both the windscreen wipers and flashing indicators.

Checking generator output

The most accurate method of checking generator output is to wire an ammeter into the main lead from the generator and then temporarily by-pass the regulator. With the engine running at about 2500–3000 RPM, the generator should produce its maximum output. A serious problem with this test, however, is that any poor connection or other failure in the ammeter circuit (or in the unit itself) could damage the generator, particularly an alternator. Any test of this nature should also be restricted to about two seconds.

A rough indication of whether a generator is charging or not, can be gained by switching on the headlamps and noting their brilliance. Now start the engine and run it at a fast idle; if the generator is charging, the lamps should become a little brighter.

Probably the easiest and most effective check the average car owner can make is to wire a voltmeter across the battery (from negative to positive terminals). With the engine running at a fast idle the reading should be 14–15 volts, whereas with the engine stopped it will be 12–13 volts (assuming the battery to be in order). A reading higher than 15 volts means that the generator is overcharging probably due to a regulator fault. If the generator is not charging the fault can be in the unit itself, in the regulator (and cut-out in dynamo systems) or in the circuit between them.

Most modern alternators are self-contained, the regulator and rectifier being housed within the body of the alternator. These regulators are solid-state electronic units with no moving parts. Older alternators and all dynamo systems use a separate control box operating on electro-mechanical principles. In some cases with these the reason for any lack of charge may be simply that the points are sticking – often a light tap on the side of the box will put things right. Do not, however, hit the plastic cover used on some control boxes. On occasions these regulator or cut-out points become oxidised, creating a high resistance between the two contacts. They can be cleaned, but care should be taken; use only a very fine contact file or glass paper. Also, the gaps are critical so remove only the oxidisation and not the metal. Both regulator and cut-out points are adjustable but the procedure can be fairly complex and should be left to an auto-electrician. Disconnect the battery before attempting any work on the control box.

Alternator faults

Although alternators are in general more reliable than dynamos they are also more complex and easily damaged; therefore, any major repairs should normally be left to an auto-electrician. However, changing brushes and cleaning the slip-rings on an alternator is a much easier operation compared to similar work on a dynamo. Access to the brush box differs considerably according to the make and model. On the Lucas ACR range the brushes are under a black moulded cover at the back of the unit. With many others the brushes or brush box are clearly visible at the back of the alternator. While on some AC Delco, Delco Remy, Denso and Mitsubishi models access to the brushes involves dismantling the alternator.

There is no set period when alternator brushes should be changes but they last much longer than those in a dynamo. This is partly because they carry only the field current of around 2–3 amps and partly because they are in contact with the smooth surface of the slip-rings. Dynamo brushes on the other hand, carry the full charging current and are in contact with a segmented commutator.

Check that the brushes (new or old) are free to move in their holders and are being pushed into contact with the slip-rings by their springs. Cleaning the slip-rings only involves wiping their surfaces with a soft rag, dampened in methylated spirits.

The majority of other alternator faults are caused by misuse such as an overtight drive belt causing a bearing to collapse or disconnecting some charging circuit lead when the engine is running which results in failure of the rectifier diode.

Dynamo faults

Many symptoms indicating a dynamo problem could, instead, be due to a fault in the voltage control box (regulator and cut-out).

To help determine which is at fault, the operation of the dynamo on the vehicle can be checked by carrying out the following simple test: disconnect the leads from the dynamo terminals. Connect a test lamp between the larger terminal on the dynamo (usually marked D) and a good earth. Then, on most dynamos including Lucas units, connect a jump lead between the smaller field terminal F and terminal D. On some other dynamos, including Bosch, the jump lead should be connected between the smaller terminal F and a good earth. Now start the engine and increase the speed gradually. If the test lamp lights up, the dynamo is operating and the trouble is probably in the wiring or the control box. No light will indicate a faulty dynamo.

Do not increase the engine speed beyond about 1000 RPM, otherwise the test lamp may blow.

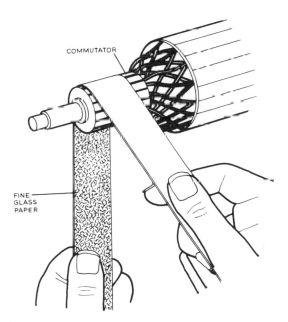

COMMUTATOR

FINE
GLASS
PAPER

Figure 10.1. Cleaning a dynamo commutator. The same treatment can be given to a starter motor commutator

The most common dynamo failures are associated with the brushgear/commutator. This can be easily checked out by first disconnecting all leads from the dyanmo, and connecting a voltmeter between the main terminal 'D' and earth. Now start the engine and slowly increase speed. The voltmeter reading should be in the region of 2–4 volts; a zero reading indicates most probably a problem with the brush/commutator arrangement, although a defective armature (unlikely) or de-polarised field (unlikely unless work has been carried out on the unit) could also result in a zero reading.

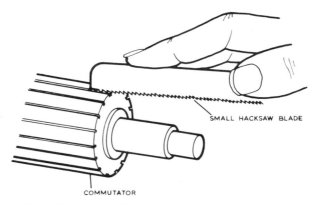

Figure 10.2. Cutting back the insulation on a dynamp commutator. This should not be done on a starter motor commutator because their brushes have a high copper content and dust from them would short out the segments

A glazed or slightly worn or scored commutator can be cleaned. In more severe cases it can be skimmed on a lathe. To clean up a slightly worn commutator first dismantle the dynamo, then with the armature clamped in a vice (with some form of soft packing) clean up the commutator using a strip of fine glass paper (*Figure 10.1*). Follow this up by cutting back the insulation between the segments, using a thin hack-saw blade or something similar (*Figure 10.2*). Clean off any resulting debris with a petrol-dampened rag.

On reassembly make sure that the brushes are free to slide in their holders and make contact with the commutator under spring pressure. If the brushes are worn and this spring pressure consequently reduced, use some form of packing between the brush and the spring as a temporary measure.

Starter system

Faults in the starter system are fully covered in Chapter 3 and are generally due to worn/sticking brushes or worn/glazed commutator. Sticking brushes and a dirty commutator should be cleaned, and worn brushes and weak brush springs should be renewed. A slightly worn commutator can be cleaned as described for a dynamo commutator above, but the insulation between the segments of a starter motor commutator should never be undercut.

Although the basic circuit layout of a starter system is straightforward (page 33), a large number of manufacturers now use a circuit, which by-passes a ballast register in the ignition system (page 54). This does not affect the starter circuit other than the need usually for an extra terminal on the solenoid.

Electrical system – general

Faults in a car's electrical system can be broadly separated into three groups: short circuits, open circuits; and high resistance circuits. Provided a logical checking sequence is adopted, locating a particular fault should not be too difficult using only a test lamp.

Short circuit

This type of fault usually takes the form of a direct leak to earth of the battery current, with a consequent high current flow through that part of the circuit affected. Normally this will result in a fuse blowing, but if any particular circuit is unfused it could lead to the cable insulating melting and causing a possible fire. The immediate action to take, should such a fault occur, is to disconnect the battery (assuming there is no fire) and then to trace the defect. One further problem which can arise, however, is that if the burnt cable is part of a loom, it may also have burnt the insulation of other cables within the same loom, resulting in additional 'short' circuits.

In many cases the source of the problem will be obvious with signs of overheating or scorching of the cable or component. It can happen, however, that due to the high current flow, the circuit may get hot and burn at some point away from the initial short. If the fault has caused a fuse to blow, connect the test lamp across the two fuse-holder clips and then re-connect the battery (*Figure 10.3*). In the absence of a fuse, connect the lamp between the vacant battery terminal and the disconnected battery cable. In both cases the lamp should come on by virtue of the short circuit, assuming any switches in the circuit to be in the 'ON' position.

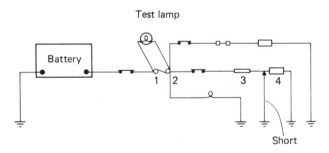

Figure 10.3. Tracing short circuit using a test lamp
1. *Connect the test lamp across the blown fuse. With all switches in the circuit closed, the lamp will glow brightly due to the short*
2. *Disconnect each cable in turn; when the light goes out or dims, the faulty circuit is located*
3. *Disconnect the suspect cable at various junction points along its length. If the lamp goes out the defect has not yet been reached; when the lamp stays on, the fault has just been passed.*
4. *Where the end component is suspected to be at fault, check this first by disconnecting its power lead, if the test lamp (across the fuse) goes out, the consumer unit is at fault. All switches in the circuit must be closed*

You now need to trace the circuit through to the next junction, where if, as usual there are a number of cables (circuits) leading from the one terminal, each one should be disconnected until the lamp goes out or burns dimly. When this happens you have located the defective circuit. Leave this cable connected and move on to the next junction or terminal and repeat the test. Carry on until eventually you will find that the lamp stays on; when this happens you have just passed the defect.

Sometimes it happens that the short is not actually in the circuit but in the end component, be it a lamp, a motor or whatever. If you suspect this, ignore the previous checks and go straight to the component. Disconnect its power source and your test lamp (connected as before) should go out. If it does not, then it is not the component at fault. The only exception to this is if the faulty component has caused damage back along the cable. Any switches in the circuit should be in the 'ON' position.

Open circuit

With this type of fault, although the end result will be much the same as a short, in that the consumer component does not do what it should, the actual defect may not be so obvious, with no signs of burning. Having said that, however, what may have started out as a short could have become an open circuit – for example, a blown fuse.

An open circuit then is a break or gap somewhere in the line, preventing the flow of an electric current. Other than a blown fuse, an open circuit could result from a relay or switch not operating, a cable pulled out from its terminal or indeed, a break in a cable. Where an open circuit has resulted from a short, then obviously it is essential to rectify the cause before doing something about the open circuit.

Tracing a defect of this type is relatively simple (see *Figure 10.4*): leave the battery connected and wire one side of the test lamp to a good earth. Then with the affected consumer component switched on, follow the circuit back from the component itself, touching the free end of the test lamp on every junction or connection in turn. If the lamp comes on brightly, you need go no further. From there on back, the circuit should be in order.

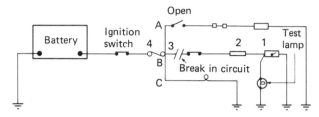

Figure 10.4. Tracing open circuit using test lamp

1. With all the switches in the circuit closed, connect the test lamp between the component power supply and a good earth. If the lamp comes on, suspect the component or its earth.

2. Where the lamp does not light, move back through the circuit connecting the test lamp from terminals or junctions to earth

3. If at some stage the lamp comes on, go no further – the defect has just been passed

4. It can be assumed that if circuits A, B and C are all out of action, the fault is either at the fuse or the power supply to it. Check on the battery side of the fuse.

Should the lamp come on at the beginning of the test, i.e. at the consumer connection, then the fault is either in the unit itself or its earth connection. Most lamps, for example, are earthed through their body/mounting screws; these can be checked by touching the free end of the test lamp on a good conductive point on the body of the suspect lamp unit. If the earth is defective, both the test lamp and the consumer lamp will come on, albeit with reduced intensity.

High resistance circuit

This type of fault has much in common with an open circuit. In fact depending upon its severity the results can be similar. Both faults are much more likely to occur at a junction of terminal than in the cable itself and both occur quite frequently at an earth connection. Probably the most common example of a high resistance is a loose battery connection, resulting in poor starter operation. Also, a defective or non-existing earth strap between the engine and chassis body can produce similar starting difficulties.

Nearly all high resistance circuits result from either loose or corroded connections/terminals. In some cases a high-resistance fault can cause some strange effects, for example, with some combined flasher/stop lamp assemblies a defect such as this can result in the stop/tail lamps blinking when the indicator switch is operated.

A high resistance circuit can be traced in much the same way as for an open circuit, except that the test lamp can vary in light intensity instead of being extinguished.

11

Diesel fuel system

The major difference between a diesel and a petrol engine is that the diesel does not have an ignition system but relies on the temperature of compressed air in the combustion chamber to ignite the fuel. This means that the fuel has to be injected into the combustion chamber at a very high pressure and in a finely atomised spray. The equipment used to do this – the fuel pump and injector(s) are manufactured to very close tolerances; with the actual pumping elements this is in the region of 0.00006 inch.

That is why cleanliness when working on the fuel system of a diesel engine is so absolutely essential; a speck of dirt the width of a human hair could cause considerable and expensive damage. For the same reason any fuel system maintenance should be carried out when specified; this will probably include draining any water from the fuel filter at certain intervals, for water can also damage the mirror-like surfaces of the pump and injector elements. A typical diesel fuel system is shown in *Figure 11.1*.

Unlike petrol, diesel fuel does not evaporate, so that any spillage on to hands or clothes can result in an unpleasant smell that lingers for some time. In addition, it can cause a rash if it comes in contact with skin; where possible use a barrier cream before starting work. Diesel fuel on shoes will make them slippery, with the consequent danger that they could slip off the pedals when you are driving.

Diesel fault finding

A diesel engine may have no ignition system but all car diesel engines are fitted with glow-plugs. These are used to boost the

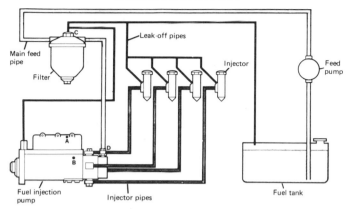

Figure 11.1. Layout of a typical diesel fuel system using the Lucas-CAV DPA distributor-type injection pump. Where the system needs venting (bleeding) through any reason, such as after running out of fuel, the following procedure should be adopted:

First slacken the vent (A) on the front of the governor-control cover (mechanical governors) or on the top of the control-gear housing (hydraulic governors). Next slacken one of the two hydraulic-head locking screws (B). If the pump is installed in such a way that one locking screw is above the other, then the higher of the two should be slackened. In later pumps a vent valve is fitted to one of these screws.

Unscrew two or three turns the vent plug (C) on the tope cover of the filter (not the return pipe to the tank). Now operate the priming lever at the fuel feed pump and when bubble free fuel issues from each venting point tighten the screws in the following order:

(1) filter-cover venting screw C; (2) head-locking screw B; (3) governor vent screw A

Next slacken the pipe union D at the pump inlet, operate the priming device, and retighten when fuel issues freely from around the threads.

Finally, slacken the unions at the injector ends of two of the high-pressure pipes from the pump. Set the accelerator in the fully-open position and ensure that the 'stop' control is in the 'run' position; now turn the engine over on the starter motor until bubble-free fuel issues from both pipes. Tighten the unions and the engine is ready to run

heat of the compressed air when starting from cold; any failure in the electrical circuit to the plugs would probably result in a no-start situation when the engine is cold, but would have no effect whatsoever in a warm engine. This and other defects of a diesel engine fuel system are shown in the fault finding chart (*Figure 11.2*). The numbers in the chart correspond to those in the text, where a more detailed explanation is given.

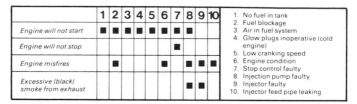

	1	2	3	4	5	6	7	8	9	10
Engine will not start	■	■	■	■	■	■	■	■		
Engine will not stop							■			
Engine misfires		■				■		■	■	■
Excessive (black) smoke from exhaust								■	■	

1. No fuel in tank
2. Fuel blockage
3. Air in fuel system
4. Glow plugs inoperative (cold engine)
5. Low cranking speed
6. Engine condition
7. Stop control faulty
8. Injection pump faulty
9. Injector faulty
10. Injector feed pipe leaking

Figure 11.2. Diesel system fault-finding chart

1. No fuel in tank

The solution to this problem is fairly obvious – put some fuel in the tank, bleed the system as necessary and take care not to let the same thing happen again.

Some pumps are self-venting, in which case all that is required is to crank the engine over on the starter motor until it fires – do not, however, operate the starter for long periods at a time. Where a non-self-venting system is used, the bleeding procedure should be given in the car's handbook. This will generally consist of first obtaining a good supply of fuel to the pump and could then involve slackening off the injector feed pipes, before cranking the engine to get a supply at each injector. The actual procedure varies from car to car, depending upon the location of the fuel system components; it is always advisable, therefore, to follow exactly the sequence given in the handbook and not to try any shortcuts.

2. Fuel blockage

This type of fault can be either a complete or partial blockage, both of which can prevent the engine from starting. A partial blockage could, however, result in fuel starvation and a misfire or a refusal to accelerate. Any blockage is most unlikely in the high-pressure side of the system (from the pump to the injectors), and is more likely in the low-pressure side at the tank pick-up or the filter.

Check for fuel flow by either slackening the bleed screw at the pump or the inlet pipe union and operating the primer pump (if fitted) or cranking the engine. Where the lift or transfer pump is integral with the injection pump, just slacken the bleed/vent screw and crank the engine. Lack of fuel at this point would indicate either a blockage or air leak in the feed pipe from the tank. Try disconnecting the inlet pipe at the filter and blowing back through it to the tank in a similar manner used on a petrol engine.

If the test proves positive and there is a supply of fuel at this point, retighten the bleed screw then slacken off one of the injector unions and crank the engine over a few times. No fuel at the slack union could be due to air in the system, a faulty stop control at the pump or a defective pump. Diesel fuel tastes even worse than petrol, so take care when blowing or sucking on fuel pipes. It is always advisable to use a length of plastic hose as a mouthpiece. Freezing weather conditions can also cause a fuel blockage due to waxing of the fuel (see page 142).

3. Air in fuel system

This problem would normally occur only if some part of the fuel system had been disconnected or the fuel tank run dry. If neither of these conditions apply, check for an air leak in the supply line. Bleed the system as necessary.

4. Glow plugs inoperative

On older cars the glow plugs were usually operated by a separate control on the dash, whereas the modern trend is to wire them in so that they operate when the 'ignition' switch is turned to the start position. With some it may entail holding the key in special 'glow' position for a few seconds – check the car's handbook for the correct cold starting procedure.

Glow-plugs seldom give trouble, although, after a high mileage the heating element can burn out. This is unlikely to happen to all of the plugs at the same time and, if only one was affected, the engine would probably start, but misfire and smoke badly until warmed up. Failure of all the plugs would almost certainly be due to a fault in the power supply. Check for a 12-volt supply at the plug terminals with an assistant holding the 'ignition' key in the glow position. On many cars the plugs have an automatic cut-out which switches off the plugs after a few seconds regardless of the key position, and this may be linked with a warning light on the dash. If the battery has enough power to satisfactorily operate the starter motor, it should have more than enough for the glow plugs.

5. Low cranking speed

If the starter motor cranking speed on a diesel engine is slow, then the heat generated by compression will also be low or, put another way, the heat loss will be greater. This could result in the temperature being insufficient to ignite the fuel. Consequently the engine will not start. The only answer in these cases is to rectify the fault (see page 37). This will probably also mean charging the battery or using slave leads from another battery, or possibly, tow-starting the car. When adopting this latter course do not forget to switch on the glow plugs before attempting to start the engine.

6. Engine condition

Any factor which affects the compression in a diesel engine car results in a no-start situation, much more so than with a petrol engine. However, as with any multi-cylinder internal combustion engine, this is more likely to be at one or possibly two cylinders, rather than on them all, in which case the engine may start but misfire especially when cold.

Reasons for lack of compression apply to both petrol or diesel – burnt valves, incorrect valve clearances, worn bores/rings or a defective cylinder-head gasket are the most probable causes. Do not try checking the compression pressures with an ordinary petrol engine compression tester. Even assuming one could be fitted in a fuel injector hole, the resulting pressure would probably blow the thing apart.

7. Stop control faulty

A diesel engine cannot be stopped simply by switching off the ignition – there is no ignition system. The method used is to cut off the supply of fuel. With most diesel-engined cars this is done by using an electrically-operated solenoid valve at the injection pump. This valve is normally held in the closed (shut-off) position by a spring, until energised (supplied with an electric current), when it opens, allowing fuel to flow to the pumping elements.

The electrical supply to the solenoid valve is taken through what, in a petrol-engined vehicle, would be termed the ignition switch. Turning this switch to the ON position causes the solenoid to be energised, so allowing a flow of fuel, whereas switching it OFF results in it interupting the fuel flow to the pumping elements, so stopping the engine. It follows, therefore, that any failure in the electrical supply to the valve would result in it not opening and the engine refusing to start, or would cause it to stop if the fault occurred while the engine was running. Check for a 12 volt supply at the valve, not forgetting that the 'ignition' must be switched on.

Sometimes a click may be heard from the solenoid valve as it is switched on or off, in which case it can be assumed to be operating. If not, the only satisfactory test is to remove it and test its operation outside the pump. Some older diesel-engined cars may have a manually-controlled fuel shut-off valve, operated from a knob on the dash. On these, check that the valve at the pump operates when the controlling knob is moved.

8. Injection pump faulty

Testing the operation and output from the fuel-injection pump requires specialised equipment, usually only found at Bosch/

CAV agents. Some indication of pump performance can be gained, however, from this simple test:

1. First ensure that the pump is being supplied with clean, air free fuel (bleed as necessary), and that the stop control is functioning as it should.
2. Next, slacken off each of the injector pipes (at the injector end) and operate the starter. Fuel should emerge, in small amounts, from each of the slackened unions. If not the pump is suspect.

Some pumps are driven by a toothed belt, which is often the same belt used for driving the camshaft of OHC engines. Although these belts are very reliable, they can occasionally suffer from incorrect adjustment, overridding the teeth or a complete breakage.

9. *Injector faulty*

Operating as they do in the pretty hostile environment within the combustion chambers, it is surprising that the injectors of a diesel engine last as long as they do. Even when they do fail, the reason is often nothing to do with the injector itself.

As with the injection pump, specialised equipment is required for checking the injectors. However, a simple test will give some idea of their performance. Remove the suspect injector from the engine after first disconnecting its feed pipe. Slacken the union at the pump end of the pipe and re-position the pipe so that the injector can be re-fitted in a clear space within the engine compartment, then re-tighten all the unions. To prevent the engine from starting during the test slacken off the unions at all the other injectors. Now with an assistant turning the engine (on the starter motor), observe the spray formation from the exposed injector – it should be symmetrical and finely atomised, with a sharp cut off – that is with no dribble. The injector should also give a discernible grunt or buzz as the fuel in injected.

Take great care when carrying out this test, for the working pressure of the fuel is such that the spray from the injector could penetrate the skin (or eyes) with disastrous results. It may be found advantageous to direct the spray into a clear jar (*Figure 11.3*). In any case, avoid any contact with the spray.

If the engine is misfiring, the faulty injector can be found by slackening each injector union in turn, while the engine is running. Do not forget to tighten each union before proceeding

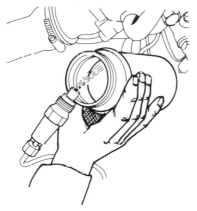

Figure 11.3. When testing a fuel injector, take care to avoid spray contacting the skin. Direct the spray into a glass jar as shown

to the next. The defective injector is the one that makes no difference in the engine note when its union is slackened. This does not necessarily mean that the injector is at fault; there could be a lack of compression on that particular cylinder, or the pumping element could be at fault.

In some cases, by holding the injector pipe, it can be felt when injection of the fuel takes place. Obviously, if injection can be felt on all the pipes except one, that is the most likely suspect.

10. Injector feed pipe leaking

This would be a fairly obvious defect because, firstly, the engine would misfire and, secondly, the escaping diesel fuel will be visible and smell. If a union is leaking, a simple tightening job may stop the leak. Should, however, the pipe be defective (cracked or split) then it will have to be replaced. There are normally two pipes at the injector; the fuel feed pipe from the pump, which is a relatively thick-walled steel pipe with screwed union at either end. The second pipe is the fuel leak-off pipe, which directs any fuel leaking past the injector, back to the tank or filter; these may be a thin-walled steel pipe or rubber with, usually, just a push-on connection at the injector.

Cold weather troubles

In very cold weather a diesel-engined vehicle may refuse to start because its fuel is frozen. The fuel does not freeze in the accepted sense – there will not be any ice forming or pipes cracking. What happens is that the paraffin hydrocarbons in the fuel separate out and begin forming into wax crystals; these can eventually clog the filter or any other restriction in the system such as a narrow passage through a union or even at a bend in a pipe. The fuel also takes on a cloudy appearance.

Oil companies usually supply both summer and winter grades of fuel, although some filling stations may still be selling the summer grade during an early cold spell. Summer grade fuel normally 'freezes' at about $-1°C$, while winter grade fuel is soluble down to about $-9°C$. The winter grade is usually suitable for most places in the British Isles. However, where temperatures below $-9°C$ are consistently met with, a fuel heater (usually operated from the vehicle battery) can be fitted or anti-coagulant additives can be added to the fuel. As a temporary measure petrol can be added to the diesel fuel. This, however, reduces the lubricity of the fuel and can damage the pump if used too frequently; at no time use more than about a 40/60 per cent mix of petrol and diesel fuel. Using petrol also increases the fire risk, although no more than is usual in a petrol-engined car.

Kerosene can also be added to diesel fuel as an antifreeze measure, but would conflict with Customs and Excise Regulations in the United Kingdom.

Appendix: useful data

Metric conversion factors

To convert	To	Multiply by	To convert	To	Multiply by
Linear measure			**Pressure**		
inches	millimetres	25·400	pound/sq.in	kilogramme/ sq. centimetre	0·070
millimetres (mm)	inches	0·039	kilogramme/ sq. centimetre (kg/cm²)	pound/sq. in (lb/in²)	14·223
feet	metres	0·305	pound/sq. in	atmospheres	0·068
metres (m)	feet	3·281	atmospheres (atm)	pounds/sq. in	14·696
miles	kilometres	1·609	bars	pound/sq. in	14·504
kilometres (km)	miles	0·621			
Square measure			**Torque**		
square inches	square millimetres	645·160	pound-feet	kilogramme- metre	0·138
square millimetres (mm²)	square inches	0·002	kilogramme- metre (kg−m)	pound-feet	7·233
square feet	square metres	0·093	pound-feet	Newton-metre	1·356
square metres (m²)	square feet	10·764	Newton-metre (Nm)	pound-feet	0·738
Cubic measure			kilogramme- metre (kg·m)	Newton-metre	9·807
cubic inches	cubic centi- metres	16·387	Newton-metre (Nm)	kilogramme- metre	0·102
cubic centi- metres (cm³)	cubic inches	0·061			
cubic inches	millilitres	16·387	**Speed**		
millilitres (ml)	cubic inches	0·061	mile/hour	kilometre/ hour	1·609
UK pints	litres	0·568	kilometre/ hour (km/h)	mile/hour	0·621
litres (l)	UK pints	1·760	feet/second	metre/second	0·305
UK gallons	litres	4·546	metre/second (m/s)	feet/second	3·281
litres (l)	UK gallons	0·220	metre/sec (m/s)	kilometre/ hour	3·600
US gallons	litres	3·785	kilometre/ hour (km/h)	metre/sec	0·278
litres (l)	US gallons	0·264			
UK gallons	US gallons	1·201	**Consumption**		
US gallons	UK gallons	0·837	mile/UK gal	kilometre/ litre	0·354
Weight			kilometre/ litre (km/l)	mile/UK gal	2·825
ounces	grammes	28·350			
grammes (g)	ounces	0·035			
pounds	kilogrammes	0·454			
kilogrammes (kg)	pounds	2·205			

miles/UK gal to litres/100 km
$$= \frac{282·473}{\text{miles/UK gal}}$$

litres/100 km to miles/UK gal
$$= \frac{282·473}{\text{litres/100 km}}$$

Temperature Conversion

$$\text{Fahrenheit} = \frac{9}{5}C + 32$$

$$\text{Centigrade} = \frac{5}{9}(F-32)$$

Decimals of an inch to millimetres

in	mm	in	mm	in	mm	in	mm
0·001	0·0254	0·026	0·6604	0·051	1·2954	0·076	1·9304
0·002	0·0508	0·027	0·6858	0·052	1·3208	0·077	1·9558
0·003	0·0762	0·028	0·7112	0·053	1·3462	0·078	1·9812
0·004	0·1016	0·029	0·7366	0·054	1·3716	0·079	2·0066
0·005	0·1270	0·030	0·7620	0·055	1·3970	0·080	2·0320
0·006	0·1524	0·031	0·7874	0·056	1·4224	0·081	2·0574
0·007	0·1778	0·032	0·8128	0·057	1·4478	0·082	2·0828
0·008	0·2032	0·033	0·8382	0·058	1·4732	0·083	2·1082
0·009	0·2286	0·034	0·8636	0·059	1·4986	0·084	2·1336
0·010	0·2540	0·035	0·8890	0·060	1·5240	0·085	2·1590
0·011	0·2794	0·036	0·9144	0·061	1·5494	0·086	2·1844
0·012	0·3048	0·037	0·9398	0·062	1·5748	0·087	2·2098
0·013	0·3302	0·038	0·9652	0·063	1·6002	0·088	2·2352
0·014	0·3556	0·039	0·9906	0·064	1·6256	0·089	2·2606
0·015	0·3810	0·040	1·0160	0·065	1·6510	0·090	2·2860
0·016	0·4064	0·041	1·0414	0·066	1·6764	0·091	2·3114
0·017	0·4318	0·042	1·0668	0·067	1·7018	0·092	2·3368
0·018	0·4572	0·043	1·0922	0·068	1·7272	0·093	2·3622
0·019	0·4826	0·044	1·1176	0·069	1·7526	0·094	2·3876
0·020	0·5080	0·045	1·1430	0·070	1·7780	0·095	2·4130
0·021	0·5334	0·046	1·1684	0·071	1·8034	0·096	2·4384
0·022	0·5588	0·047	1·1938	0·072	1·8288	0·097	2·4638
0·023	0·5842	0·048	1·2192	0·073	1·8542	0·098	2·4892
0·024	0·6096	0·049	1·2446	0·074	1·8796	0·099	2·5146
0·025	0·6350	0·050	1·2700	0·075	1·9050	0·100	2·5400

Decimals of an inch to millimetres

in	mm.	in	mm	in	mm	in	mm
0·11	2·794	0·36	9·144	0·61	15·494	0·86	21·844
0·12	3·048	0·37	9·398	0·62	15·748	0·87	22·098
0·13	3·302	0·38	9·652	0·63	16·002	0·88	22·352
0·14	3·556	0·39	9·906	0·64	16·256	0·89	22·606
0·15	3·810	0·40	10·160	0·65	16·510	0·90	22·860
0·16	4·064	0·41	10·414	0·66	16·764	0·91	23·114
0·17	4·318	0·42	10·668	0·67	17·018	0·92	23·368
0·18	4·572	0·43	10·922	0·68	17·272	0·93	23·622
0·19	4·826	0·44	11·176	0·69	17·526	0·94	23·876
0·20	5·080	0·45	11·430	0·70	17·780	0·95	24·130
0·21	5·334	0·46	11·684	0 71	18·034	0·96	24·384
0·22	5·588	0·47	11·938	0·72	18·288	0·97	24·638
0·23	5·842	0·48	12·192	0·73	18·542	0·98	24·892
0·24	6·096	0·49	12·446	0·74	18·796	0·99	25·146
0·25	6·350	0·50	12·700	0·75	19·050	1·00	25·400
0·26	6·604	0·51	12·954	0·76	19·304	2·00	50·800
0·27	6·858	0 52	13·208	0·77	19 558	3·00	76·200
0·28	7·112	0·53	13·462	0·78	19·812	4·00	101·600
0·29	7·366	0·54	13 710	0·79	20·066	5·00	127·000
0·30	7·620	0·55	13·970	0·80	20·320	6·00	152·400
0·31	7·874	0·56	14·224	0·81	20·574	7·00	177·800
0·32	8·128	0·57	14·478	0·82	20·828	8·00	203·200
0·33	8·382	0·58	14·732	0·83	21·082	9·00	228·600
0·34	8·636	0·59	14·986	0·84	21·336	10·00	254·000
0·35	8·890	0 00	15·240	0·85	21·590	11·00	279·400

Miles to kilometres

miles	km	miles	km	miles	km	miles	km
1	1·609	26	41·843	51	82·077	76	122·310
2	3·219	27	43·452	52	83·686	77	123·919
3	4·828	28	45·062	53	85·295	78	125·529
4	6·437	29	46·671	54	86·905	79	127·138
5	8·047	30	48·280	55	88·514	80	128·748
6	9·656	31	49·890	56	90·123	81	130·357
7	11·265	32	51·499	57	91·733	82	131·966
8	12·875	33	53·108	58	93·342	83	133·576
9	14·484	34	54·718	59	94·951	84	135·185
10	16·093	35	56·327	60	96·561	85	136·794
11	17·703	36	57·936	61	98·170	86	138·404
12	19·312	37	59·546	62	99·779	87	140·013
13	20·921	38	61·155	63	101·389	88	141·622
14	22·531	39	62·764	64	102·998	89	143·232
15	24·140	40	64·374	65	104·607	90	144·841
16	25·750	41	65·983	66	106·217	91	146·450
17	27·359	42	67·592	67	107·826	92	148·060
18	28·968	43	69·202	68	109·435	93	149·669
19	30·578	44	70·811	69	111·045	94	151·278
20	32·187	45	72·420	70	112·654	95	152·888
21	33·796	46	74·030	71	114·263	96	154·497
22	35·406	47	75·639	72	115·873	97	156·106
23	37·015	48	77·249	73	117·482	98	157·716
24	38·624	49	78·858	74	119·091	99	159·325
25	40·234	50	80·467	75	120·701	100	160·934

Miles to kilometres

miles	km	miles	km	miles	km	miles	km
110	177·028	360	579·364	610	981·700	860	1384·036
120	193·121	370	595·457	620	997·793	870	1400·129
130	209·215	380	611·551	630	1013·887	880	1416·223
140	225·308	390	627·644	640	1029·980	890	1432·316
150	241·402	400	643·738	650	1046·074	900	1448·410
160	257·495	410	659·831	660	1062·167	910	1464·503
170	273·588	420	675·924	670	1078·260	920	1480·596
180	289·682	430	692·018	680	1094·354	930	1496·690
190	305·775	440	708·111	690	1110·447	940	1512·783
200	321·869	450	724·205	700	1126·541	950	1528·877
210	337·962	460	740·298	710	1142·634	960	1544·970
220	354·056	470	756·392	720	1158·728	970	1561·064
230	370·149	480	772·485	730	1174·821	980	1577·157
240	386·243	490	788·579	740	1190·915	990	1593·251
250	402·336	500	804·672	750	1207·008	1000	1609·344
260	418·429	510	820·765	760	1223·101	2000	3218·688
270	434·523	520	836·859	770	1239·195	3000	4828·032
280	450·616	530	852·952	780	1255·288	4000	6437·376
290	466·710	540	869·046	790	1271·382	5000	8046·720
300	482·803	550	885·139	800	1287·475	6000	9646·064
310	498·897	560	901·233	810	1303·569	7000	11265·408
320	514·990	570	917·326	820	1319·662	8000	12874·752
330	531·084	580	933·420	830	1335·756	9000	14484·096
340	547·177	590	949·513	840	1351·849	10000	16093·440
350	563·270	600	965·606	850	1367·942	25000	40233·600

Kilometres to miles

km	miles	km	miles	km	miles	km	miles
1	0·621	26	16·156	51	31·690	76	47·224
2	1·243	27	16·777	52	32·311	77	47·846
3	1·864	28	17·398	53	32·933	78	48·467
4	2·486	29	18·020	54	33·554	79	49·088
5	3·107	30	18·641	55	34·175	80	49·710
6	3·728	31	19·263	56	34·797	81	50·331
7	4·350	32	19·884	57	35·418	82	50·952
8	4·971	33	20·505	58	36·040	83	51·574
9	5·592	34	21·123	59	36·661	84	52·195
10	6·214	35	21·748	60	37·282	85	52·817
11	6·835	36	22·369	61	37·904	86	53·438
12	7·457	37	22·991	62	38·525	87	54·059
13	8·078	38	23·612	63	39·146	88	54·681
14	8·699	39	24·234	64	39·768	89	55·302
15	9·321	40	24·855	65	40·389	90	55·923
16	9·942	41	25·476	66	41·011	91	56·545
17	10·563	42	26·098	67	41·632	92	57·166
18	11·185	43	26·719	68	42·253	93	57·788
19	11·806	44	27·340	69	42·875	94	58·409
20	12·427	45	27·962	70	43·496	95	59·030
21	13·049	46	28·583	71	44·117	96	59·652
22	13·670	47	29·204	72	44·739	97	60·273
23	14·292	48	29·826	73	45·360	98	60·894
24	14·913	49	30·447	74	45·982	99	61·516
25	15·534	50	31·068	75	46·603	100	62·137

Kilometres to miles

km	miles	km	miles	km	miles	km	miles
110	68·351	360	223·694	610	379·036	860	534·379
120	74·565	370	229·907	620	385·250	870	540·593
130	80·778	380	236·121	630	391·464	880	546·806
140	86·992	390	242·335	640	397·677	890	553·020
150	93·206	400	248·548	650	403·891	900	559·234
160	99·419	410	254·762	660	410·105	910	565·448
170	105·633	420	260·976	670	416·319	920	571·661
180	111·847	430	267·190	680	422·532	930	577·875
190	118·060	440	273·403	690	428·746	940	584·089
200	124·274	450	279·617	700	434·960	950	590·302
210	130·488	460	285·831	710	441·173	960	596·516
220	136·702	470	292·044	720	447·387	970	602·730
230	142·915	480	298·258	730	453·601	980	608·944
240	149·129	490	304·472	740	459·815	990	615·157
250	155·343	500	310·686	750	466·028	1000	621·371
260	161·556	510	316·899	760	472·242	2000	1242·742
270	167·770	520	323·113	770	478·456	3000	1864·113
280	173·984	530	329·327	780	484·669	4000	2485·484
290	180·198	540	335·540	790	490·883	5000	3106·055
300	186·411	550	341·754	800	497·097	6000	3728·226
310	192·625	560	347·968	810	503·311	7000	4349·597
320	198·839	570	354·181	820	509·524	8000	4970·968
330	205·052	580	360·395	830	515·738	9000	5592·339
340	211·266	590	366·609	840	521·952	10000	6213·710
350	217·480	600	372·823	850	528·165	25000	15534·275

Litres to UK gallons

l	UK gal	l	UK gal	l	UK gal	l	UK gal
1	0·2200	26	5·7192	51	11·2184	76	16·7176
2	0·4399	27	5·9392	52	11·4384	77	16·9376
3	0·6599	28	6·1591	53	11·6584	78	17·1576
4	0·8799	29	6·3791	54	11·8783	79	17·3776
5	1·0998	30	6·5991	55	12·0983	80	17·5975
6	1·3198	31	6·8190	56	12·3183	81	17·8175
7	1·5398	32	7·0390	57	12·5382	82	18·0375
8	1·7598	33	7·2590	58	12·7582	83	18·2574
9	1·9797	34	7·4789	59	12·9782	84	18·4774
10	2·1997	35	7·6989	60	13·1981	85	18·6974
11	2·4197	36	7·9189	61	13·4181	86	18·9173
12	2·6396	37	8·1389	62	13·6381	87	19·1373
13	2·8596	38	8·3588	63	13·8580	88	19·3573
14	3·0796	39	8·5788	64	14·0780	89	19·5772
15	3·2995	40	8·7988	65	14·2980	90	19·7972
16	3·5195	41	9·0187	66	14·5180	91	20·0172
17	3·7395	42	9·2387	67	14·7379	92	20·2371
18	3·9595	43	9·4587	68	14·9579	93	20·4571
19	4·1794	44	9·6786	69	15·1779	94	20·6771
20	4·3994	45	9·8986	70	15·3978	95	20·8971
21	4·6193	46	10·1186	71	15·6178	96	21·1170
22	4·8393	47	10·3385	72	15·8378	97	21·3370
23	5·0593	48	10·5585	73	16·0578	98	21·5570
24	5·2793	49	10·7785	74	16·2777	99	21·7769
25	5·4992	50	10·9985	75	16·4977	100	21·9969

English	Italiano	Français	Deutsch	Español
Blinking light	lampeggiatore	clignotant	Blinklicht	intermittente
Brake fluid	l'olio dei freni	l'huile de freins	Bremsflüssigkeit	aceite de los frenos
Brakes	freni	freins	Bremser	frenos
Bulb	lampadina	ampoule	Birne	bombilla
Carburettor	carburatore	carburateur	Vergaser	carburador
Clutch	frizione	embrayage	Kupplung	embrague
Coil	bobina	bobine	Zündspule	bobina
Condenser	condensatore	condensateur	Kondensator	condensador
Contact breaker	ruttore	rupteur	Unterbrecher	ruptor
Differential	differenziale	différentiel	Ausgleichgetriebe	differencial
Distributor	distributore	distributeur	Verteiler	distruidor
Engine	motore	moteur	Motor	motor
Fan-belt	cinghia del ventilatore	courroie du ventilateur	Keilriemen	correa del ventilador
Filter	filtro	filtre	Filter	filtro
Fuel pump	pompa di alimentazione	pompe d'alimentation	Kraftstoffpumpe	bomba de alimentacion
Gasket	guarnizione	joint	Dichtung	junta
Gearbox	cambio	boîte de vitesses	Getriebe	cambio
Generator	generatore	générateur	Generator	dinamo
Head (cylinder)	testate	tête	Zylinderkopf	culata
Headlamp	faro	phare	Scheinwerfer	faro
Hose	tubazione	tuyauterie	Leitung	tubo
Leads	cavetti	fils	Zündkabel	cables
Multigrade oil	olio multigrade	huile multigrade	Mehrbereichs-oel	aceite multgrado
Oil pressure	pressione dell'olio	pression de l'huile	Oeldruck	presion del aceite
Oil sump	coppa cell'olio	carter inférieur	Oelwanne	cubeta
Pads	pasticche	plaquettes	Brems	pastillas
Radiator	radiatore	radiateur	Kühler	radiator
Radiator cap	tappo del radiatore	bouchon du radiateur	Kühlerverschluss	tapon del radiator
Sparking plugs	candele	bougies	Zündkerzen	bujias
Starter motor	motorino d'avviamento	démarreur	Anlasser	motor de arranque
Steering	sterzo	direction	Lenkung	volante
Stop lamps	fanalino stop	stops	Bremslicht	luz de stop
Transmission shaft	albero di transmissions	arbre de transmission	Gelenkwelle	arbol de transmission
Tyres	pneumatici	pneus	Reifen	neumaticos
Valve	valvola	clapet	Ventil	valvula
Wheels	ruota	roues	Räder	ruedas
Windscreen wiper	tergicristallo	essuie-glace	Scheibenwischer	limpia parabriasas

Index